ON THE WING

ON THE WING

A HISTORY OF THE WINDSOR SPITFIRES

BOB DUFF &
JIM PARKER

BIBLIOASIS

FIRST EDITION

Library and Archives Canada Cataloguing in Publication

Duff, Bob

On the wing : a history of the Windsor Spitfires / Bob Duff and Jim Parker.

Includes bibliographical references and index.
ISBN 978-1-926845-20-3 (bound).—ISBN 978-1-926845-19-7 (pbk.)

1. Windsor Spitfires (Hockey team)—History. 2. Ontario Hockey League—History. 3. Hockey—Ontario—Windsor Region—History. I. Parker, Jim, 1964- II. Title.

GV848.W45D83 2010 796.962'620971332 C2010-906975-7

Edited by Daniel Wells.
Cover design by Bill Douglas.

Canada Council for the Arts | Conseil des Arts du Canada
Canadian Heritage | Patrimoine canadien
ONTARIO ARTS COUNCIL
CONSEIL DES ARTS DE L'ONTARIO

Biblioasis acknowledges the ongoing financial support of the Government of Canada through The Canada Council for the Arts, Canadian Heritage, the Book Publishing Industry Development Program (BPIDP); and the Government of Ontario through the Ontario Arts Council.

PRINTED AND BOUND IN CANADA

This book is dedicated to all loyal Spitfires fans who have stuck with this team through thick and thin and good and bad, and were rewarded for their loyalty by receiving junior hockey's greatest prize, two years in a row.

Contents

Marcel Pronovost, 1981. (WS)

Foreword

WINDSOR IS MY SECOND HOME. I WAS BORN in Lac la Tortue, Que., but I've spent the majority of my life in Windsor. I always tell people that I was adopted by Windsor.

It all started by accident, or coincidence, I guess you could say. My journey to Windsor began in the winter of 1947. The Wilson brothers, Larry and Johnny, played for a high school team and they also played for Shawinigan, the same team as me.

The year before, I was centre on the second line and we won the provincial midget championship. The next year, they put me back on defence because I was the biggest kid. Marcel Cote, who was a Detroit Red Wings scout, watched the two Wilsons play for their English high school, and then he came to Shawinigan to watch them play again. And that's when he saw me. In those days, the scouts depended more on the arena managers to let them know who could play.

Detroit signed all three of us to C forms and brought us to Ontario for training camp in the fall of 1947. We went to training camp at the old rink in Waterloo and were told that we were going to go to Galt to play junior in the OHA. And then halfway through the camp, they said, "You're going to Windsor." The Wings had transferred their sponsorship agreement to Windsor. The Butcher brothers owned the team, Lloyd Pollock was the manager and Jimmy Skinner the coach.

That's how I came to Windsor, and how I became a Spitfire. My mother once said to me, "If we hadn't let you go to Windsor at 16, what would you have done?" And I told her, "I would have gone anyway." She said, "That's what I thought."

Coming to Windsor to play for the Spitfires was the best thing that ever happened to me, but I have to tell you, at first, it was an eye-opener. I remember the first time I saw the rink, the old Windsor Arena. It looked like they'd cut the end of the ice surface off to put in more seats. I liked that, though, because I was a hitter.

We had to come down the stairs to the ice surface from the dressing room. The shortness of the ice and the high boards really caught my attention, and how old the building was. I came out of Shawinigan, in a building that was built in 1937, so it was quite new. I was a little bit spoiled.

Regardless, Windsor was the right place for me to be at that time in my life. Boy, did I ever get to play a lot of hockey. Besides playing for the Spitfires in the OHA Junior A Series, I was also playing for Detroit Auto Club in the senior International Hockey League. I played 52 games in 1947-48 and another 51 in 1948-49. At the end of that year, they somehow got it arranged so that I played for the Windsor Hettche Spitfires in the Allan Cup.

I went to training camp with the Red Wings the next year and I was assigned to Omaha. I played the whole season for Omaha. I was rookie of the year and at the end of the year – I played that night and then the next day – I was on a plane coming to Detroit. That was the year that Gordie Howe got hurt and was out for the rest of the Stanley Cup playoffs and they put Red Kelly up front, and put me on defence with Leo Reise. We won the Cup. We beat the New York Rangers in Game 7 of the final in overtime.

Marcel Pronovost (white shirt) playing for Detroit Auto Club against the Windsor Spitfires in an IHL game at Windsor Arena during the 1948-49 season. (MP)

The following season, I suffered a broken cheekbone in training camp, then broke my ankle early in the season. Detroit GM Jack Adams assigned me to Indianapolis to get back into shape. I played 34 games there, and then came back up to Detroit, and that was it. I played there for the next 14 years until I was traded to Toronto, and then I played five years in Toronto with the Maple Leafs.

Early in my Detroit career, once my wife and I had a family, we decided to buy a home and settle in Windsor. That was 1953. We wanted our children to be educated in Canada. So Windsor continued to play a major role in my and my family's lives. Even when I was traded to Toronto in 1965, there was a Windsor element to the whole process. I was driving across the Ambassador Bridge from Detroit back to Windsor when I heard the news on the radio that I had been dealt to the Leafs.

When I went to Toronto, I didn't think I'd ever get back to Windsor. I finished my NHL playing career with the Maple Leafs in 1970, then accepted a position as playing-coach with Toronto's Tulsa farm club in the Central Hockey League. From there, I took a position as coach of the Chicago Cougars in the fledgling World Hockey Association, coached the Hull Festivals of the Quebec Major Junior League, then Punch Imlach, my old Toronto coach, hired me to coach the Buffalo Sabres.

After I left Buffalo, I went back to Hull, then I was offered a coaching position with the Red Wings in 1979. Just like that, I was back in Windsor. And soon, back with the Spitfires. After leaving Detroit, I was hired to coach Windsor in 1981.

Something, it seemed, was always pulling me back to the city. In 1985, I was behind the bench as the Belle River Canadiens captured the OHA Jr. C title. That was the most focussed group of young men I've ever worked with. All I had to do was give them a little advice and open the gate.

I went into scouting, working with the NHL's Central Scouting Bureau. Windsor was – and is – the perfect location for an NHL scout. You can get to all brands of hockey – junior, college, NHL, and minor pro – all within a short distance of the city.

I was working with NHL Central Scouting, and Max McNab, who was general manager with the New Jersey Devils – Lou Lamoriello, the current GM, had just come on board with the team at the time – through Jim Gregory at Central Scouting, contacted me about a scouting position with the club. I've worked for them for the last 20 years.

The best years, really, have been since I've

Spitfires defenceman Marcel Pronovost crashes the Guelph Biltmores' net during a 6-1 Windsor victory in a 1948-49 OHA Junior A game at Windsor Arena. (MP)

joined the New Jersey Devils. I was part of the club's scouting staff for Stanley Cup wins in 1995, 2000 and 2003. Working with Lou Lamoriello, it's so enjoyable. He's such a competent man and he's very loyal to his employees. And the job has allowed me to remain in Windsor.

There was something special in every Stanley Cup, really, and those championships I've won with New Jersey have been added to the five Stanley Cups I won as a player – four with Detroit in 1949-50, 1951-52, 1953-54 and 1954-55, and another title with the Leafs in 1966-67. Four times, I was named an NHL all-star and I played in the NHL all-star game 11 times. In 1978, when I was inducted into the Hockey Hall of Fame, that was such a memorable evening, because my parents were able to be there and share it with me.

I don't think any of it would have been possible without Windsor. Windsor gave me the opportunity to get to the National Hockey League and play in Detroit for a beautiful organization with good management and good players. I played with Leo Reise and Bob Goldham as defence partners and with Gordie Howe, Teddy Lindsay and Red Kelly as teammates. They were very important people in my life.

Between playing and coaching and scouting, I don't think anyone saw more Spitfires games at Windsor Arena than I did. In 2004, I was inducted into the Windsor/Essex County Sports Hall of Fame and in 2005, the Spitfires recognized me by raising my No. 4 to the rafters as an honoured number. They were real honours for me and I have to admit, kind of caught me by surprise. I don't get emotional, but in the case of each of those gestures, it was appreciated.

It's funny you know, because Windsor, it was the only place I ever wore a number other than three. The second year I was here, the Spitfires gave me No. 3. In Omaha, they gave me three. When I went to Indianapolis, they gave me three. In Detroit, the lower berths on the train went to the lower-numbered players. So I took Bill Quackenbush's No. 3 when he was traded to Boston.

Hockey has provided me with a good living and Windsor has provided me with a home, and a lifetime of great memories. I think the town you play junior in always kind of becomes your second home. You're taken in by a family and treated like one of their own and the whole town gets to know who you are. Windsor is a blue-collar town and the town I'm from is also a blue-collar town. I guess that's why I've always felt at home in Windsor.

Marcel Pronovost
October, 2010

Windsor Spitfires Jim Hay (15), George Ouellette (6), Johnny Wilson (9) and Larry Wilson (10) help Dave O'Meara defend his goal during a 6-5 loss to the Omaha Knights of the United States Hockey League in a 1948 exhibition game. (MP)

Introduction

TODAY THE REIGNING TWO-TIME MEMORIAL Cup champion Windsor Spitfires are the talk of the junior hockey world for their outstanding achievements on the ice. But there was a time in Windsor when "out" was the only place you could play hockey.

Outdoors, that is.

Until the construction of Windsor Arena, which opened in 1925, places to play hockey in the City of Roses were few and far between. Many early leagues were contested on outdoor ice pads, and the outcomes of seasons were determined by the whims of Mother Nature.

One of the first true hockey stars to ply his trade in Windsor skated on these outdoor rinks, years after skating alongside hockey legends in the battle for Lord Stanley's mug. Ernie Liffiton was a left-winger with the 1907-08 Stanley Cup champion Montreal Wanderers, a powerhouse club with several future Hall of Famers in the line-up. Riley Hern tended goal, while Ernie (Moose) Johnson and Art Ross manned defensive positions. Forwards included Tom Hooper, Ernie Russell and Bruce Stuart. Dickie Boon, the team's coach, also earned Hall of Fame enshrinement.

Years later, Liffiton's other profession brought him to Windsor. "My dad worked for a consortium of Dominion Bridge and Canadian Bridge in Montreal," Ernie Liffiton Jr. explained in a 2004 interview. "He had a chance to come down here with Canadian Bridge Company, so in 1916, we moved to Windsor."

Ernie Liffiton Sr. did the steel work for both the Ambassador Bridge and the Detroit-Windsor Tunnel. It's a safe bet that he was the only Stanley Cup winner on either job.

He kept playing while in Windsor, even though the level of hockey wasn't what he was accustomed to.

During the 1919-20 season, Liffiton Sr., then 35, played for the Border Cities Stars of the Detroit Hockey League. A Jan. 12, 1920 game report in the *Border Cities Star* praised Liffiton's skill as his club humbled West Warren by a 7-1 count.

"A feature of the game was the rushing of Liffiton, who was holding down right defence for the Stars. Despite the slushy conditions of the ice, he could carry the puck and his work provided the fans with a sample of hockey as it is played in the top divisions in Canada. There is not a point of the game that he does not know."

Hockey took a quantum leap forward in Windsor when Windsor Arena, then known as the Border Cities Arena, opened its doors in 1925. At the time, it was considered an architectural structure of the highest order.

"Windsor's much-mooted artificial ice arena is at last a reality – a vast monument of concrete and steel dedicated to the greatest athletic pastime in the captivity of sportdom," wrote Deane Van Luven in the Sept. 5, 1925 *Border Cities Star*. "At Wyandotte Street and McDougall Ave. there stands a palace of hockey that would command the respect and admiration of expert critics anywhere in this country.

"One year ago today, the Border Cities, as a unit, was as far removed from participation in hockey, organized hockey that is, as a grasshopper from getting a nomination to the city council. No longer may the rest of Canada point scornfully to the heart of Essex County and refer

(Left)
The Windsor Bulldogs were a minor-pro team which played in the CanPro and International Leagues from 1927-36. (TTSA)

(Right)
Detroit Red Wings GM Jack Adams brought NHL sponsorship to the Spitfires in 1947. (MP)

to our neighbourhood as a place wherein shinny is played on somebody's backyard."

The first ice surface was laid down in the rink in early November of 1925. "Surely, Santa Claus has arrived a month ahead of schedule," noted the Nov. 7, 1925 edition of the *The Border Cities Star*. "Windsor and its surrounding municipalities have hoped that one day, an artificial ice stadium would grace its lands. For years, borderites carried their skates to open-air rinks, where at the pleasure of old man weather, it was possible at times to skate on hard ice."

The National Hockey League's New York Americans downed the reigning Stanley Cup champion Victoria Cougars of the Western Hockey League 1-0 in the opening game at Windsor Arena. The Windsor Hornets joined the Ontario Hockey Association's senior circuit that season, including future NHLers Fred Brown and Marvin (Cy) Wentworth in their lineup.

The following fall, big-time pro hockey graced Windsor for the first time. The Detroit Cougars – today the Red Wings – joined the NHL in 1926, but absent an NHL-calibre rink of their own, played their home games during the 1926-27 campaign at Windsor Arena. Detroit opened its NHL history there Nov. 18, 1926 with a 2-0 loss to the Boston Bruins.

Three nights earlier, the Hamilton Tigers had edged the Windsor Hornets 2-1 in the inaugural game of the new Canadian Professional Hockey League, a minor-pro loop that served as a farm system for NHL teams. Windsor's club was renamed the Bulldogs a year later, and in 1930, the league was renamed the International League. Windsor skated in the league until 1936, winning championships in the 1928-29 and 1935-36 seasons. Among the more prominent names to don a Windsor sweater during this time period were Hall of Fame goaltender Clint Benedict, Leighton (Hap) Emms, Normie Smith, and Dave Kerr.

In 1945, the end of World War II brought normalcy back to the lives of people across North America and the local hockey ranks were swelling with players as soldiers steadily returned from overseas. The Michigan-Ontario League, a prominent senior loop prior to the outbreak of the war, had faded away with much more significant battles needing to be fought, but now, area hockey people were putting the pieces together to bring the league back to life.

A Dec. 5, 1945 meeting at Windsor's Norton Palmer Hotel was attended by Jack Adams, coach-GM of the Detroit Red Wings, Fred Huber, the Wings director of public relations, and several local hockey dignitaries including Lloyd Pollock and Len Loree. It was announced that the league would return, with four franchises – Windsor Spitfires, Windsor Gotfredsons, Detroit Auto Club and Detroit Bright's Goodyears – and with a new name, the International Amateur Hockey League, later shortened to the International Hockey League when it became a pro organization.

That first season began Dec. 21, 1945, and consisted of 15 games, with Friday doubleheaders at Windsor Arena and Monday twinbills at the Olympia in Detroit. The Spits and Gotfredsons tied 4-4 opening night at Windsor Arena, while the Auto Club, eventual champions of that inaugural campaign, outscored Bright's 12-9. Windsor teams took two IHL titles, one by the Spitfires in 1946-47 and one by the Hettche Spitfires in 1948-49.

Windsor made its first foray into junior A hockey in 1946, when the original Spitfires were born. They skated in the OHA Junior A series through the 1952-53 season, reaching the league finals in 1947-48 and 1949-50. The Spitfires served as a sponsored club of the Red Wings and in 1950-51, goaltender Glenn Hall won the Red Tilson Memorial Trophy as MVP of the league.

The Bulldogs returned to prominence in 1953, when Windsor joined the OHA Senior A series. Former Spitfires such as Bobby Brown, Gord Haidy and Irwin Gross were all stars for the Bulldogs, who brought an Allan Cup to the city when they beat the Winnipeg Maroons in 1962-63. The Bulldogs also took Windsor to the world, touring Russia the following season.

The Bulldogs played in the IHL in 1963-64, then big-time hockey took another hiatus from Windsor until 1971, when the Spitfires re-emerged as a member of the Tier II Southern Ontario Junior Hockey League. Led by coach Wayne Maxner, the Spitfires won the 1973-74 SOJHL title, posting a 39-15-8 record with a lineup that included future NHL referee Bill McCreary.

A year later, Windsor was accepted again into the OHA Junior A ranks. The Spitfires joined the OHA Junior A Series, forerunner to the Ontario Hockey League, as an expansion franchise in 1975. Doug Johnston was Windsor's first coach, but was replaced by Maxner before season's end. Maxner guided Windsor to the league finals in 1979-80. In 1980-81, Windsor centre Ernie Godden set a league record that still stands when he scored 87 goals.

Peter Karmanos purchased the franchise in 1984, renaming the team the Compuware Spitfires, and in 1988, under the tutelage of coach Tom Webster and led by captain Adam Graves, the Spitfires won their first OHL title and reached the Memorial Cup final before falling 7-6 to the Medicine Hat Tigers.

A group headed by Steve Riolo acquired the Spitfires in 1989, and in 2001-02, reached the conference finals for the first time since that 1988 championship season. In 1994, defenceman Ed Jovanovski became the first Spitfire to go first overall in the NHL entry draft when he was selected by the Florida Panthers. Riolo eventually acquired controlling interest in the franchise and in 2006, sold the team to current owners Bob Boughner, Warren Rychel and Peter Dobrich.

Under their leadership, the Spitfires have produced talent such as NHL first round draft picks Greg Nemisz, Josh Bailey, Ryan Ellis, Cam Fowler, and Taylor Hall, who in 2010 joined Jovanovski as the only Spitfires to top the NHL draft when he was taken first overall by the Edmonton Oilers.

Playing out of the 6,500-seat WFCU Centre, which opened in 2008, Windsor has grown into the envy of major junior franchises, winning Memorial Cup titles in 2008-09, and 2009-10, just the seventh team to capture successive crowns.

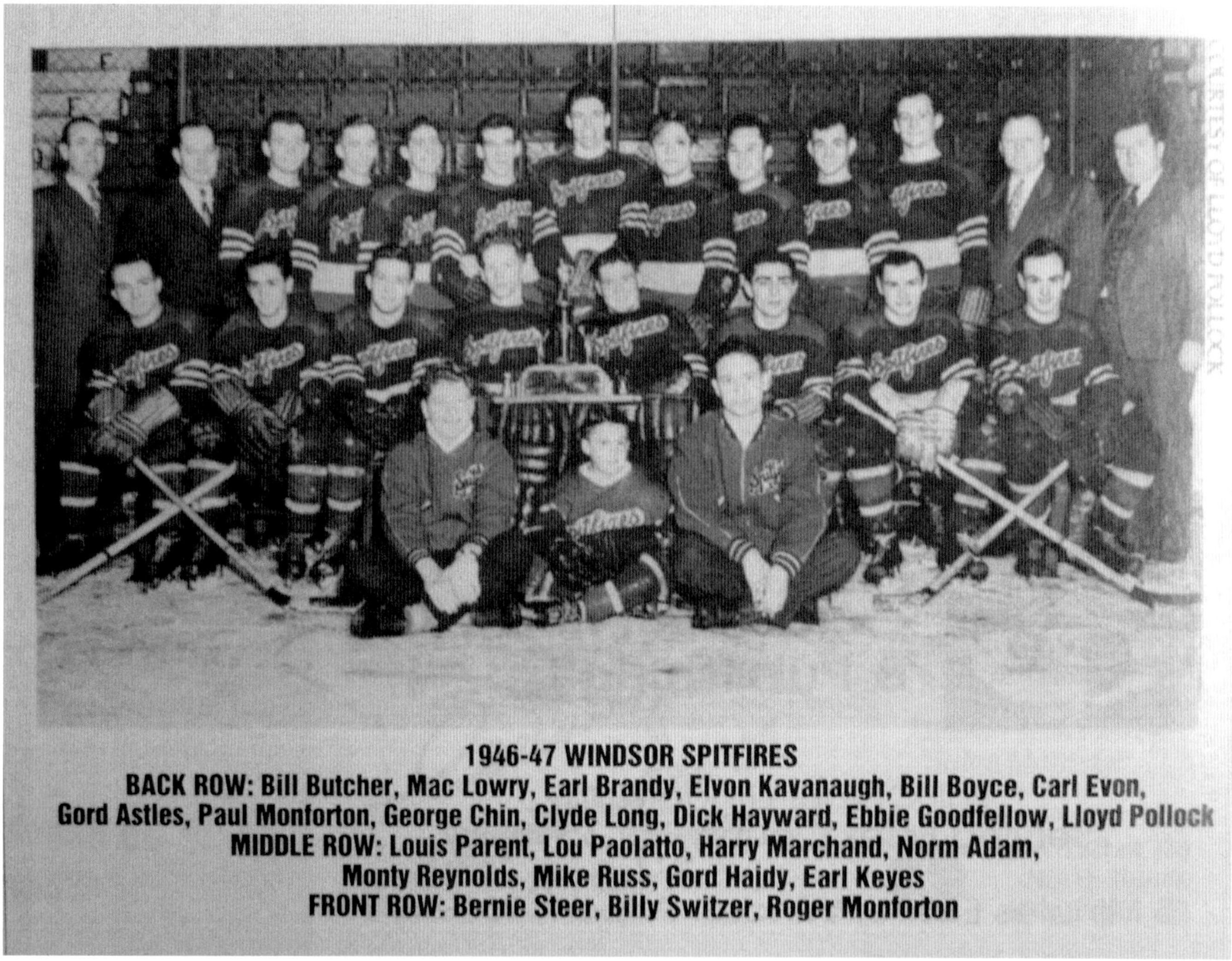

The original Spitfires team that competed in the OHA Junior A series during the 1946-47 season. (TTSA)

ONE

The Spitfires Take Flight

YOU COULD SAY THAT THE OPERATORS OF THE Windsor Spitfires were a cocky bunch.

On May 1, 1946, they called a press conference in Windsor, during which two items were on the agenda.

The first item of business: former National Hockey League star Ebbie Goodfellow, who played across the Detroit River for the Detroit Red Wings from 1929-43, was named coach of the Windsor Spitfires for the 1946-47 season. But the big news that day was where they intended the team to play: the Spitfires had applied to the Ontario Hockey Association to be granted Junior A classification.

Now, generally, this is how it works – first, you get a franchise. Then, you hire a coach. But the Spitfires, who'd been a strong, competitive entry in the OHA junior B ranks for several seasons, felt they were a lock to make the leap to the junior A ranks.

In fact, Spitfires general manager Lloyd Pollock felt the addition of a quality hockey man such as Goodfellow to the fold would only make the OHA's rubber stamp of approval easier to achieve.

"I think we are lucky to be able to get such a man," Pollock told the *Windsor Star* of Goodfellow, winner of the Hart Trophy as the NHL's Most Valuable Player during the 1939-40 season. "It became necessary to find a new pilot when (previous coach) Jack Dent, who, along with myself, started the Spitfires, resigned to take over the post of director of public relations for the Windsor Arena."

The two men had put the wheels in motion to seek a junior A franchise when Dent was offered his new position. "Dent and myself had already submitted an application for junior A ranking in the OHA before he resigned," Pollock explained. "Now, with Goodfellow at the helm, we are hoping to be able to give Windsor hockey fans the best teenaged-team they have ever had in these parts.

"To do this, we know that it will be necessary to add strength to the team we had last year. With this idea in mind, we are prepared to bring in several new players."

Up until this point, Windsor and area players seeking their fortunes in high-level hockey were forced to take their game elsewhere. Windsor-born goaltender Harvie Teno and defenceman Clarence Drouillard left town and won a Memorial Cup with the St. Michael's Majors in 1933-34.

The Spitfires were hoping to put junior hockey on the map in the Rose City, but were seeking special dispensation from the OHA in order to help ease the team's transition. "In seeking admittance to the junior A division of the OHA, we asked to be given a bye until the start of the playoffs," Pollock said. "However, we do hope to be able to book exhibition games throughout the season with such teams as (the) St. Michael's College Majors, Galt Red Wings, Oshawa, and the rest, so that the fans will be able to see for themselves how we stack up against the cream of the junior crop."

During the 1945-46 season the OHA Junior A Series consisted of eight teams – Toronto St. Michael's, Galt, the Oshawa Generals, St. Catharines Falcons, Toronto Marlboros, Toronto Young Rangers, Barrie Flyers, and Hamilton Lloyds.

New coach, Ebbie Goodfellow (centre) is shown discussing plans for next winter along with the team's former coach, Jack Dent (left) and team manager Lloyd Pollock (right). (WS)

If the OHA wanted Windsor as part of this fold, it was going to make the Spitfires stew through a hot, steamy summer before giving their answer.

"I had a devil of a time getting into the A league," Pollock recalled in a 1992 interview with the *Star*. "I made I don't know how many trips to Toronto to try and convince them. They thought Windsor was too far to come."

The league's answer finally came one September 8. "Junior A hockey, the big time of Canada's national amateur sport, will become a reality for Windsor fans this winter," Ken Johnson reported in the *Windsor Star*. "The Windsor Spitfires, (tentatively) granted admission to the junior A division of the Ontario Hockey Association last June, yesterday became a definite member of the 10-team provincial group."

The Stratford Kroehlers were awarded a franchise as well, keeping even numbers in the league. But while Windsor was in, Dent and Pollock didn't get everything they wanted. There would be no exhibition slate to allow Windsor an adjustment period. The Spitfires would be full-fledged members of the league, expected to partake in regular-season play, though because of the distance to Windsor the Spitfires were given an 18-game slate, while other teams played a 36-game season.

"The Spitfires will play each team in the circuit once around, each game counting for four points," Johnson explained. "The Spitfires will have nine home games (at Windsor Arena) and will make nine road trips. Tentative plans call for the schedule to begin around the first of November.

"The club will be built around the junior-age players left from last year's junior B entry and will be strengthened by a few imports."

Shot Down In Opener

Training camp opened for the expansion Spitfires in early October. They had just one problem and it was a major one. In those days prior to the entry draft, junior clubs were generally affiliated with National Hockey League teams, meaning players were often supplied to the club by their sponsoring NHL franchise.

The Spitfires had no NHL affiliation, meaning coach Ebbie Goodfellow and GM Lloyd Pollock were left to scrape together a squad on their own.

"We had about four guys from out of town and the rest of us were area kids," recalled defenceman Dick Hayward, an original Spitfire and one of those local players. Hayward was a product of the local minor-hockey system, playing the previous season for Dayus Roofing in the Windsor Juvenile League.

Hayward, goalie Monty Reynolds, defenceman Carl Evon and forwards Gord Haidy, Earl

Keyes, Harry Marchand and captain Paul Monforton were all Windsor boys. Brothers Stan and Leon Gaudreault came to the city from Quebec, while Elvon Kavanagh was from South Porcupine, Ont., George Chin from Lucknow, Ont., Clyde Long from Owen Sound and Gord Astles from London.

Of that bunch, Haidy, a member of the Windsor/Essex County Sports Hall of Fame, was the one who moved onto bigger things, eventually skating one game in the NHL with the Detroit Red Wings.

"I had played for the safety patrol team the year before," Haidy, who led the Spitfires with 23 goals and 30 points that season, recalled in a 1992 interview with the *Windsor Star*. "Our first year in the league was tough, but we knew what we were in for. Other teams were sponsored by NHL clubs and that meant they had 15 good hockey players.

"We didn't even have a trainer. Our trainer was the equipment man. He'd give you an aspirin and tell you you were all right. We played hurt. We played with separated shoulders. You couldn't afford to lose a guy."

Harry Marchand played for the Spitfires in the Windsor City League, IHL and OHA Junior A series. (MP)

The team they faced on opening night, Nov. 2, 1946 at Windsor Arena was none other than the Toronto St. Michael's Majors, Memorial Cup finalists the previous spring after winning the OHA Junior A Series regular-season title with a 26-2-0 slate. An affiliate club of the Toronto Maple Leafs, they were loaded with talent. They were coached by a former NHL legend, Joe Primeau, who centred the Leafs' famed Kid Line of the 1930s between Charlie Conacher and Harvey (Busher) Jackson.

"St. Mike's, nearly half of them turned pro after that season," Hayward said. "Just about every one of them went on to something."

Leonard (Red) Kelly, who'd later win eight Stanley Cups with the Wings and Leafs, was on the ice in a St. Mike's sweater that night. So was Fleming Mackell, a two-time Cup winner with the Leafs, and Ben Woit, a three-time Cup champ in Detroit. Les Costello won a Stanley Cup with Toronto before turning to the priesthood, and later founded the Flying Fathers, a team of hockey-playing priests who raised millions of dollars for charitable causes.

Ed Sandford, Ed Harrison, Rudy Migay, Ray Hannigan and John McLellan were other St. Mike's players who'd later make their mark on hockey's biggest stage.

The first sentence in the *Windsor Star*'s preview of the game said it all: "Coach Ebbie Goodfellow and manager Lloyd Pollock can only sit back and hope now."

But there was little reason to hold out hope.

It began innocently enough, a pair of McLellan goals spotting St. Mike's a 2-0 first-period advantage. The Majors upped their edge to 6-0 after two periods, then exploded for nine third-period goals and a stunning 15-0 shutout triumph.

Migay finished with a hat-trick and two helpers, while Mackell tallied twice and set up three other scores. Amazingly, Kelly, a Hockey Hall of Famer who enjoyed a 20-season NHL career with the Wings and Leafs, was limited to a solitary assist on the game's final goal.

Windsor Star reporter Ken Johnson succinctly summed up the night: "Recipe: Take 13 of the best teenaged hockey players you can find. Dress

Dick Hayward was a defenceman with the original Spitfires Junior A team in 1946-47. (Rich Hayward)

GM Lloyd Pollock (left) and coach Jimmy Skinner (right) talk strategy with Spitfires forward Bob Rawlyk in 1948. (WS)

them in blue uniforms. Play them against a band of youngsters inexperienced in Ontario's premier hockey league.

"The result: A 15-0 score."

Hayward saw no reason to expunge the memory of that night. Instead of the final score, he prefered to recall the thunderous ovation the Windsor Arena crowd of 4,062 gave the Spits as they took the ice.

"When we skated out that first time, the place was full," he said. "We had good crowds all the way through that season."

After an 0-5-1 start, the Spitfires finally found the win column thanks to a 28-save shutout performance by Reynolds in a 4-0 whitewash of the Stratford Kroehlers Dec. 14, 1946 at Windsor Arena. Mike Russ netted the first game-winning goal in franchise history.

Windsor finished that season 5-12-1, good enough for seventh place and to finish ahead of three other teams – St. Catharines, Hamilton and the Toronto Young Rangers.

"It was great," Hayward said. "I don't have any bad moments from it at all, just fond memories.

"It was something new. We were just kids from here and we were travelling all over. We even played at Maple Leaf Gardens."

Mr. Spitfire

Lloyd Pollock was often described as one of the greatest things that ever happened to Windsor athletics.

Pollock and Jack Dent were chiefly responsible for the existence of the Spitfires. Pollock obtained a franchise from the Ontario Hockey Association for a fee of $500, while Dent took care of outfitting the new club, purchasing uniforms for just $100.

"They were the ones who got local junior hockey started," Windsor sports historian Tony Techko said of Dent and Pollock in a 1993 interview with the *Windsor Star*.

Born July 26, 1909 in Pine River, Ont., Pollock worked for Canadian Pacific Railway, transferring to Windsor in the mid-1930s. Not long after that, he made his first foray into local hockey, serving as secretary-treasurer of the Windsor City Hockey League. A great planner and administrator, Pollock spent seven seasons as general manager of the Spitfires and developed a close friendship with Jack Adams, who was general manager of the Detroit Red Wings at the time.

That friendship eventually led the Red Wings to move their junior affiliation from Galt to Windsor in 1947.

After his Spitfire days, Pollock was elected president of the Ontario Hockey Association in

1961 and to the same post with the Canadian Amateur Hockey Association in 1968.

In 1983, Pollock was inducted into the Windsor/Essex County Sports Hall of Fame in the founders category. He died in 1993 at the age of 84.

Spitfires Legend: Gord Haidy

Gord Haidy led the 1946-47 Spitfires in scoring with 23 goals and 30 points, and later starred for the Windsor Bulldogs seniors.
(WS)

In an era when to reach the elite level of professional sport you were required to act like a child and speak only when spoken to, Gord Haidy was, to put it politely, a non-conformist.

"Haidy had everything going for him," recalled Detroit Red Wings legend Gordie Howe.

Everything except tact.

"(Detroit general manager) Jack Adams disliked people who smoked cigars and, you know, touched the alcoholic beverages," Howe explained. "Now we all would have a beer now and then. The only difference between Gord and a lot of the guys was that they'd do it where nobody would see them."

The man who was the first to play a starring role while wearing a Windsor Spitfires' sweater definitely walked to his own beat, a fact he later recognized held him back from reaching the heights of stardom in the NHL.

"He told me he missed a meeting to discuss a contract with Jack Adams and Adams was so furious he told my dad he'd never play in the NHL," Gord's son Marty Haidy explained. "Chicago wanted him, but the Wings wouldn't release him."

Haidy played one NHL game for the Detroit Red Wings – a 1950 Stanley Cup semifinal contest against the Toronto Maple Leafs. The following fall, he returned his contract offer unsigned, angering Adams. "We didn't hit it off, that's all," Haidy once explained to the *Windsor Star*, "I'm probably the one to blame. I was kind of a fiery little punk at the time and he was the boss."

Hall of Fame broadcaster Budd Lynch, who handled play-by-play for both the Spitfires and the Red Wings, recalled another unfortunate incident that may have affected Haidy's NHL opportunities.

"Jack had Haidy come up (from Indianapolis of the American Hockey League) for a game on a Sunday," Lynch said. "Haidy gets to the railway station in the afternoon and goes right to the Olympia."

When he arrived, Haidy realized he'd left something very important behind. He'd forgotten his skates in Indianapolis. Detroit trainer (Ross) Lefty Wilson fit Haidy for another pair, but when word got to Adams that Haidy had forgot his blades, the Detroit GM ordered coach Tommy Ivan to bench the rookie.

"Haidy sat on the bench, never got on the ice and afterwards, Jack handed him return railway tickets to Indianapolis," Lynch recalled. "There's a kid who could have made it, who should have made it."

On the ice, Haidy was a rugged right winger with soft hands and a hard head.

Haidy was the leading scorer for Windsor during the two seasons he played for the Spitfires and became the property of the Wings when they made the club a sponsored junior affiliate in 1947. Haidy played Junior B for the Spitfires and was the only player to stay with the club when the Spits moved to Junior A in 1946. He led the club in scoring with 23-7-30 totals during the 1946-47 campaign and netted a team-high 38 goals the following season.

(Left) Gord Haidy celebrates a Spitfires' win with several of his teammates. (MP)

(Right) Both Gord Haidy (right) and Wheatley's Glen Skov (left) played with the Spitfires and the Detroit Red Wings. (WS)

In 1948, he joined the Indianapolis Capitals of the AHL and won a league title with them a year later. Haidy also had minor-league stints with New Westminster and Buffalo before returning to Windsor to play with the Senior Bulldogs.

In a 1955 story about Haidy's season with the Bulldogs, *Windsor Star* sportswriter Jack Dulmage noted that, "Haidy's ways have clearly mellowed. He picked up only six misconducts."

Though his aggressive style in the field of play earned him professional offers from the Detroit Red Wings as well as several major-league baseball clubs, Haidy wasn't one to boast.

"My dad never talked much about himself," Marty Haidy said. "He'd tell stories, but they were usually about other guys he played with. I found out more about his playing days from people like (former Spitfires) Jimmy Skinner, Marcel Pronovost and Johnny Wilson. They spoke highly of him, which is something I'm proud of."

One such tale involved Haidy and Howe accepting invitations to the Detroit Tigers' training camp in the late 1940s. Adams would have none of it and told the pair to pack in the ball games or they'd never play hockey again.

On the diamond, he was equally dominant. Haidy earned pro offers from the Cincinnati Reds, Philadelphia Phillies, Pittsburgh Pirates and St. Louis Cardinals, but turned them all down for his first love, hockey.

"I figured I'd get more of a chance in hockey," Haidy said. "I was going right to the American Hockey League. In ball, you go down to one of those low minor leagues for a few hundred dollars a month. And in those days, a Canadian ballplayer had to be some kind of superstar to get a break."

Haidy's No. 11 sweater was made an honoured number by the Spitfires in 2005 and hangs from the rafters at the WFCU Centre. He died in 2004 at the age of 76.

Gord Haidy Spitfires Stats

SEASON	GP	G	A	P	PIM
1946-47	15	23	7	30	15
1947-48	25	38	19	57	43

Getting Their Wings

The fortunes of the Spitfires took a 180-degree turn in the right direction June 13, 1947, when the Detroit Red Wings announced that they would sponsor the Spitfires as their OHA Junior A club beginning with the 1947-48 campaign.

One week earlier, the Wings had ended their sponsorship deal with the Galt Red Wings, the team they'd worked with the previous five seasons. Windsor made perfect sense as Detroit's top Ontario junior squad due to the proximity of the two border cities and the close relationship between Red Wings GM Jack Adams and Spitfire GM Lloyd Pollock.

"The support of the Detroit organization is expected to help both organizations considerably," wrote the *Windsor Star*.

The Spitfires would receive the assistance of the Detroit scouting staff in finding players, and in turn, the Wings could easily keeps tabs on these players.

In fact, Detroit GM Jack Adams assembled his own little empire of prospects in the Detroit-Windsor area. The Red Wings operated the six-team International Hockey League and a senior amateur loop with three clubs in Detroit – the Bright's Goodyears, Metal Mouldings and the Auto Club – as well as the Hettche Spitfires and Staffords in Windsor, and the Toledo Mercurys. Seeing a golden opportunity, Adams began using the IHL to further the development of young Red Wings prospects.

"Jack Adams was a pretty shrewd hockey man," remembered former NHL player and coach Johnny Wilson, a Detroit resident who played for the Spitfires in the OHA and IHL.

"What he did was take all of us who were playing junior with the Spitfires (in the OHA) and divide us up among the IHL teams. The guy you beat the crap out of one night would be your best buddy the next night. We sometimes played five games a week. The year we won it all (with the 1948-49 Hettche Spitfires in the IHL), we must have played a hundred games."

Things also improved immensely for the junior Spitfires through their association with the Wings. Jimmy Skinner came in to coach Windsor, whose roster blossomed to include future NHLers like Jim (Red Eye) Hay, Gord Haidy, Doug McKay, and the Wilson brothers, Larry and John. They finished first overall during the 1947-48 regular season.

A high-powered offence that produced a league-high 231 goals was paced by second-year Spitfire Haidy's 38 goals.

Larry Wilson formed a potent Spitfires forward unit in 1948-49 along with his brother Johnny and Bob Rawlyk. (MP)

Johnny Wilson scored 54 goals in two seasons as a Spitfire. (MP)

Brothers Larry and Johnny Wilson (9) celebrate a Spitfires goal against the Toronto St. Michael's Majors. (MP)

Johnny (9) and Larry Wilson (10) tussle along the boards in an IHL game with the Windsor Hettche Spitfires. (MP)

Windsor's Wilsons

For years, the picture occupied a place of honour on the west wall of Windsor Arena near centre ice, not far from the main doors to the rink.

Larry Wilson posed proudly in his Windsor Spitfire uniform, flanked on one side by his brother Johnny and on the other by Bob Rawlyk.

Larry and his brother Johnny were Spitfire teammates from 1947-49 before both went on to play and later coach in the NHL. Larry's Windsor-born son Ron is currently coach of the Toronto Maple Leafs.

Johnny, a left winger, was fourth on the club in goals (23) and points (51) and third in assists (28) that first season. The following campaign, Larry, a centre, emerged as an offensive force, finishing third in club scoring with 23-38-61 totals. Johnny was fifth on the team with 51 points, including 31 goals. They formed a potent scoring line along with Rawlyk, and eventually, their family came to call Windsor home.

"When we came to Windsor to play junior, the first time my dad came to visit, he absolutely loved the city," Johnny Wilson said. "He decided they were going to move away from Shawinigan Falls, Quebec.

"He got a job at General Motors and we moved to Windsor."

Ted and Caroline Wilson purchased a home on Lincoln Road, not far from Ottawa Street.

Larry Wilson died in 1979. Johnny Wilson, 81, makes his home in the Detroit suburbs.

Many Wilson family members remain in the Windsor area. "We had a lot of family here, so we were always coming back to visit relatives," Ron Wilson said.

Every so often, Ron Wilson returns to town and takes a ride down memory lane.

"I'm a sentimental sort, kind of a Field of Dreams guy," he said. "Every couple of years, I like to come back and just drive around the area, looking for old street names, recalling old memories."

Marching To The Finals

Atop the standings, Windsor entered the 1947-48 playoffs as favourites, so it wasn't any surprise at all when the second-year Spitfires found themselves in the final facing the third-place Barrie Flyers for the OHA Jr. A title.

But it wasn't to be for Windsor.

"With any championship team, you need the right people, the right chemistry and a few breaks," said Marcel Pronovost, a defenceman with the Spitfire team which lost the 1948 OHA Jr. A final series to the Flyers.

"We had the right people. The only ingredient we were missing was goaltending."

But it hadn't started out that way. At the beginning of the season a young 17-year-old phenom was between the pipes, the likes of which no one had ever before seen. Terry Sawchuck started the first three games and won them all. It looked as if he had the ability to carry the team to great heights, including, possibly, a Memorial Cup.

Then, it happened.

On Nov. 2, 1947, Spitfire coach Jimmy Skinner received a call from Detroit Red Wings GM Jack Adams, informing him that Harvey Jessiman, goalie for Detroit's USHL farm club in Omaha, Nebraska., had been sold to Philadelphia of the AHL and his spot in Omaha would be filled by Sawchuk, who won the AHL's rookie award that year.

"If we keep Terry, we go all the way," Pronovost said, shaking his head, as he thought about what might have been. "At the end of the year, what let us down was our goaltending."

Spitfires coach Jimmy Skinner also remembered the devastation of that call, but it was a call he knew would come sooner rather than later, almost from the first moment he saw Sawchuk between the posts.

"A few games into the season, Jack Adams calls me and says 'I've got some bad news Jim, we've got to move Sawchuk to Omaha,'" Skinner recalled. "I wasn't surprised, though, because I figured he should have been there in the first place.

"He was only 17, but even then, he was outstanding."

Terry Sawchuk won all three of his starts in the Spitfires goal in 1947-48 before the Detroit Red Wings turned him pro. (WS)

Sawchuk would go on to an NHL career that produced 103 shutouts, four Stanley Cups and a trio of Vezina Trophies en route to a Hockey Hall of Fame induction.

The first time Pronovost met Sawchuk that fall in Windsor, there was no indication of the enduring friendship that would develop between the two men.

"He was aloof and distant," Pronovost recalled of that original meeting with Sawchuk.

He was also the best goalie the Spitfires had ever seen.

"Reflexes, angles – he had it all and he also had a lot of guts," Skinner said. "He was fearless in the net and extremely confident.

"He'd always say to the guys, 'Get me a couple and we'll win.' And he meant it. He didn't say it in a bragging kind of way. He was just that confident."

Gord Buckley and Ivan Walmsley attempted to fill the void left by Sawchuk's departure. Walmsley got the call in the playoffs, going 6-6 and posting an unimpressive 4.16 GAA.

Despite the disadvantage between the pipes, Windsor still opened a quick 2-0 lead against Barrie. Then the Flyers stormed back, thanks to some great goaltending from future Toronto Maple Leaf Gil Mayer, who posted two shutouts as Barrie won the next four games to take the series.

After leaving the Spitfires, Terry Sawchuk won the Calder Trophy as the NHL's top rookie in 1950-51. (WS)

Pronovost indicated that the five Stanley Cups he won in a Hall of Fame 20-year career with Detroit and Toronto never made up for the lost shot at the Memorial Cup.

"In junior, you don't have that much time to win it," he said. "That makes it special."

Spitfires Legend: Marcel Pronovost

Marcel Pronovost still remembers the stark jolt he received upon walking through the doors of ancient Windsor Arena for the first time.

"The shortness of the ice and the high boards really caught my attention," Pronovost said. "And how old the building was."

A native of Lac-de-Tortue, Que., Pronovost first came to the City of Roses in 1947 as a 17-year-old hopeful. "I was supposed to go to Galt, which was where Detroit's junior farm club was then," Pronovost said. "At the last minute, Lloyd Pollock and the Butcher brothers got the club moved to Windsor."

Pronovost, freshly signed to the standard C-form National Hockey League contract by the Detroit Red Wings, arrived from his Quebec home to play defence for the Windsor Spitfires, the Detroit-sponsored club in the Ontario Hockey Association's junior A series.

"I came out of Shawinigan, in a building that was built in 1937, so it was quite new," Pronovost said. "I was a little bit spoiled."

Little did he know at the time that Windsor would come to play such a significant role in his life.

More than 60 years later, Pronovost has witnessed plenty of hockey, much of it in Windsor.

"It's provided me with a good living," Pronovost says modestly of the game he so loves.

Not to mention a litany of honours and achievements that place Pronovost alongside the all-time greats of the game.

The Windsor resident won five Stanley Cups as a player – four with Detroit and one with the Toronto Maple Leafs. Four times he was named an NHL All-Star and he played in the league's

Marcel Pronovost (centre) enjoys a sunny day with the Wilson brothers Larry (left) and Johnny (right). All three came to Windsor from Shawinigan Falls, Quebec. (MP)

Top: Coach Jimmy Skinner instructs three of his players – Johnny Wilson (left), Larry Wilson (centre) and Marcel Pronovost. (MP)

Bottom: Spitfires Francis O'Grady (left), Marcel Pronovost (centre) and George Ouellette (right) work the boards at Windsor Arena. (MP)

all-star game 11 times. In 1978, Pronovost was inducted into the Hockey Hall of Fame.

"The best years, really, have been since I've joined the New Jersey Devils," said Pronovost, who's been part of the club's scouting staff for Stanley Cup wins in 1995, 2000 and 2003. "Working with (Devils GM) Lou Lamoriello, it's so enjoyable. He's such a competent man and he's very loyal to his employees."

The job has also permitted him to remain in Windsor, which Pronovost views as his adopted hometown. "Most of my life has been spent in Windsor," Pronovost said. "I think the town you play junior in always kind of becomes your second home. You're taken in by a family and treated like one of their own and the whole town gets to know who you are.

"Windsor is a blue-collar town and the town I'm from is also a blue-collar town. I guess that's why I've always felt at home in Windsor."

As a Red Wings player from 1949-65, Pronovost ultimately called Windsor home, wanting his children to be educated in Canada. "We settled into Windsor in 1953," he said.

A 1965 trade to the Leafs moved him from Windsor for a time. Pronovost returned to the city when named coach of the Wings during the 1979-80 season. He later coached the Spitfires from 1981-83.

You'll usually still find him in the arena at Spitfires games, hard at work within the game he loves so much.

The Spitfires honoured Pronovost in 2005 by hanging his No. 4 from the rafters.

Marcel Pronovost Spitfires Stats

SEASON	GP	G	A	P	PIM
1947-48	33	6	18	24	61
1948-49	42	14	21	35	135

Spitfires coach Jimmy Skinner holds a game-winning puck amidst his players. To his immediate left is future Hall of Fame coach Al Arbour. (WS)

Wings Edge Spitfires

Today, such contests would be considered foolhardy. Back in the day, they were commonplace.

Exhibition games between National Hockey League teams and their junior affiliates, that is.

The Detroit Red Wings often crossed the border to Windsor Arena for a mid-season showdown with the Windsor Spitfires, at the time among Detroit-sponsored clubs in the era prior to the invocation of the amateur draft.

One such night was Feb. 19, 1949.

The reason for these games was twofold. First, they served as better tune-ups than practices during the NHL's six-team era, when week-long gaps between regular-season games weren't uncommon. Secondly, they generally benefited charitable causes.

The Windsor Junior Hockey League was the benefactor as the Wings arrived in town on this occasion and $1,300 was raised via gate receipts produced by the crowd of 2,170.

The Wings, who were in first place in the NHL, showed up armed to the hilt. Harry Lumley started in goal, while (Black) Jack Stewart, Red Kelly and Bill Quackenbush patrolled the blue-line. The forward unit that opened the game was Detroit's vaunted Production Line of Sid Abel, Gordie Howe and Ted Lindsay.

In an effort to even matters out, the Wings loaned defenceman Lee Fogolin Sr. and centre George Gee to the Spitfires, and it seemed to help when Marcel Pronovost set the pro-Spitfires crowd abuzz, burying the rebound of a Larry Wilson shot to put Windsor in front at 7:37 of the opening frame.

Before the period was over though, Howe tallied twice and the Wings carried a 2-1 advantage to the dressing room.

When Howe completed his hat-trick in the second period, it appeared as if the Wings might be on their way to a rout. But John Taylor pulled one back for Windsor to narrow the margin to 3-2 after 40 minutes.

Abel and Bud Poile scored quickly in the third period to make it 5-2 Detroit, but if people thought the game was over, they were wrong. Johnny Wilson narrowed the gap to 5-3, beating

Detroit back-up goalie Jim Shirley on a penalty shot.

Within three minutes, the Spitfires had tied the score on goals by Gee and Johnny Wilson. Finally, with 5:45 left in the game, Abel dented the twine for the game-winner, allowing the Wings to escape with a hard-fought 6-5 decision.

Afterwards, both coaches expressed satisfaction with the exercise.

"This was as good a workout as we've had in a long time," Detroit coach Tommy Ivan said.

Mr. Skinner

He is perhaps best remembered for the sloppy kiss that he planted on the Stanley Cup as rookie coach of the Detroit Red Wings in the spring of 1955. But Jimmy Skinner cut his coaching teeth behind the bench of the Spitfires.

A teacher at heart, it was those days working with prospects that he embraced most fondly.

"I've had so many thrills in hockey, but I'm proudest of seeing 27 or 28 of the kids I coached make it into pro hockey," said Skinner, who called Windsor home for 62 years.

"That's the most important thing I ever did in hockey."

A native of Selkirk, Man., Skinner coached the Wings from 1954-58, then served as chief scout, director of Detroit's farm system and GM until his 1982 retirement. Skinner's hockey career started as a Junior A player in Winnipeg and he later player senior A with Flin Flon.

"I played games for Flin Flon and then worked in the mines for 56 cents an hour," Skinner recalled in an interview with the *Windsor Star*. "Players would take any job to play hockey then."

Skinner turned pro with Detroit, playing in the Wings' farm system for Omaha and Indianapolis. His leadership skills became apparent, and he captained both teams, and Wings general manager Jack Adams also saw qualities in Skinner that led him into coaching. He put Skinner in charge of the Spitfires when they became a Detroit-sponsored junior club in 1947.

Hall of Fame broadcaster Budd Lynch, who handled Spitfires play-by-play duties during

Jimmy Skinner coached the Spitfires to the 1948 and 1950 OHA Junior A finals, and led Detroit to a Stanley Cup in 1955. (WS)

Skinner's tenure, remembered the competitive side of Skinner.

"I remember we did a game in Barrie . . . and our broadcasting location was a crossbeam over the ice," Lynch noted in his autobiography, *My Life: From Normandy to Hockeytown*. "There's this skirmish by the Spitfires bench. I remember saying, 'I think there's two gendarmes in this whole place, and one of them is over by (Windsor coach) Jimmy Skinner and he's about to discover that Skinner is a lefthander.'"

Skinner guided the club's fortunes until the 1953 move of the team to Hamilton, leading Windsor to a pair of first-place finishes and two league final appearances.

"Hockey has been good to me," Skinner said shortly before his 2007 death at the age of 90. "I've met a lot of nice people and they don't forget you."

Skinner was inducted into the Windsor/Essex County Sports Hall of Fame in 2006. He is also a member of the Detroit Red Wings Hall of Fame, the Flin Flon Hockey Hall of Fame and the Manitoba Hockey Hall of Fame.

(Above Left) Goalie Ivan Walmsley, and forwards George Ouellette and Bruce Giesebrecht defend the Spitfires' goal during a game from the 1947-48 season. (MP)

(Above Right) Doug McKay played in the 1948 OHA Junior A final with Windsor and the 1950 Stanley Cup final with Detroit. (MP)

Brotherly Battle

Teammates battling for a league scoring crown isn't all that unusual.

Teammates who are also brothers scrapping for a scoring title is a little bit more out of the ordinary. But this is exactly what unfolded at Windsor Arena during the 1948-49 Ontario Hockey Association Junior A season.

Not since Doug (1942-43) and Max (1945-46, 1946-47) Bentley shared three NHL scoring titles with the Chicago Blackhawks had hockey seen a sibling rivalry like the duel between Windsor Spitfires forwards Bert and Bruce Giesebrecht.

"Bert and Bruce Giesebrecht, the Petawawa (Ont.) lads have been in the forefront of scoring operations since the start of the 1948-49 season and at this stage are so far ahead of the rest of the pack, it seems only a question of which of the pair will cop the silverware," noted Jack Dulmage in the Jan. 29, 1949 edition of the *Windsor Star.*

All season long, they were neck and neck among the scoring leaders, and as the season drew near its close it became apparent that not only would one of them wear the crown, but it would also be a record-setting performance.

On Jan. 29, Bert stood atop the race with 38-41-79 totals, followed closely by Bruce with 15-41-76 numbers.

Both were poised to surpass the previous league single-season standard of 82 points established by Fleming Mackell of the Toronto St. Michael's Majors in 1946-47.

The Spitfires travelled to Toronto Jan. 30 for a date with the Marlboros and Bert garnered a goal and an assist in a 6-5 win to move within a point of Mackell's mark. On Feb. 2, during a 6-2 triumph over the Barrie Flyers at Windsor Arena, Bert set up a goal by Bruce and he'd equalled the league single-season points standard.

Next up was a Feb. 5 home date with the Galt Rockets and an appointment with history.

There were 3,100 on hand at Windsor Arena and although Doug McKay's four-goal night paced the way to a 12-3 drubbing of the Rockets, all eyes were on the Giesebrechts.

Bruce did the early scoring, setting up a goal by McKay and tallying another himself. Both brothers were held off the scoresheet during the second frame, but 2:32 into the final period, Bert took a feed from McKay and whipped a shot past Galt goalie Slim Sommerville for his record 83rd point.

Windsor would go on to clinch top spot in the league for the second season in succession.

The 1947-48 club was the first Spitfires team to play for the OHA Junior A title.

FRONT ROW: Walter (Gunzo) Humeniuk; Ivan Walmsley; Gord Haidy; John Taylor; Jim Uniac; Gord Buckley.

MIDDLE ROW: Mac Lowry, Bill Butcher; Larry Wilson; Johnny Wilson; Doug McKay; George Ouellette; Lloyd Pollock; Jimmy Skinner.

BACK ROW: Cameron Church; Bruce Giesebrecht; Max Quackenbush; Bert Giesebrecht; Skip Frezell; Jim Hay; Marcel Pronovost. (MP)

Bert Giesebrecht finished the season with a league-record 93 points. Bert's 47 goals were a league-leading number as well, while Bruce Giesebrecht's final totals of 42-47-89 also surpassed the previous league standard.

Bert Giesebrecht became the first Spitfire to wear an OHA Jr. A scoring crown, but his hold on the mark was short-lived. The following season, Earl (Dutch) Reibel of the Spitfires collected a league-record 53 goals and 129 points.

Dutch Master

Reibel had already surpassed Giesebrecht's total with an assist in a Jan. 25 game and was setting sights on the magical 100-point plateau.

There were 5,200 fans on hand at Windsor Arena Feb. 8 as the Spitfires took the ice to face the Guelph Mad Hatters. As much as they were also there to see Reibel's shot at history, another subplot to the night was that the Spitfires had gone unbeaten on home ice since they lost 6-2 to the same Mad Hatters on Dec. 14, 1949.

The night didn't start out as one of promise. Guelph's Gerry Theberge and Ron Plumb scored during the game's first 5:55 of play to grab an early 2-0 advantage. From there, though, Windsor goalie Glenn Hall shut the door, blocking 31 shots and the Spitfires went to the attack.

The line of Glen Skov, Reibel and Eddie Stankiewicz had been the league's most dominant trio all year long and this game would be no different. Irwin Gross cut Guelph's lead in half before the period ended and then Skov, Reibel and Stankiewicz took control in the second frame.

Skov tied the game, then John Bailey made it 3-2 Windsor, with Reibel assisting on both goals to reach 99 points for the season. Then Reibel took a feed from Gross and lifted a 20-foot backhander past Guelph goalie Dennis Mooney at 14:10 of the period and attained the century mark. Skov scored twice more to complete his seventh hat-trick of the season and Windsor skated off the ice 6-2 winners.

The Reibel-Stankiewicz-Skov trio finished the game with eight points. While Reibel was the first to get there, for the season, all three would reach the 100-point plateau, ,with both Skov and Stankiewicz collecting 102 points.

Reibel finished the season with the scoring title and 129 points, but his hold on the record didn't last long. Guelph's Ken Laufman garnered 139 points during the 1951-52 season.

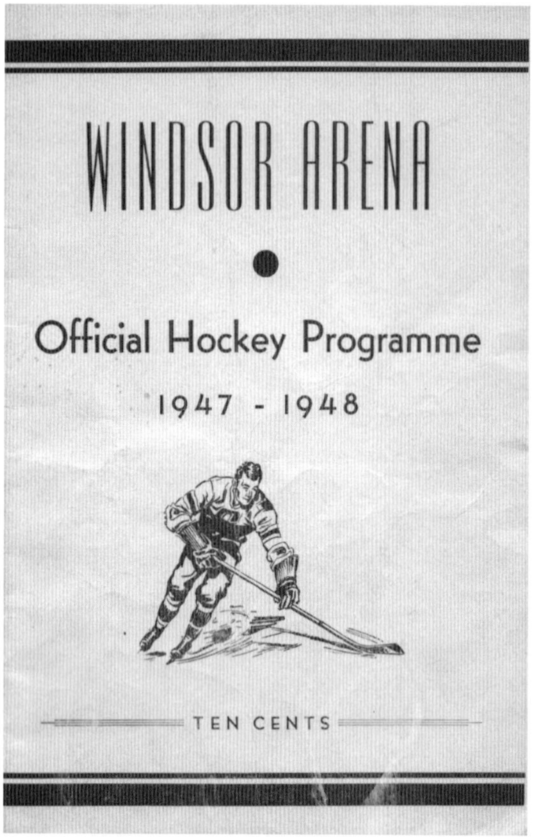

Windsor Arena program, 1948. (MP)

Crouch with 72 shots. Stankiewicz added another pair of goals in the final frame, while Reibel gathered two more helpers.

That left Stankiewicz with a seven-goal, eight-point game and 50 goals for the season, while Reibel produced a 10-point night that virtually assured him of the OHA Jr. A scoring crown.

Entering the game, Reibel, who'd collected a solitary assist in Windsor's previous game against Stratford, sat at 114 points, one ahead of George Armstrong of the Toronto Marlboros. Armstrong had enjoyed a seven-point performance in the Marlies' 9-4 victory over Barrie earlier in the day.

Lost in the impressive performances by Stankiewicz and Reibel was a big night for linemate Glen Skov, who garnered three goals and three assists. It was his eighth hat-trick of the season.

In total, the trio accounted for 24 of Windsor's 31 scoring points in the game.

Stanky's Seven Spot

The Ontario Hockey Association Junior A series playoffs were a scant week away when the Windsor Spitfires played host to the Oshawa Generals before 3,200 the night of Feb. 18, 1950, in what in terms of the standings was a meaningless game.

That didn't stop the Spitfires from putting on an unforgettable show.

It started just 1:11 into the game when Eddie Stankiewicz slammed the rebound of an Earl (Dutch) Reibel shot past Generals goalie Jack Crouch, launching both Windsor players toward record-setting nights.

By the end of the opening period it was 4-1 Windsor, Stankiewicz potting a second goal and Reibel collecting a goal and two more assists.

Early in the second period, Oshawa scored twice to narrow Windsor's margin to 4-3, but then the floodgates opened and the frame ended with Windsor in front 11-3. Stankiewicz buried three goals in this period, while Reibel was good for a goal and three assists.

Windsor completed a 14-6 victory, peppering

Another Finals Failure

Two years removed from their first title shot, in 1950, the Spitfires were back at it again, battling with the Guelph Biltmores for OHA Jr. A honours.

Again, Windsor was the favorite. Again, the Spitfires came up short.

"We had a great hockey club that year," recalled former NHLer Glen Skov, who captained that 1949-50 Spitfires team. "I thought we had a pretty good shot to win the Memorial Cup."

The Biltmores, led by Hall of Famer Andy Bathgate, downed an injury-riddled Windsor squad in six games.

Unlike the 1947-48 team, puckstopping wasn't an issue. The Spitfires had goaltending, and plenty of it, in the form of future NHL great Glenn Hall. Hall backstopped the club to a second-place finish behind Toronto.

It wasn't easy, though. Early in the season, the OHA ruled Windsor had one too many import players on its roster, and wiped out all the club's wins, dropping them from second all the way to the basement.

Elmer Skov played for the Spitfires, as did his brothers Glen and Art. (WS)

"We went right back to zero points," Skov remembered. "But we fought our way back. And that helped get the fans behind us even more."

A powerful offence helped Windsor fight back, led by Earl (Dutch) Reibel, whose 129 points set a league scoring record. Reibel scored 53 times, as did Eddie Stankiewicz, who later was to become, albeit briefly, the coach of the reborn Spitfires in the 1970s. Skov chipped in with 52 goals.

Jim (Red Eye) Hay was the only leftover player from the 1947-48 squad. Jimmy Skinner remained behind the bench. Among his players was Vic Howe, Gordie's younger brother.

Guelph opened a 2-0 lead in the series on home ice, as Windsor was forced to play without Skov, forward Bob Bailey and defenceman Lloyd Hinchberger, all injured.

"We had to bring up other players from junior B," Skov said. Among the callups was a young defenceman named Al Arbour.

Windsor quickly struck back to win two on home ice, but were upset at home in Game Five. It was their first home-ice loss since December. Frank Bathgate, Andy's brother and a future Windsor Bulldog senior, scored in overtime to give Guelph a 3-2 win in Game Six and clinch the series.

Interleague Intrigue

The 1950 visit of the Montreal Jr. Canadiens as part of a crossover of exhibition games between junior clubs of Ontario and Quebec brought the defending Memorial Cup champions to Windsor Arena.

Since there was little interaction between junior leagues other than in the Memorial Cup playdowns, even an exhibition series such as this one had hockey fans curious to see how the rivals stacked up against each other.

Winners of the Canadian junior crown the previous spring, the junior Habs suited up some players who would become household names later in the decade as the parent Montreal Canadiens captured five consecutive Stanley Cups from 1956-60.

Leading the way was left-winger Dickie Moore. Later an NHL scoring champion, Moore led the Quebec Junior Amateur Hockey Association with 44-47-91 totals in 1949-50. Centre Don Marshall was another Baby Hab destined for a lengthy and successful NHL career, while a third member of the club's forward crew – Scotty Bowman – made his name working behind NHL benches. Montreal's coach was Sam Pollock, the man who later brought Bowman to Montreal to coach the Canadiens to five Stanley Cup titles between 1973-79.

The Spitfires who would oppose them weren't exactly slouches, having reached the Ontario Hockey Association Junior A final in 1949-50 before falling to Guelph in six games. In goal, they were backstopped by a future Hockey Hall of Famer in Glenn Hall. Playing in front of Hall were the likes of Al Arbour, John Muckler, Jim (Red Eye) Hay, Jim Anderson, Earl Johnson, Irwin Gross and Elmer Skov.

The three-game set opened Oct. 5 at Windsor Arena and was witnessed by a disappointing gathering of 1,500, but those who did show up were in for a treat, as the Spitfires humbled the Habs 4-1.

Glenn Hall won the Red Tilson Trophy as most outstanding player of the OHA Junior A series in 1950-51. (WS)

Outshooting the junior Canadiens by a 36-20 margin, Windsor grabbed the lead 1:27 into the contest on a goal by Gross. Ken Kiddie knotted the count on a Montreal powerplay and that's the way it ended after one period. Martin Zorica tallied the game winner early in the second period and Eddie Joss added a pair of third-period markers for Windsor.

The series shifted to Sarnia the next night and the Montrealers pulled even, gaining the measure of the Spitfires by a 2-1 count, setting the stage for the series decider back at the Barn.

The third game was a tense, defensive struggle witnessed by 1,400 and was scoreless through two frames. Just past the one-minute mark of the third period, Johnson gave Windsor the lead and before the stanza was eight minutes old, scores by Anderson and John Offidani upped Windsor's advantage to 3-0. Dave McCready broke Hall's shutout bid with nine minutes to play, but Windsor's 3-1 victory gave the Spitfires a solid decision over the Memorial Cup champs in the series and brought bragging rights to the OHA.

Spitfires Legend: Glenn Hall

He came to be known in hockey circles as Mr. Goalie during a hall of fame career, but during the 1950-51 Ontario Hockey Association Junior A season, Mr. Zero would have been a more appropriate handle for Spitfires goalie Glenn Hall.

Posting six shutouts that season, Hall established a club record that remains on the books to this day. He was especially stingy during the month of January, hanging up three goose eggs.

Hall already had two shutouts on his ledger for the campaign when the Toronto Marlboros came to Windsor Arena Jan. 3 to play the Spitfires. Before 3,500 fans, Hall turned aside 28 shots, 12 of the saves coming in the final frame. Meanwhile, the line of Jim Anderson, Irwin Gross and Elder Thomas handled the scoring, the latter two setting up Anderson for a pair of tallies in Windsor's 2-0 victory over the first-place Marlies.

Hall kept another clean sheet Jan. 21 as the Spitfires moved into a three-way tie for first place with the Marlboros and Barrie Flyers thanks to a 2-0 win over the Flyers before 4,900, the largest Windsor Arena crowd to see a Spits game so far during the season.

Hall was sensational, blocking 40 shots – 16 in the first period, 14 in the second and 10 in the third – while Gross scored once and set up the other goal by Thomas. "The 19-year-old wonder from Humboldt (Sask.) delivered one of his finest games," Jack Dulmage wrote in the *Star* of Hall.

"In Glenn Hall, the Windsor club has a goalie who has been the backbone of the club," added *Windsor Star* sports columnist Doug Vaughan. "For this corner's money, Hall is the best goaltender in the tough OHA loop this winter."

Three nights later, Hall was at it again, turning aside 27 shots as the Spitfires whitewashed the Stratford Kroehlers 6-0 before 2,500 at Windsor Arena. Hall's fifth shutout of the season moved Windsor back into a first-place tie with the Marlies.

Hall finished his compilation of zeroes on the road Feb. 13 with a 3-0 win at St. Catharines. He turned aside 35 shots, including one from the stick of Pierre Pilote – later Hall's teammate on a Stanley Cup winner in Chicago – that led to stitches in Hall's face. Following a 10-minute absence for repairs, Hall returned to the net and completed his shutout.

"The announcer at the game said that I was unconscious and carried off the ice, but that was never true," Hall growls, still bitter at this attempt to disparage his courage.

"I skated off on my own.

"I was kind of lucky, actually," Hall remembered. "The puck hit me right around the eye. I got one stitch in the eye, one in the side of the nose and a couple below the eye."

Combined with his 31-11-1 record, the six shutouts helped Hall become the first Spitfire to win the Red Tilson Award as the league's most outstanding player.

Looking back, Hall is puzzled that he'd be the one to hold the Spitfires shutout mark.

"The funny thing was, I didn't get that many shutouts," Hall said.

By the time he was done playing in 1971, Hall would become quite familiar with the digit, though.

His 84 career shutouts rank him fourth on the NHL's all-time list. An enshrinee in the Hockey Hall of Fame, Hall played in eight Stanley Cup finals, winning with Chicago in 1960-61, was selected to six NHL First All-Star Teams, won three Vezina Trophies and captured the Conn Smythe Trophy as Stanley Cup MVP in 1968. He is also the owner of one of sport's most unassailable records.

For 502 consecutive National Hockey League regular-season games, Hall stood in front of the Chicago Blackhawks net without relief.

Glenn Hall Spitfires Stats

SEASON	GPI	GA	SO	GAA	W-L-T
1949-50	43	152	0	3.41	31-11-1
1950-51	54	167	6	3.09	32-18-4

Glenn Hall. Windsor Spitfires' goalie, shows the trend in summer suiting. (WS)

The Three Coaches

Comedy provided the Three Stooges. Music gave us the Three Tenors.

During the 1951-52 season, the Windsor Spitfires suited up the Three Coaches.

Oh, they weren't coaches then, just three teenaged defencemen who dreamed of greatness in the NHL, and all of them would earn it behind an NHL bench.

Al Arbour was the veteran of the trio, in his third of four seasons with the Spitfires. John Muckler was in his second season as a Spitfire, and Don Cherry was a Windsor rookie.

In his four decades as a player and coach in the NHL, Arbour travelled down the road to the Stanley Cup final 13 times, winning eight – four each as player and coach.

Prior to taking the New York Islanders from expansion club to Cup winner, before he was the solid, steady, bespectacled defenceman who played with four different clubs (Detroit, Toronto, Chicago, St. Louis) in the Stanley Cup finals, Arbour was a Spitfire. "He was a tall, skinny kid back then," remembered Muckler, who coached the Edmonton Oilers to a trio of Stanley Cups. "At first, he was a forward."

Arbour made the move to the blue-line and it became apparent that this would become his home. "He turned blocking shots into an artform," Muckler said. "Al was one of the best at doing this."

The innovative style which he would later employ as a coach was present during his playing days. Arbour took to wearing football pants under his hockey uniform, to help absorb the blows from flying vulcanized rubber.

A Spitfire for 18 games during the 1951-52 season, Cherry, who coached Boston in two Stanley Cup finals before gaining icon status on Hockey Night In Canada's Coach's Corner, recollected that he lived with the Skovs at 1964 Francois Road.

"Mrs. Skov used to make us porridge every morning," Cherry said. "I loved Windsor. I had such a grand time, I had to borrow $25 from (GM Lloyd) Pollock for the train home."

Cherry, paired along the blue-line with Arbour, garnered three assists in 18 games and 30 penalty minutes, none of which were assessed for rendering someone unconscious the night Windsor goalie Dennis Riggin was injured.

"I was in the penalty box, as usual, and this lady came up to me and said, 'What happened to the young goalie?'" Cherry recalled. "I said, 'They think his back's broken,' and she fainted."

Turned out the lady was Riggin's aunt.

Hold Those Tigers

Off to an abysmal 3-18-2 start to the 1951-52 season, Spitfires coach Jimmy Skinner tendered his resignation on December 14, 1952. "I felt that my resignation would be in the best interests of the club and the fans," Skinner told Jack Dulmage of the *Windsor Star*. "The team hasn't been going well and there's been much criticism. It just seemed that the time had come for me to step aside."

Len Wilson, a member of the Spitfires board of directors, took over on an interim basis until Windsor-born former pro Mickey Drouillard, who'd played in the minor leagues with the Windsor Bulldogs, was named coach December 19, 1952.

The change behind the bench didn't help much, though. Windsor stumbled home 9-42-3, ninth in the ten-team league. Finishing behind the Spitfires were the Oshawa Generals, along with Windsor also an affiliate club of the NHL's Detroit Red Wings.

After years of success as part of the Wings' system, the Spitfires suddenly found the prospects cupboard to be bare, and there was speculation that Skinner's resignation was the first step in the break-up between the two franchises.

"We are intent only on the problems of the immediate future," Spitfires president Bill Butcher said. "As to next season, there has been no definite contemplation, but as of now, we are still connected with the parent Red Wings."

Windsor remained a Detroit satellite entering the 1952-53 OHA Junior A season, and Skinner returned to coach the team, but things didn't get much better. The Spitfires concluded a disappointing campaign by dropping a 6-5 home-ice decision to the Galt Black Hawks on March 1, 1953. Eighth in the standings at 16-35-5, it was the second straight season that the Spitfires had missed the playoffs.

Little did anyone know at the time that it would be another 22 years before a Windsor team would again be seen in junior A action.

On June 5, 1953, the *Windsor Star* reported that plans were in the works to relocate the Spitfires franchise to Hamilton. Windsor manager Lloyd Pollock applied for the transfer of the Spitfires franchise to Hamilton at an OHA meeting one day earlier, but the decision was postponed until July 16.

The day of reckoning came, and it brought bad news for Windsor. "The Ontario Hockey Association granted Hamilton a franchise to run a team in the Junior A League," the Canadian Press reported July 16, 1953. "Hamilton will replace the Windsor Spitfires in the nine-team loop."

The Hamilton team would be known as the Tiger Cubs and would assume Windsor's role as the OHA Junior A-sponsored club of the Detroit Red Wings.

Apparently, a disagreement between Detroit GM Jack Adams and Butcher, who was also owner of Windsor Arena, led to the death of Windsor's original junior A franchise.

Championship Bulldogs

FRONT ROW: Walter Pawlyshyn, Wayne Rutledge, Bill Mitchell, Bill Baksi, (General Manager), Lou Bendo (Captain), Harry Watson (Coach), Irwin Gross, Monty Reynolds, Joe Klukay.

CENTRE ROW: Jim Kimmerly (Assistant Manager), Norm Foster, Tom Micallef, Jean Marc Asselin, Jacques Begin, Tom Walker, Jerry Serviss, Bud Hillman, Jack Costello, Bobby Brown, Sam Fox (president of Windsor Arena).

BACK ROW: Kirk Scott (Assistant Trainer), Real Chevrefils, Bill Pring, Jim Josephson, Bill Mitchell (Trainer).

(TTSA)

Putting Bite in Bulldogs

In 1963 – a decade after the original Spitfires franchise left town for Hamilton – several of those old Spitfires teamed up to give Windsor a remarkable hockey achievement.

That spring, the Windsor Bulldogs downed the Winnipeg Maroons to earn the Allan Cup, symbolic of the senior hockey championship of Canada.

Right-winger Bobby Brown (1950-53), centre Irwin Gross (1949-51) and goaltender Monty Reynolds (1946-47) were all former Spitfires who helped the Bulldogs cop their national crown.

During the regular season, Brown led the team with 41 goals, while Gross was the leader in assists (69) and points (102). In Allan Cup play, Brown again topped the team with

15 goals, while Gross dished out a club-leading 25 helpers included among a team-best of 31 points.

Spitfires Legend: Irwin Gross

Irwin Gross played junior, senior and professional hockey for teams in Windsor. (WS)

Searching for a way to relay the magnificence of his former Windsor Bulldogs teammate Irwin Gross to an audience never privileged to have seen him play, Jack Costello drew upon a modern-day icon.

"He was a lot like Steve Yzerman," Costello said, "but without the fiery temperament."

Gross was the linchpin for the Bulldogs' 1963 Allan Cup team, someone who came to the city as a teenager to play for the Spitfires, making both a name and a home for himself.

That Bulldogs team included five former National Hockey League players. Joe Klukay won four Stanley Cups with the Toronto Maple Leafs. Real Chevrefils scored 31 times for the 1956-57 Boston Bruins.

Regardless, the club's leading scorer during that championship season was Gross, who accumulated an impressive 102 points in just 45 games and 31 more in 13 Allan Cup games.

Gross won four league scoring titles during his career, three of them with the Bulldogs.

Born in Melville, Sask., Gross launched his junior career with Humboldt of the Saskatchewan Junior League, winning his first scoring title with them in 1948-49.

He played two seasons for the Spitfires, collecting 42 goals and 87 points in 1949-50, then following up with team-leading 37-45-82 totals in 1950-51.

Jerry Serviss, another member of that championship Bulldogs squad, grew up in nearby Moose Jaw, and saw plenty of the young Gross in action.

"You look at the list of players who played in the leagues he was in – guys who went on to long careers in the NHL – yet he was the one on top of the points at the end of the season," Serviss said, noting it was likely Gross's lack of world-class speed that kept him from the NHL.

Detroit Red Wings general manager Jack Adams brought two players from that Humboldt team east to play junior for the Spitfires – Gross and a netminder by the name of Glenn Hall.

Gross also later played for the Bulldogs when the club joined the International Hockey League in 1963-64, meaning he represented Windsor in the junior, senior and professional ranks.

Playing for Shawinigan in the Quebec League, Gross was the only person besides Jean Beliveau to gain an MVP vote during the 1952-53 season.

Quebec coach Punch Imlach was so impressed with Gross that when the parent Montreal Canadiens brought Beliveau up to the big leagues for good the following fall, Imlach traded five players to Shawinigan to acquire Gross.

That spring, he helped the Aces capture the Edinborough Cup title as champions of minor-pro hockey, scoring the Cup-clinching goal against Hall, who was in goal for the Edmonton Flyers.

With that Windsor Allan Cup team, Gross played centre on the club's top forward unit between wingers Bobby Brown and Tom Walker.

"There was no line anywhere in senior hockey that could compare to them," Serviss said.

Gross's puck skills were what made the trio click.

"Tommy Walker and Bobby Brown were great players in their own right, but they benefitted greatly from Irwin's puck-moving and stickhandling skills," Costello said. "He had an uncanny ability to pass the puck and work his way out of trouble."

Blessed with movie-star good looks, Gross's wife Dawn was a former Miss Windsor whom he met while playing for the Spitfires. A centre of note, he never sought to be a centre of attention.

"He was always a team-first guy," Serviss recalled.

It's here where they most see the parallels to Yzerman.

"He would never brag about himself and I always thought that was a feather in his cap," Costello said. "And he was always having the guys over to his house to build camaraderie."

A scoring leader. And a leader of men.

The Wings had Stevie Y.

The Bulldogs, and the Spitfires, had Irwin G.

Irwin Gross Spitfires Stats

SEASON	GP	G	A	P	PIM
1949-50	48	42	45	87	53
1950-51	53	37	45	82	107

Spitfires Tidbits

Whistle Blower

Among those who played with the original Spitfires in 1946-47 was Art Skov, a junior B callup who debuted Jan. 20, 1947 in a 12-4 win at Hamilton. Skov made it to the NHL, working 1,023 games as an NHL official between 1956-75.

Ebb and Flow

Ebbie Goodfellow, first coach of the Spitfires, left his post shortly after the conclusion of Windsor's first season in March of 1947 to accept the head coaching position with the AHL's St. Louis Flyers.

Taking Flight

Tom McGrattan became the first Spitfires product to play in the NHL. He tended goal for the Detroit Red Wings Nov. 9, 1947, replacing the injured Harry Lumley in the third period of a 6-0 loss to the Toronto Maple Leafs. It was McGrattan's only NHL appearance.

The Other Brother

Vic Howe, a right-winger with the 1949-50 Spitfires, was the younger brother of Mr. Hockey himself, the one and only Gordie Howe.

Just Joss-ing

Centre Eddie Joss played with the Spitfires from 1949-51. He finished second in the club in scoring with 75 points in 1950-51. His grandson Terry Joss tended goal for the Spitfires from 1995-97.

Lions Den

Defenceman Al Arbour played in Windsor's last game of the 1952-53 season, then left directly for Washington, D.C. to suit up for the Eastern League's Lions, launching a pro playing career that lasted until 1971 and included 1,213 NHL games.

Fast Work

Spitfires GM Lloyd Pollock joined the OHA executive on June 3, 1953. The next day at league meetings, he proposed the move of the Spitfires franchise to Hamilton.

You Otter Know

The original Windsor Spitfires franchise remains part of the OHL. After moving to become the Hamilton Tiger Cubs in 1953, it later became the Hamilton Red Wings in 1960, the Hamilton Fincups in 1974, the St. Catharines Fincups in 1976, the Hamilton Fincups again in 1977, the Brantford Alexanders in 1978, the Hamilton Steelhawks in 1984, the Niagara Falls Thunder in 1988, and since 1996, has been the Erie Otters.

The Spitfires returned to major junior hockey in 1975 following a 22-year absence. (TTSA)

TWO

Rebirth of the Squadron

JUNIOR HOCKEY WAS A LONG TIME RETURNING to Windsor following the departure of the Spitfires to Hamilton in 1953. In 1971, the Spitfires were reborn as a Tier II junior club competing in the Southern Ontario Junior A Hockey League, and were a success, winning a league title under coach Wayne Maxner during the 1973-74 season.

Clearly, though, the city longed for what it once had – major junior hockey, the best of the best in the development ranks. "The fans in this city deserve it after the encouragement they've given us over the past four years," Spitfires owner Fred Sorrell told the *Windsor Star*.

Back in the Show

Windsor's wish finally came true February 10, 1975, when governors of the Ontario Hockey Association Major Junior A Series unanimously voted to award Windsor an expansion franchise.

Only one year earlier, a similar bid by Windsor co-owners Fred Sorrell, Brian Beach, Al McLaren and Cal Parent was rejected by the OHA, which was of the opinion that Windsor Arena was not up to snuff as a major junior facility. Dimensions of the rink's ice surface were 175 feet by 75 feet, and OHA minimum standards called for ice surfaces measuring 190x85.

"They offered no commitment last season that our standards could be met, so they were rejected," OHA commissioner Clarence (Tubby) Schmalz explained to the *Windsor Star*. "But this year, we feel they have the commitment, and that swung the vote in their favour.

"We felt their prior application placed them at the top of the list, and we felt on the whole, that we have an obligation to Windsor."

The clincher was a letter from Windsor Arena Ltd. president Lou Bendo. "He stated that he would do anything reasonable to see that a major A franchise could be located in this city," Beach said. "We certainly don't anticipate any problems meeting these standards.

"I feel the OHA must agree with this assessment of the situation, otherwise they wouldn't have accepted the application after turning it down last year."

Opening Night Jitters

The past was on hand to welcome the future, but it was the present that sent everyone home bitterly disappointed.

Windsor officially returned to major junior hockey Sept. 25, 1975, as the expansion Spitfires played host to the Oshawa Generals in the Ontario Hockey Association Junior A Series season opener at Windsor Arena.

There was cautious optimism around the city after the rookie-laden Spitfires rolled to a 9-1-1 mark in exhibition play. A crowd of 4,335 packed the Barn and to add to the festive atmosphere, many past stars from Windsor's previous stint in the league were on hand for the grand opening ceremonies.

Among the former Spitfires in attendance were Hockey Hall of Famer Marcel Pronovost, Gord Haidy, Ray Adam, Doug McKay, Ivan Walmsley, Dennis Riggin, Bruce Giesebrecht,

Windsor Spitfires, 1974-75

FRONT ROW: Gary Armstrong, Bill McCreary, Floyd St. Cyr, Jim Butcher (Coach), Doug Nowels, Hugh Mitchell (Captain), Scott Miller.

CENTRE ROW: Wally Tatomir (Trainer), John Riley, Mark Miller, Chuck Bosnyak, Yves Plouffe, Ian Campbell, Gerry McLean, Rod Beilhartz, Wayne Young, Ray Dugal.

THIRD ROW: Mike Sovie, John Tavella, Bruce Boyd, George Armstrong, Mark Smith, Randy Kozar, Colin Thompson. (WSHC)

Bobby Brown and Elmer Skov. Lou Bendo represented the alumni of the senior Windsor Bulldogs and former Detroit Red Wing Bill Gadsby also participated in the celebration. Other dignitaries present included president Cliffe Phillips, Hugh MacLean and Windsor's Harvie Teno, representing the OHA executive, and OHA Jr. A commissioner Clarence (Tubby) Schmalz.

When the puck dropped, the party soon ended. Oshawa took a bit of time to get its bearings, but once the Generals did, they steamrolled the Spitfires.

Future Toronto Maple Leaf Paul Gardner opened the scoring for Oshawa nine minutes into the game and by the 11:29 mark of the second period, the Generals had increased their advantage to 7-0.

At that point, Windsor coach Doug Johnston replaced starting goalie Wayne Mills with Bob Parent and that seemed to stem the tide. The Generals didn't score again until firing three more goals home in the game's final three minutes, recording a 10-1 shellacking of Windsor.

Rolly Hedges tallied the lone goal for the Spitfires.

Windsor Arena left its mark on the game as well. It was still scoreless in the opening frame when a pane of glass at the south end of the rink was jarred loose. Arena maintenance workers required 18 minutes to complete repairs before action resumed on the ice.

Afterwards, Johnston was suitably disconsolate, offering up a sense of foreboding of what was to come for the young Spits during the 1975-76 season.

"You get nights like that," he told the *Windsor Star*'s Marty Knack. "The worst thing is, Oshawa's not going to be one of the better clubs."

Miller Time

Scott Miller could best be described as the first superstar of the modern-era Spitfires. In fact, Miller's star shone with the club even before the Spitfires found their way back into the major-junior ranks, playing for the team for three seasons in the Southern Ontario Junior A Hockey League.

A Spitfire from 1972-76, Miller scored 117 goals in a Windsor uniform. He was named first captain of the team during that inaugural 1975-76 campaign, finishing the season with 24-34-58 totals in 56 games.

After his playing days, Miller moved into the family sporting goods business, and today still operates the shop in his hometown of Essex.

The Spitfires retired Miller's No. 23 sweater and each year, the team honours the player who shows the most determination and dedication with the Scott Miller Award.

Scott Miller was the captain when the Spitfires returned to the major junior ranks in 1975-76. (WSHC)

Charlie's Haul

Charlie Skjodt was a 19-year-old rookie Spitfires forward during the team's first season back in the OHA Junior A Series in 1975-76.

"I think I was a late-bloomer," Skjodt said. Drafted by Peterborough, Skjodt's offensive style didn't fit with Roger Neilson's plans.

"I was done," Skjodt said. "No one was going to take a 19-year-old and give me a chance."

The Spitfires proved willing to give him that chance and Skojdt, playing centre between Scott Miller and Ted Bonham, responded with a team-leading 41 goals, which stood as the club standard for rookies until Taylor Hall netted 45 goals in 2007-08.

"Windsor was always a second home to me," Skjodt said. "I'll always be thankful for the opportunity to play in Windsor, because otherwise I don't think I would have gotten a chance."

Drafted by the Toronto Maple Leafs in 1976, Skjodt never played in the NHL, but enjoyed a 10-season minor-pro career.

Spitfires Legend: Mark Renaud

Mark Renaud doesn't recollect that things were difficult for the expansion 1975-76 Windsor Spitfires. In fact, he views being an original member of his hometown junior team as a true honour.

"It was nice to be part of the first team, as much as we struggled," Renaud said. "There's a lot of fond memories. When I look back on it now, it means a great deal. You sort of don't have a handle on it when you go through it at the time."

Renaud was trying out for a junior B team when Spitfires general manager Doug Johnston invited him to the OHL expansion club's training camp as a walk-on. Only 16, he played all 66 games, putting up 3-15-18 numbers.

"It was a real struggle that year and I made the team because we weren't very strong," Renaud said. "We got beat 10-1 by Oshawa in our opener.

"It was exciting though because there was a real buzz about the team being back in the OHL. We drew huge crowds when teams like the Toronto Marlies came into town.

Mark Renaud was a Spitfires rookie in 1975-76, the club's first season back in major junior hockey. (WS)

"I loved getting a chance to play in my hometown for the Spitfires. They gave me an opportunity in hockey."

Renaud played just the one season in Windsor, moving to the Niagara Falls Flyers the following campaign. He went on to skate in 152 National Hockey League games with the Hartford Whalers and Buffalo Sabres, scoring six goals and 56 points.

His first NHL goal was registered against the Edmonton Oilers and goaltender Eddie Mio, a Windsor native who played for the Spitfires in Tier II junior. "I just turned and fired it at the net, didn't even look before shooting," Renaud said. "Someone collided with the goalie (Mio) and the puck slid into the wide-open net."

Though his NHL time was brief, Renaud was afforded the opportunity to team with some of the legends of the game. "My first year in Hartford, I got to play with Gordie Howe and his two sons (Mark and Marty)," Renaud said. "Dave Keon was also on that team and Bobby Hull was with the Whalers for a bit that season too. It was quite the roster. That was a great thrill.

"After I left Hartford for Buffalo, I got to play with Gilbert Perreault. He was just an incredible player. Just being able to say I played with those guys is pretty nice.

"I tell people I was a good American (Hockey) League player. I was a good skater and I could handle the puck, but I was small. Just getting the opportunity to play in the NHL, that was my greatest thrill."

That, and playing for his hometown team. "It was a tough year," Renaud said of that 1975-76 campaign. "It was so long ago, but I always feel like a Spitfire."

Renaud's son Mickey captained the Spitfires and was drafted by the Calgary Flames, but died of a heart ailment in 2008.

Mark Renaud was a 2009 inductee into the Windsor/Essex County Sports Hall of Fame.

Mark Renaud Spitfires Stats

SEASON	GP	G	A	P	PIM
1975-76	66	3	15	18	42

End of the Nightmare Start

Among the record-setting performances established over the years at Windsor Arena, this may be the one most people choose to forget.

When the Spitfires wrapped up the 1975-76 Ontario Hockey Association Junior A Series season, their inaugural campaign in the loop, they did so by fishing more pucks out of their net than any team in the history of the league.

The red light went on behind the Windsor net a total of 470 times, nine of those occasions coming during the final home game of the season, a 9-7 shootout with the Ottawa 67's March 11, 1976 before 2,315, which naturally saw the Spitfires finish up on the short end of the score.

Things were so bleak for the club that they utilized seven affiliate players in that final home game to fill in for injuries and suspended players. Meanwhile, trainer Wally Tatomir worked the bench in place of coach Wayne Maxner, who was off on a scouting mission to bolster the club's hopes for the 1976-77 season.

Maxner had only been named the coach a month earlier when Doug Johnston was let go, one of many moves the Spitfires made during an expansion campaign that saw Windsor post a dismal 12-50-4 record.

Wayne Maxner coached the Spitfires in a record 564 games. (WS)

Off the ice, there was speculation of losses in excess of $40,000 during that first season and even as the club took the ice for that final home game, there was talk of major changes.

The *Windsor Star* reported that Spitfires president Brian Beach was denying rumours that the club was about to be sold to a group headed by current co-owner Fred Sorrell and his two Wheels roller skating rink business associates, Chuck Faubert and Jaroslav L. Glos.

"I have nothing to say," said Sorrell, who owned the team along with Beach, Cal Parent and Al McLaren. "I am not going to contribute to rumours."

Change was also prevalent on the ice. Searching for answers, the club suited up no less than 44 players during the season. Only four of them – Charlie Skjodt, Guy Losier, Mark Renaud and Joel Quenneville – dressed for all 66 regular-season games.

Skojdt led the team in scoring with 41 goals and 89 points, while Losier was next with 28 goals and 77 points.

Windsor finished its season with road dates at Kingston and Peterborough. The Canadians hammered the Spitfires 9-1 at Kingston, Windsor getting its only goal from Gary Purdon. A 7-3 defeat followed the next night against the Petes. Quenneville tallied the final goal of Windsor's first season.

Fittingly, the loss was Windsor's 13th in a row, another ominous digit in a season that was filled with bad luck.

The Max Factor

Had he kept driving, who knows where he would have ended up?

It's a thought that Wayne Maxner often ponders in quiet moments.

He realizes what Windsor has meant to his life.

"Part of me is still there," Maxner said.

Maxner was a veteran professional player, with 62 games of National Hockey League experience for the Boston Bruins on his resumé, when he rumbled into Windsor the afternoon of Sept. 9, 1973, en route to training camp in Victoria, B.C. with the Los Angeles Kings.

The trip ended right there and another journey began.

On Aug. 29, Jerry Serviss stepped down as boss of the Southern Ontario Junior Hockey

Wayne Maxner served three separate stints behind the Windsor bench. (WS)

League club, accepting a position as coach of the International Hockey League's Flint Generals. On Sept. 8, the Spitfires announced that Eddie Stankiewicz, a prominent Spitfires player in the early 1950s, had accepted the position as coach.

Less than 48 hours later, citing personal reasons, Stankiewicz tendered his resignation, right about the time that Maxner rolled into town.

"I used to run a summer hockey school in Halifax," Maxner said. At the end of the clinic, he'd use his connections to garner invites to Ontario Hockey Association Junior A camps for a couple of his top protégés.

That year, Vic Whynott and Johnny Verran reported to the London Knights and coach Bill Long, Maxner's longtime friend. "One of the kids' dads, Harry Verran and I, we flew into Toronto and drove down to London," Maxner recalled. "London had a working agreement with Windsor at the time and when we got to London, Bill Long told us he'd sent the two kids to Windsor, so we just kept going down the highway."

Shortly after he arrived at the rink, someone asked if he was Wayne Maxner. Answering in the affirmative, he was quickly shuttled off to a private room for a meeting with team ownership. Later, he was taken to dinner.

"(The coaching offer) really caught me off guard," Maxner remembered. He took the Windsor job and a legend was born.

The Max factor.

Maxner guided the Spitfires to an SOJHL title that season. "I'll never forget that they told me the team was pretty much set," Maxner said. "We had two goaltenders, were set on defence and had a number of forwards returning.

"I didn't listen very well. I made 12 moves. Pretty soon, I had two new goaltenders, a couple of new defencemen and a few forwards and we were very fortunate to win the championship.

"That was a very exciting year." The performance earned Maxner a job with the Quebec Major Junior Hockey League's Hull Festivals. But no matter how often he left, some magical force kept pulling him back.

Maxner returned late in the 1975-76 season, Windsor's first in major junior and four seasons later, led the club to its first championship final. After a stint in charge of the Detroit Red Wings, he was back again in 1983-84.

His final run was as Spitfire coach/general manager from 1991-93. In total, Maxner sat behind the Spitfire bench for 564 games, more than any coach. Only Tom Webster (294) guided the club to more victories than Maxner (267).

"I still have a tape that someone at Channel 9 put together for me of my Spitfire years and I watch it all the time," Maxner said. "That's one tape that I'll never give up or lend. I met a lot of great people. I can still see Mrs. Freeman up there yelling on game night. I'll never forget my time in Windsor.

"I still keep in touch with a lot of people in Windsor. I remember interviewing Steve Horne (the Spits director of marketing) when we first hired him and he's still on the job." Vince Bassman, an OHL governor for the club during Steve Riolo's tenure as owner of the Spitfires, remains Maxner's accountant.

"A lot of positive things came out of my stay in Windsor," said Maxner, who's never lost sight of what that trip down the 401 meant to his hockey future.

Spitfires Legend: Brad Smith

Even though it was only a brief opportunity, Brad Smith has never forgotten what it meant to be an original Windsor Spitfire.

"It was a thrill to play for your hometown team, especially the first year back in Major A," Smith said. "You just wanted to be part of it, because it's your home. You grew up there playing minor hockey, you went to school there, you lived there.

"It was very exciting."

After Windsor was granted its franchise in the OHA Junior A Series, the team was permitted to protect a group of local midget-aged players to help build a nucleus. "The owners came in and at that time, they got to protect eight players from the area," Smith said.

"I remember a friend of mine called and said, 'I got a call. They protected me.' I thought my phone was going to ring, but it didn't ring until an hour later.

"I remember going to training camp. I worked hard all summer and I led the team in scoring (during scrimmages) and I was cut before the exhibition games. It was a frustrating thing, because I thought I did really well and had prepared myself."

Smith came up three times from junior B that season, producing 4-2-6 totals in four games before suffering a broken ankle that ended his season. "I remember I got called up, scored a goal and then got sent back to junior B," Smith said. "Then I called up about two weeks later and I scored three goals and an assist. I thought I was all set and after the game, I was sent back to junior B."

Smith made it for good the following season and during the 1976-77 campaign, led the Spitfires with 37 goals and 90 points. He was part of Windsor's first playoff series win over the Kitchener Rangers, which led to a second-round meeting with the defending Memorial Cup champion St. Catharines Fincups.

"I'll never forget playing in Game 6 at Windsor Arena," said Smith, who coached the Spitfires from 1989-90. "I was sitting on the bench looking around the rink and I couldn't see a single seat. They were sitting even in the stairways.

"I always tell people I was a Spitfire."

Brad Smith played for and later coached the Spitfires. (WS)

Selected in the fourth round of the NHL Amateur Draft by the Vancouver Canucks in 1978, Smith played 222 NHL games with the Canucks, Atlanta Flames, Detroit Red Wings and Toronto Maple Leafs, earning the nickname Motor City Smitty.

"I was very fortunate to play most of my career in Detroit and Toronto, close to home so my parents could see many of my games," said Smith, who finished with 28 goals and 62 points.

"It was such an honour to wear a Red Wings' jersey, growing up just across the river, and then to retire as a Maple Leaf. For a mediocre player, I had a great NHL career."

Elected to the Windsor/Essex County Sports Hall of Fame in 2009, today Smith works as director of player personnel for the Colorado Avalanche.

Brad Smith Spitfires Stats

SEASON	GP	G	A	P	PIM
1975-76	4	4	2	6	4
1976-77	66	37	53	90	154
1977-78	20	18	16	34	39

Brief Appearance

En route to greatness, Tecumseh's Tim Kerr's first taste of big-time junior hockey came in a 1976-77 fling with the Spitfires. Kerr played Jr. B hockey for the Windsor Royals and moved up to the Spitfires as a midget-aged player. In nine games, he fired two goals and had four assists.

"He was a dominant player, a big kid, much bigger than other kids in Junior B," said Jim Peck, Kerr's coach with the Royals. "He wasn't outstanding as far as being a really big scorer in those days."

Brad Smith was a teammate of Kerr that year and an opponent on other occasions in both the OHL and NHL. "One time, we played in Kitchener and won 5-2," Smith said. "Timmy got two goals and one assist and you could see right there that one day he was going to be a great player."

Kerr was selected by Kingston in the midget draft in 1977 and scored 71 goals in three seasons with the Canadians. However, he went unclaimed in the NHL entry draft and Philadelphia signed him to a free-agent contract in October, 1979.

The knock against Kerr at the time was that he was a great scorer, but a bad skater. Kerr worked hard to improve his skating ability and it paid dividends. Kerr scored at least 50 goals each season from 1983-87, making him just the fourth NHL player to do so. In the process, he established a reputation as one of the game's toughest players. You could hit him with a stick, punch him in the face, but you weren't going to move him from the slot.

"He's the perfect example of what you can accomplish by working hard," Smith said. "He worked for what he wanted and secured that so-called pot of gold at the end of the rainbow."

1977-78 OHL All-Star Game

There were 3,361 in attendance at Windsor Arena the night of Feb. 8, 1978 to watch Wayne Gretzky and the Leyden Division take on the Emms Division in the Ontario Major Junior Hockey League's All-Star Game, but it was a future 700-goal scorer in the National Hockey League who stole the spotlight.

Playing on a line with Spitfires left-winger Gerry Leroux and Toronto Marlboros centre Gary Dillon, Mike Gartner of the Niagara Falls Flyers scored two goals – one of them short-handed – and collected an assist as the Emms Division edged the Leyden Division 6-4 in the Ontario Major Junior Hockey League All-Star Game.

"I don't have as much talent as the other guys, but I work hard," claimed Gartner, who enjoyed a Hockey Hall of Fame career that saw him pot 708 goals.

Gartner was named outstanding player for the Emms Division, but it was Spitfires captain Joel Quenneville who registered the game-winning goal. Serving as captain of the Emms squad, Quenneville, who partnered on defence with future Detroit Red Wing Willie Huber of the Hamilton Fincups, scored on a low slapshot from a faceoff to snap a 4-4 tie at 5:17 of the third period.

"The harder you shoot, the more breaks you are going to get," Quenneville said.

It looked as if the Emms would run away with the game when they fashioned a 3-0 first-period lead on goals from Hamilton's Jay Johnston, Gartner and Dino Ciccarelli of the London Knights. Interestingly, it was the first goal scored all season by Fincups blue-liner Johnston.

Meanwhile, London goalie Pat Riggin, son of former Spitfires goalie Dennis Riggin, completely closed the door during his 20 minutes of work, but the Leyden squad woke up in the second period. Former Spitfires draft pick Jim Fox of the Ottawa 67s, Keith Acton of the Peterborough Petes and Mike Pidgeon of the Oshawa Generals scored to get them back in the game and only a goal by Leroux kept the Emms ahead heading into the final frame.

Just 1:16 into the final frame, Gretzky of the Sault Ste. Marie Greyhounds scored on a long slapshot to tie the count at 4-4, setting the stage for Quenneville's heroics.

"We played well in the first and third periods," Quenneville said. "(Spitfires coach-GM Wayne Maxner, who coached the Emms team) gave us hell after the second for not finishing our checks."

Gretzky, who skated on a line with Fox and Tony McKegney of the Kingston Canadians, finished with a goal and an assist and was voted the Leyden's most outstanding player.

Joel Quenneville jumped right from the Spitfires to the Toronto Maple Leafs in 1978. (TTSA)

Spitfires defenceman Joel Quenneville signs autographs for adoring youngsters. (WS, 1979)

Spitfires Legend: Joel Quenneville

Joel Quenneville doesn't have to think for long to come up with his favourite memory of playing for the Spitfires.

"I remember Mrs. Freeman (the button lady) up in the corner of the rink," Quenneville said. "She was at all the games. I'd be coming in on the point and she'd be standing up there, getting all excited."

An original with the expansion Spitfires in 1975-76, Quenneville remembered how his Spitfires teams took on the flavour of ancient, tiny Windsor Arena. "It was a tough building to come into and we'd had tough teams a couple of the years that I was here," he said.

"Personality was probably the best thing about the building. I still can't believe they played in it as long as they did. That's probably the most amazing thing. I remember when we played, it was like, 'It's still going?' Even then.

"When you think of all the games that were played there, it's amazing. Not too many buildings have the memories that it does. A lot of great hockey players, a lot of great games and the greatest fans."

Quenneville, a local product of Windsor's Riverside Minor Hockey Association, was one of those great players. During the 1977-78 season, he established single-season marks for a Spitfires defenceman than remain on the books today, collecting 27-76-103 totals.

"It was one of those years when everything went well," recalled Quenneville, who captained the Spitfires. "We had a good team and I benefitted from that.

"I have more memories of my days in junior than I do as a pro. Going to school, heading to practice, hanging out with the guys and the long bus trips are all part of the shared experience and they've stuck with me."

Quenneville was a 1978 third-round draft choice of the Toronto Maple Leafs. Following a 13-season NHL playing career with the Leafs, Hartford Whalers, Colorado Rockies and Washington Capitals, Quenneville turned to coaching, guiding the fortunes of the St. Louis Blues and Colorado Avalanche before leading the Chicago Blackhawks to the 2009-10 Stanley Cup championship.

After the triumph, Quenneville shared the moment with the fans he'd grown up perform-

Windsor and Hamilton exchange unpleasantries during a 1978 game. (WS)

ing in front of, bringing Lord Stanley's mug to Windsor's Canada Day parade, where it joined the Memorial Cup won by the Spitfires.

"I don't know if they've ever been together, the Memorial Cup and the Stanley Cup in the same parade," Quenneville said.

Quenneville, Bob Pulford and Jacques Lemaire are the only men to have played 800 NHL games and coached 800 NHL games. He was inducted into the Windsor/Essex County Sports Hall of Fame in 2002 and his No. 6 sweater was made an honoured number by the Spitfires in 2001.

Joel Quenneville Spitfires Stats

SEASON	GP	G	A	P	PIM
1975-76	66	15	33	48	61
1976-77	65	19	59	78	169
1977-78	66	27	76	103	114

Best of Seven Again

Three times, the Spitfires and the London Knights went to Game 7 to decide a playoff series between the two clubs. In those three series, the home team won Game 7 twice each.

How's that again?

That's right, London and Windsor played four Game 7 showdowns in three series.

During the second round of the 1979 Ontario Major Junior Hockey League playoffs, London rallied for a 3-3 tie before 5,270 at London Gardens in Game 7 of their eight-point series – junior teams didn't play overtime back then – to take the set 8-6 in a contest appropriately played April 1, because things were about to get very foolish.

Windsor filed a protest because Dean Hopkins, who set up London's last two goals, had been assessed a spearing major in the second period by referee Jim Lever and the Spitfires believed the rules called for Hopkins to be assessed a match penalty, which entailed ejection from the game. The OMJHL protest committee agreed and ordered a Game 7 replay.

This time, the Spitfires were 3-2 winners. Afterward, London filed another protest, insisting that Lever, who officiated both games, had been suspended by the league for blowing the Hopkins call and should not have handled the whistle in the second game.

The league rejected London's protest and Windsor began its third-round series against Niagara Falls. Then London called in the lawyers.

The Knights threatened legal action and the OMJHL buckled like a tin can under a car tire, wiping out the start of the Niagara Falls-Windsor set and ordering a three-team, round-robin semifinal, which Niagara Falls won.

"We played each other 27 times between exhibition, regular season and the playoffs," said Wayne Maxner, Windsor's coach that season. "We finished 13-13-1. The whole season was close."

Windsor Spitfires yearbooks for the 1977-78 and 1978-79 seasons. (WSHC)

1980 finals

For the first time since the franchise was reborn in 1975, the Spitfires finished on top of the standings, winning the 1979-80 Emms Division regular-season title by four points over the Toronto Marlboros with a 36-31-1 slate.

Offensively, the Spitfires were led by the forward unit of Blair Barnes (130), Brent Jarrett (118) and Paul Gagne (101), who combined for 349 points. Team captain and current Boston Bruins coach Claude Julien anchored the blue-line, and two goalies headed toward NHL careers, Shawn MacKenzie and Roland Melanson, handled the puckstopping duties.

"I'll never forget playing here," McKenzie said of his time with the Spitfires.

Windsor is also a city that Julien holds dear. He was a defenceman with the Spitfires from 1978-81. "Windsor was definitely a place I enjoyed," Julien said. "I still come back every once in a while to visit friends.

"Everything in your life when you're involved in hockey, whether it's as a player or coaching, there's always something that impacts you. I was there in the days when Wayne Maxner was a coach, a guy who definitely got the most out of his players."

Maxner got the utmost out of his team that spring. Windsor downed Niagara Falls 4-1 in the quarter-finals, then captured a thrilling seven-game semifinal from the Brantford Alexanders.

Former Spitfires coach Tony Curtale was a defenceman with the Alexanders in that memorable Game 7 battle, which the Spitfires took by a 5-4 count at Windsor Arena.

"Blair Barnes scored the game winner," Curtale recalled. "I remember because I was on the ice at the time and I had to put my hands over my ears because the crowd was so loud. I've never heard a crowd that loud."

Julien felt that decisive Game 7 performance reflected what that Spitfire club was all about.

"We were a character team," Julien said. "I think I grew as a player there. Everywhere you stop, you take a little bit from everybody.

There's no doubt that Windsor had an impact on me."

The Spitfires faced the Peterborough Petes, the OHL's best team, in the final, and that was where Windsor met its match. The Petes swept the Spitfires in four games.

"We had a good year, but Peterborough had a really strong team," said Ernie Godden, a forward with the 1979-80 Spitfires.

Spitfires Legend: Blair Barnes

Blair Barnes held forth as Windsor's career scoring leader from 1980-94. (WSHC)

For years, Blair Barnes was the answer to a pair of trivia questions.

He was the last player chosen in the 1979 NHL entry draft, considered by many to have been the deepest draft in history. And, he was the Spitfires' career scoring leader.

The latter mark held forth from 1980 through 1994, when Bill Bowler finally surpassed Barnes's totals. "Obviously I was pretty proud of that record," Barnes said at the time. "But it's 13 years old and records are made to be broken. He must be a pretty good hockey player."

There's no doubt that Barnes was a pretty good hockey player, producing 127 goals and 296 points in 198 games as a Spitfires centre between 1977-80. The five-foot-11, 190-pound right-winger still ranks second on the club's all-time points list and third in goals.

He played a big, strong game," said former Windsor teammate Ernie Godden, who played two years with Barnes. "You never had to tell him to pick up his game. He always came to the rink ready to play."

Barnes was drafted in the sixth round (126th overall) by the Edmonton Oilers in the 1979 NHL draft, the same draft in which the Oilers claimed Kevin Lowe, Glenn Anderson and Mark Messier, cornerstones of the club's dynasty that won five Stanley Cups. But Barnes played his lone NHL game with the Los Angeles Kings during the 1982-83 campaign.

Retiring following the 1983-84 season, Barnes scored 99 goals in his minor-league career.

Barnes was known for his bulldozing skating style, as well as his powerful slapshot. His 63 goals in 1978-79 stood as the club record until Godden set the current OHL record of 87 goals in 1980-81.

"He wasn't a finesse player," Godden told the *Windsor Star*. "He was a grinding, solid winger. I'll remember him coming down the right wing and booming that slapshot."

Barnes was also a popular player in the Spitfires' dressing room. "I remember coming back from a game in Toronto my second season in Windsor and we stopped the bus at his parents' house in Mississauga," Godden said. "The whole team went in and his parents fed us all. We all signed the wall going down to the basement."

After hanging up his skates, Barnes relocated to Chicago, where he worked for a major brewery. He died in 2010.

Blair Barnes Spitfires Stats

SEASON	GP	G	A	P	PIM
1977-78	65	22	26	48	163
1978-79	67	42	76	118	195
1979-80	66	63	67	130	98

Spitfires scoring sensation Ernie Godden is flanked by defencemen Kevin Pitel (left) and Craig Muni (right). (WS, 1981)

Godden's Snipe Hunt

A crowd of frenzied Windsor Spitfires fans witnessed Ernie Godden make Ontario Hockey League history.

Or did they?

Nearly 30 years later, even Godden isn't sure.

The night of March 12, 1981, Godden fired four goals during a 12-5 rout of the London Knights at the Barn. According to the OHL, that gave Godden 85 goals on the season, moving him past the league record of 81 tallied by Peter Lee of the Ottawa 67s during the 1975-76 campaign.

It was the second occasion in the span of four days that Godden was told he'd established a new single-season standard for goal-scoring.

Initially, a two-goal performance March 8 in a 7-4 loss at Brantford supposedly gave Godden 82 for the season. But after further review, league officials determined that a goal credited to Godden's total earlier in the season should have actually been an assist and they reduced his season total to 81.

"I broke the record twice," Godden said. "I still don't understand it. They said they gave me an assist, but on the play they were talking about, I know I scored that goal. It went in off my stick."

The entire episode grew even more surreal when, during the warmup for the London game, Knights goalie Frank Caprice was injured. "They didn't have a backup goalie," Godden recalled.

London right-winger Jim Edgerton was forced to don the pads, making the net a much easier target for Godden to hit.

He finished that season with 87 goals, still the OHL single-season mark. It was a record campaign that was set into motion via a negotiation between shooter and coach.

"I went to (Spitfires coach) Ron Harris at the start of the season and said, 'I'm a goal scorer,'" Godden recalled. "'I don't want to check this season. I want to score goals.'

"Before the first game, he said, 'OK, let's see what you got.' After the first period, he said, 'Alright, we'll do it your way.' I have to give Ron Harris a lot of credit for that season. He really gave me the opportunity to produce offensively."

Godden produced more multi-goal games that season (24) than games in which he failed to register a goal (18). He tallied 35 times on the power play and 10 more while Windsor was shorthanded. His longest goalless drought was three games.

"I loved playing for the Spitfires," Godden said. "It was an unbelievable season and I'm convinced the fans at Windsor Arena played a big role. They were unbelievable, even in the warm-ups, as the record got closer.

"I'm sure I got more pumped up than I normally would for a home game."

Spitfires Legend: Ernie Godden

Ernie Godden's 87-goal season for Windsor in 1980-81 remains the OHL single-season record. (TTSA)

Like Glenn Hall's 502 straight games in an NHL goal, or Joe DiMaggio's 56-game hitting streak, it's a mark that seems to have gained a life of its own.

Ernie Godden's OHL-record 87-goal season with the 1980-81 Spitfires.

"I hope no one breaks the record," said Wayne Maxner, who coached Godden with the Spitfires. "I love Ernie Godden. I hope he keeps the record forever."

Maxner is not alone in this emotional embrace of Ernie. The Ernie Godden Fan Club on MySpace consists of 22 members, with an additional 48 on Facebook, who list themselves as, "A group to praise the great Ernie."

Godden's mark is definitely unique for its combination of achievement and endurance. Godden has held forth as the OHL's supreme single-season scorer a year longer than Wayne Gretzky's 92-goal campaign has reigned over the National Hockey League.

"It's something that's gained me a lot of attention over the years," Godden said. "Every other year, the Hockey Hall of Fame puts up a display to recognize my record. A fellow I know, a bigwig at General Motors, he told me he saw me in the Hall of Fame."

Not that it appears to matter to him. "Records are made to be broken," Godden said. "I'm kind of surprised that I've held it for this long."

It's all pretty heady stuff for a guy whose NHL career lasted all of five games.

Smallish by NHL standards at five-foot-eight, 160 pounds, Godden was selected 55th overall in the 1981 NHL entry draft by the Toronto Maple Leafs.

He tallied a goal and an assist with the Leafs in that five-game stint during the 1981-82 season. It's the one part of his hockey career that still leaves Godden irritated.

"It was the wrong team and the wrong time," he said. "I asked the Leafs to trade me, but they said I was too much of a drawing card for their farm team, so they wouldn't move me.

"I just wanted a chance to play in the NHL somewhere."

Offered a termination contract by the Leafs in 1984, Godden instead signed with Klagenfurter AC of the Austrian League, where he produced the third 30-goal campaign of his pro career.

"That was the mistake I made," Godden said. "Other guys like Craig Muni and Lee Norwood, they signed termination contracts the same season, went to new teams the next year and enjoyed long careers. I went to Austria and I wrecked my knee."

Only 24, Godden was done in pro hockey. A terminal manager for Allied Automotive, Godden, a father of four, remains heavily involved in hockey as vice-president of travel for Amherstburg minor hockey and coaching his son Ernie Jr.

"I've got my own kids playing hockey and that's what's keeping me busy," Godden said.

Nearly three decades later, Spitfires fans continue to get a kick out of Godden's enduring place in hockey history.

The Spitfires and Belleville Bulls duke it out during a 1983 game. (WS)

Ernie Godden Spitfires Stats

SEASON	GP	G	A	P	PIM
1978-79	64	25	31	56	165
1979-80	62	40	41	81	158
1980-81	68	87	66	153	185

0-20 Vision

It started innocuously enough, with a 5-3 setback to the Wolves Nov. 6, 1982 at Sudbury. But it would be another 20 games and Christmas would nearly come before the Spitfires would again attain a victory, a club record for futility that remains on the books today.

The same Wolves were at Windsor Arena Dec. 20, 1982. Spitfires goalie Kevin Hamlin dropped the gloves with Sudbury forward Tim Hrynewich 13 minutes into the game, setting the tone for an 8-2 explosion that finally brought a halt to Windsor's painful skid after 20 consecutive losses.

"It's sure a relief to get it over with," Spitfires forward Claude Loiselle told the *Windsor Star*'s Dave Hall. It truly was a team effort that ended the slump. A dozen Windsor players figured in the scoring. The line of Loiselle, Gus Greco and Todd Hooey collected eight points, while the Greg Gravel-Paul Lawless-Jim Olsson trio was good for seven points. The George Finn-Pat Lahey-Paul MacDermid unit added five points.

"I'm very pleased for my players, because they've been suffering through all of this," Windsor coach Marcel Pronovost said. "We refused to panic, although I came close to it a couple of times."

Amazingly, the Spitfires rallied to make the playoffs, but were swept by the North Bay Centennials.

Gravel's Gravy

On the night he set the rink on fire, Windsor Spitfires forward Greg Gravel sounded more like a frustrated fisherman.

He was obsessed with the ones that got away.

"Forget the ones that went in and listen to me for a minute," Gravel explained to the *Windsor Star*'s Dave Hall shortly after his record six-assist, nine-point output as Windsor outscored the Sudbury Wolves 10-7 at Windsor Arena the night of Oct. 28, 1982. "Don't get me wrong, I'm happy we won – you wouldn't believe how much – but missing chances is the kind of sloppy play we've been guilty of all year.

"I missed three breakaways and two other easy chances when I could have put the game away. Those can cause sleepless nights no matter what else you do."

Even on nights when a fellow sets a pair of

Spitfires captain Todd Gill (6) drops the gloves with Sault Ste. Marie's Jim Aldred. (WS)

club records that remain on the books to this day.

In the long history of the Spitfires franchise, no other player has ever recorded as many helpers or picked up as many points as Gravel registered in that game. He set up linemate Paul Lawless for four of Windsor's 10 goals.

"An exceptional performance," was how Spitfires coach Marcel Pronovost described Gravel's effort.

Windsor led the game by an 8-2 count before allowing a Sudbury rally that nearly cost the Spitfires the contest, narrowing the Windsor advantage to 9-7. Lawless finished the job, burying a rebound from one of those trio of breakaway chances that Gravel failed to convert.

The battle provided a scorefest and a slugfest, featuring 326 penalty minutes, 253 of which were assessed by referee Dave Lynch during the first period alone, a frame that took an hour to play. In total, the game lasted three hours.

There were 20 majors, 13 misconducts and six game misconducts handed out and at one point, seven Spitfires and six Wolves occupied the penalty box at the same time. Windsor took advantage of the mayhem, potting six power-play goals.

In other words, the 1,300 fans in attendance at the old Barn got to see a little bit of everything. Including a record-setting performance that has never seen an equal during Windsor's history.

Spitfires Legend: Todd Gill

Constant upheaval in the front office. Many coaches. Several general managers. An organization where mediocrity wasn't just accepted, it had become the benchmark of the franchise.

When the Toronto Maple Leafs claimed defenceman Todd Gill from Windsor with the 25th pick of the 1984 NHL entry draft, he was already well-versed in what life would hold for him as a Leaf.

"I think we had eight coaches and three ownership changes when I was with the Spitfires," said Gill, who played three seasons in Windsor from 1982-85. "I guess it was good preparation for Toronto.'"

Regardless, the Brockville, Ont. native has nothing but fond memories of Windsor.

"We played in a great old rink in front of what I would say are the best fans in the OHL," Gill said. "I met a lot of great people, Windsor had an excellent school system.

"The only regret I have is that I don't get back to the area as much as I'd like to."

He got to spend much more time near Windsor later in his NHL career, when Gill was acquired by the Detroit Red Wings, much to the delight of his old Spitfire billet. Terry Byrnes was Gill's billet when Gill was playing for the Spitfires. Byrnes was a huge Red Wings fan.

When Gill arrived in Detroit in 1999, among the first people he contacted was Byrnes. "When I called, the first thing he said to me was, 'Well, it took you 15 years, but you finally got it right,'" Gill said.

Gill, who played his last NHL season in 2002-03, today is coach, GM and owner of the Brockville Braves of the Central Junior Hockey League.

"I'm too busy," Gill said. "I need another day in the week."

Todd Gill Spitfires Stats

SEASON	GP	G	A	P	PIM
1982-83	70	12	24	36	108
1983-84	68	9	48	57	184
1984-85	53	17	40	57	148

The Next Gretzky

History repeated itself at Windsor Arena in the fall of 1983 when the Spitfires acquired centre Keith Gretzky, younger brother of the Great One, Wayne Gretzky, from the Brantford Alexanders.

Three decades earlier, Windsor had suited up Vic Howe, younger sibling of Mr. Hockey, Gordie Howe, during the 1949-50 season.

At 17 in 1984-85, the younger Gretzky produced team-leading 31-62-93 numbers and was selected by the Buffalo Sabres in the third round of the NHL entry draft.

"He knows a lot about the game," former Spitfires teammate Wilf Payne told the *Windsor Star*. "He soaked up everything when he was playing."

Larry Mavety, who acquired Gretzky from Windsor for his Belleville Bulls during the 1985-86 season, also praised his hockey IQ. "He lived and breathed hockey when he was here," Mavety said. "He learned a lot from his father (Walter)."

Keith Gretzky played six seasons in the minor pro ranks, always pursued by his big brother's imposing shadow. "It's tough to live up to what Wayne's done," Keith acknowledged. "Nobody has."

Keith Gretzky led the Spitfires in scoring during the 1984-85 season with 31 goals and 93 points. (WS)

Spitfires Tidbits

Super Six

Even though the expansion Spitfires won just 10 games in 1975-76, six of them later played in the NHL – defencemen Chris Kotsopoulos, Joel Quenneville and Mark Renaud, left-winger Mike Dwyer, right-winger Brad Smith and goaltender Bob Parent.

Young American

Spitfires defenceman Richie Dunn, a future NHLer, played for the United States in the 1977 world junior championship. Dunn also played for Team USA in the 1981 Canada Cup.

Turkish Delight

Seeking an NHL comeback, former Boston Bruins star Derek Sanderson skated with the Spitfires in February of 1978. Nicknamed the Turk, Sanderson was hoping to sign with the cross-border Detroit Red Wings, but instead joined the Pittsburgh Penguins in March.

First One

Left-winger Paul Gagne, selected 19th overall by the Colorado Rockies in 1980, was the first Spitfire ever taken in the opening round of the NHL entry draft.

Memorial Memories

Windsor didn't make it to the Memorial Cup until 1988, but the Memorial Cup made it to Windsor Arena in 1981. In the days before the host city gained automatic entry into the tournament, the Cornwall Royals defended their title with an 8-2 win over the Kitchener Rangers. The Victoria Cougars also participated in the event, which was contested from May 3-15.

Movie Star

Racki, the thug who tormented Rob Lowe's character in the 1986 hockey movie *Youngblood*, was portrayed by George Finn, who led the Spitfires with 224 penalty minutes in 1981-82.

Backup Plan

Canadian actor Keanu Reeves, star of such films as *Speed* and *The Matrix*, played goal at Toronto's De La Salle High School and claims in his Hollywood bio that he turned down a tryout with the Spitfires before he turned to acting.

The 1987-88 Windsor Compuware Spitfires, first Windsor team to play in the Memorial Cup tournament. (TTSA)

THREE

The Compuware Era

IN JANUARY OF 1984, PETER KARMANOS, owner of the Detroit-based Compuware Systems, made an unsuccessful bid to acquire an Ontario Hockey League expansion franchise for Detroit to play in an arena he planned to construct in the northeast area of Detroit. Undaunted, Karmanos turned his attention to acquiring an existing OHL team, and on May 17, 1984, announced he'd purchased the Windsor Spitfires. Windsor had only recently undergone an ownership change of its own. Fred Sorrell, part of the ownership group since the Spitfires returned to major junior hockey in 1975, sold the club less than a year earlier to John McHale, a Nepean, Ontario-based businessman.

"It was very difficult to be involved from such a distance," McHale told the *Ottawa Citizen*. "We suffered a substantial loss."

Former NHL goalie Jim Rutherford was named general manager of the newly-christened Windsor Compuware Spitfires, and immediately set out to prepare for the upcoming OHL midget draft.

Little did Windsor know that the Spitfires were about to embark on their greatest era since the original Spitfires were born in 1946.

Peter Karmanos, Jr., Chairman and CEO of Compuware Corporation. (WS)

The New Boss

Peter Karmanos made his fortune in computer software, but his true passion had always been hockey. His Compuware organization owned a solid hockey reputation in the U.S., producing such NHLers as Pat LaFontaine, Alfie Turcotte and Al Iafrate from among its 200 minor hockey participants in the Detroit area.

In six seasons – from 1979-80 to 1984-85 – Compuware's minor hockey empire collected seven national age-class championships in the United States. In 1985, Compuware won national junior, midget and peewee titles and finished as runner-up in the bantam division.

Now they were determined to make consistent winners of the Spitfires. "I've made a long-term commitment to Windsor," Karmanos told the *Windsor Star*.

According to Spitfires GM Jim Rutherford, Karmanos was someone who brought in quality people and delegated authority accordingly. "Our success starts at the top with Pete and filters right through the organization," Rutherford said. "He hires the best people available and doesn't interfere."

The Button Lady

For more than three decades, Eleanor Freeman was better known as Windsor Arena's Button Lady, because of her hockey button-covered coat.

Within the confines of Windsor Arena, Freeman was perhaps the most well-known and beloved figure not on the ice. "I have so many great memories," Freeman told the *Windsor Star*. While her vocal support was recognized when the Compuware Spitfires honoured her with a gold airplane as their No. 1 fan in 1985, it was Freeman's coat that made her a local celebrity.

She's never counted the number of buttons she collected, but her coat was covered in hundreds of pictures and pins. "People would walk up and ask to put new pins on me," said Freeman, who started her collection by buying Spits buttons for her children.

"They'd ask to take pictures with me. I remember a 12-year-old boy wanted me to sign his program. It made me feel so good to have people come up and talk to me."

In 2005, the city of Windsor honoured Freeman's commitment to the team by commemorating a mural to be painted of her on the outside of Windsor Arena.

Trailer Park Boy

From an early stage in life, Mike Volpe recognized that his future would be fashioned around four-letter words. As a young goaltending hopeful with the Windsor Spitfires, his two passions were film and stopping the puck.

Who knew at the time that he'd be able to combine the two into one of the wildest phenomenons ever to hit Canadian television?

Better known today as executive producer of the Trailer Park Boys – the smash hit Canadian-made program built around the misadventures of Julian, Ricky and Bubbles, three foul-mouthed petty thieves – Volpe was at one time a Spitfires goalie.

Sometimes, even Volpe still finds it difficult to fathom the unusual path that took him from the goal crease at Windsor Arena to the fictional Sunnyvale Trailer Park. Drafted by the Spitfires, he attended training camp in the fall of 1984.

"The team had just been taken over by Compuware," Volpe remembered. "Jim Rutherford was GM and Mark Craig was the coach. I made the team at 17 as backup to Alan Perry, but decided to go home to Halifax and went to St. Mary's University to play."

That's when Volpe's life took its first unusual turn. The New York Islanders selected him 223rd overall that spring in the NHL entry draft. "When I got drafted by the Islanders out of Canadian university hockey, that really caught me by surprise," Volpe said. "The first thing they told me was they wanted me playing junior hockey."

Volpe spent two seasons in the OHL with the Kitchener Rangers and Toronto Marlboros, opening the door to Volpe's other love.

"I'd always wanted to go to film school and the trade to the Marlies gave me the opportunity to enrol in the fine arts program at York University," Volpe said. "Talk about living two extremes of existence. I was spending my days at school with all these artsy, film-school students, then I'd head to Maple Leaf Gardens for practice and games."

At 19, Volpe returned to the Maritimes, earning a law degree from Dalhousie University and was called to the Nova Scotia bar in 1993, all the while continuing his hockey career. In 1994, he backstopped the senior Truro, N.S., Bearcats to the Allan Cup semifinals.

His first legal job was serving as general counsel for a film company, opening that door up once more to Volpe. "It was kind of like, 'It's now or never,'" Volpe said of the opportunity to move into the film industry.

He started his own company, Topsail Entertainment, and produced the critically-acclaimed Black Harbour for the CBC. Then he hit the motherlode with the Trailer Park Boys.

Mike Clattenburg, director of the Trailer Park Boys, originated the characters in a black-and-white independent film and Barrie Dunn, a fellow entertainment lawyer and producer better known to fans of the show as Ricky's dad, produced it. The first time Volpe saw the film, he instantly saw something special.

"I just knew there was going to be a segment of the population that was going to dig this," said Volpe, who, in combination with Dunn and Clattenburg, created the concept for bringing the Boys to television.

Windsor's Kevin Kerr (17) delivers a knuckle sandwich to Hamilton's Shayne Corson. (WS)

Windsor's Crash Davis

Kevin Kerr performed on the ice alongside the likes of Gretzky, Sakic, Forsberg and Vezina.

Keith Gretzky, Brian Sakic, Martin Forsberg and Steve Vezina, that is.

A minor-league legend, Kerr played for 18 seasons without skating in a single NHL game, but ended his career with 677 goals, which stood as the mark for minor-pro hockey until 2008.

Kerr called seven different leagues and 16 cities home. He was a Bullfrog, a Jackal, a Vulture, a Roadrunner, a Mallard, a Mustang and a Bull, among other creatures. He won a Calder Cup American Hockey League title with the 1993-94 Portland Pirates.

"Not playing in the NHL, sure it was a disappointment," Kerr said. "But I wouldn't trade my career for anyone else's."

Kerr played for the Compuware Spitfires from 1984-87, twice topping the 20-goal plateau, and bettering 260 penalty minutes in each of his three seasons. "It seems eons ago that I played in Windsor," Kerr said. "I still think about Windsor a lot. I had some good times playing for the Spits."

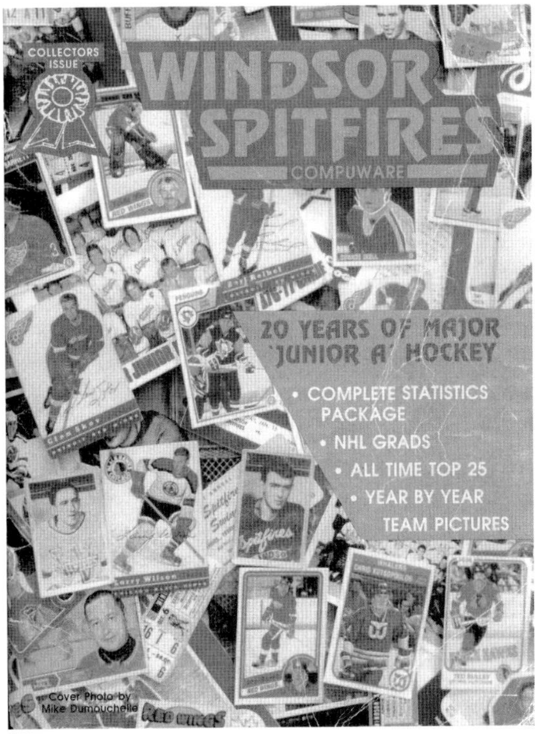

Issued in 1988, this book commemorated Windsor's 20th season in major junior hockey. (WSHC)

The Web Master

While he was plying his trade as a professional hockey player, first in the National Hockey League and later in the fledgling World Hockey Association, Tom Webster had an inkling of what life after hockey might hold for him.

"I often thought about becoming a teacher," Webster said. "Some teachers that I had as a kid were big influences on me. I think this job is very closely related to teaching in a classroom."

Hired to coach the Spitfires prior to the 1986-87 season, it became apparent over the years that one lesson Webster didn't learn was that you can never go home again. No matter how many times he has left, he always seems to find his way back home to Essex County.

"This area really has become very close to my heart," said Webster, who served three separate stints as coach of the Spitfires and still makes his

Spitfires Mike James (7), David Bowman (8), Steve Ott (14) and Paul Giallanardo (3) listen to instructions from coach Tom Webster during Windsor's 2002 run to the OHL conference finals. (DH)

home in the area today while working as a scout for the NHL's Calgary Flames.

Born in Kirkland Lake, Ont., Webster met his wife Carol and settled in Niagara Falls, Ont., but Essex County is the area that Webster considers home. "There's definitely something that keeps pulling me back here," he said.

As a player, he won a Memorial Cup with the Niagara Falls Flyers in 1964-65 and a Stanley Cup with the Boston Bruins in 1969-70. Acquired by the Detroit Red Wings in 1970, Webster was the road roommate of Gordie Howe during Mr. Hockey's last season in a Detroit uniform.

That was a year of upheaval in the Detroit club. Ned Harkness was the new coach-GM and his master plan was to take Howe, in his 26th and final season as a Red Wing, and move him to defence, placing Webster in Howe's right wing spot with Alex Delvecchio and Frank Mahovlich. "The experiment didn't last too long," Webster said.

Webster went from Detroit to the California Golden Seals, and later to the WHA with the New England Whalers.

Born with spondylolisthesis, a vertebrae problem, Webster endured a trio of spinal fusion surgeries during his playing days. He wears a scar across his stomach from the third, which had to be done from the front, because the fusion refused to take from the back.

After taking a year off to recover, The Red Wings signed Webster as a free agent in 1979. He went to camp but says he was, "a step behind everybody and too many pounds overweight" and was assigned to Detroit's Adirondack American League farm club.

"I wasn't playing at all and I didn't think it was right that I was taking a spot away from a young prospect," Webster said.

Former Spitfire Larry Wilson, who was to have been the Adirondack coach, had died just before the start of the season and Bill Purcell was brought in to run the team. "I offered to become an assistant coach and play when I was needed," Webster said. "(Detroit GM) Ted (Lindsay) agreed to it. Not long after that, Purcell got fired and J.P. Leblanc and I were named co-coaches."

Webster coached in the AHL, winning the championship in Adirondack in 1981, in the International League with Salt Lake City and in the Central League with Tulsa, capturing the 1984 title with the club that became known as the 'Orphan Oilers.'

"The team had local ownership and midway through the season, they just ran out of money," Webster said. "The league didn't want us to fold, so they all got together and decided to keep us going."

Basing the team out of Denver and housing them in an area hotel, Tulsa played its remaining 40 games and the entire playoff schedule on the road, en route to the title.

As coach of the Los Angeles Kings from 1989-92, Webster could look down his bench and send Wayne Gretzky over the boards, and admired the determination that The Great One brought to the rink each night. "He knew going into every game that everything the other team did was going to be designed to check him," Webster said. "He thrived on that challenge, he overcame and made it happen."

Webster brought a similar passion to the challenges of his job. "Tommy can be an intense coach," Rutherford said. "Whenever Tommy was tough on a player, he did so in the best interests of that player's future, but sometimes, the player didn't see it that way."

Eventually, though, they'd come to see the light. "There were times when we all felt like throwing something at him," former Spitfires captain Adam Graves admitted. "He'd yell and scream, but it was always constructive and it's all to make you a better player."

Webster won more games (264) than any Spitfires coach and led the club to its first OHL title and Memorial Cup final in 1987-88.

Adam Graves captained the Spitfires to the 1987-88 OHL title. (TTSA)

Spitfires Legend: Adam Graves

Few players in the history of the Spitfires organization invoke the sort of heartfelt passion from fans that is always offered up to Adam Graves.

When Graves returned to Windsor in 2009 as honourary captain for the OHL All-Star Game, he was as mobbed by autograph hounds as was the other honourary captain, a fellow named Steve Yzerman.

From the moment he arrived in Windsor in 1985 as the club's top draft pick, it was apparent that Graves was someone cut from a special mold.

A star in every right, he always put team first, sought to help others succeed and ensure they felt part of it all. Graves thrives in such an environment because it is everything that he is about as a human being.

"There are some guys who just want to help somebody out," said Charlie Huddy, a teammate of Graves in the NHL. "Gravy's one of those guys."

On the ice, Graves is all business. Away from the rink, he is all heart. A man filled with genuine kindness, for whom doing it the right way is the only way.

He's had good teachers. Robert and Lynda Graves opened their home to foster children, giving those who had lost hope a chance to call someplace home, to feel the sensation of being loved.

"I think if there is one thing my dad instilled in me, it was to always do the best at what you did and to treat people the way you want to be treated," Graves said of his childhood. "That's the way I've tried to live my life, by focusing on doing the right thing. Sure, I've made mistakes . . . but my heart has always been in the right place."

On the ice, there was little the man who captained the Spitfires to the 1987-88 OHL title and Memorial Cup final didn't do right.

"I was lucky enough to win a Calder Cup (AHL title with Adirondack) in 1989," Graves said, part of the three-year odyssey of success from 1988-90 which saw him win an OHL title (with Windsor), a World Junior crown (with Canada) and a Stanley Cup (with Edmonton). He later won a second Stanley Cup with the New York Rangers and enjoyed a 50-goal season in a New York uniform.

Graves and former Spitfires teammate Peter DeBoer both own shares of the OHL's Oshawa Generals, and he remains involved with the NHL as development coach with the Rangers. "I'm involved with rookie camp, training camp, the draft, all of that," he said. "I'm doing specific cross sections with the whole organization. I'm lucky enough to be a plumber in all of those areas.

"If you're part of the game, you're lucky."

Like most Spitfires fans, Graves teared up as he watched the club win the 2009 Memorial Cup, the first in franchise history. "It's hard to put it into words, how proud I was in watching, as a Spitfire myself, the team – especially the way they came through the adversity they had to endure – and then to get into the Memorial Cup, and then to be counted out in a lot of ways, and then to battle back," Graves said.

"It's tough to win like that without leadership from guys who obviously played the game, but played the game with heart and soul. I'm talking about Rychs (Spitfires GM Warren Rychel) and Boogie (Spitfires coach Bob Boughner) and I do believe that's what carried that team through the tough times and to the Memorial Cup.

"I can't think of a better, more appropriate city to win it."

It's hard to think of someone who personifies what it means to be a Spitfire more than Graves.

Adam Graves Spitfires Stats

SEASON	GP	G	A	P	PIM
1985-86	65	27	37	64	35
1986-87	66	45	55	100	70
1987-88	37	28	32	60	107

American Made

Among the offshoots of Compuware's purchase of the Spitfires was that it seemed to spark an upswing in U.S.-born players opting to skate in the OHL. Compuware helped sell the league because of their high profile in U.S. minor hockey.

"I guess we've helped a little in that regard, but it's still up to individual teams to convince players they have a sound program," Spitfires GM Jim Rutherford told the *Windsor Star*. "We can't help convince a player about the merits of any other team but our own."

Windsor was prominent among teams with Americans on its roster. Goalies Alan Perry (Providence, R.I.) and Pat Jablonski (Toledo, Ohio), defenceman Mark Kurzawski (Chicago), and forwards Mike Wolak (Utica, N.Y.), Ian O'Rear (Detroit), Brad Stepan (Hastings, Minn.), and Ron Jones (Detroit) all played for the Spitfires under Compuware's ownership.

Sock It To Him

Canada and Russia brawled in the infamous Piestany Punch-Up during the 1987 world junior hockey championship, and a Spitfire was in the middle of the fray.

Spitfires trainer Wally Tatomir, working the tournament as Canada's assistant trainer, acknowledged after the fact that he'd decked the Russian assistant coach during the brawl.

"I was holding three of our guys back from jumping over the boards, and at the same time hollering at the (Russian) assistant coach to hold their guys back," Tatomir told the *Windsor Star*. "He was just laughing at me.

"I gave him one shot, right on the face, and he went down."

"I'm not proud of the whole thing, but I don't feel bad. I felt it was the right thing to do at the time."

Both the Canadian and Russian teams were disqualified from the tournament.

A Tale of Two Seasons

With Tom Webster behind the bench, the Spitfires broke from the gate 16-7-1 to start the 1986-87 season and found themselves leading the Emms Division.

On November 26, 1986, things changed dramatically when Webster was hired to coach the NHL's New York Rangers. "We're all trying to improve ourselves, we're all trying to do what's best for our careers and in that respect, Tom's no different," Spitfires defenceman Paul Maurice told the *Windsor Star*. "Selfishly, I wanted Tom to come back to Windsor because it would be great for the team, plus I think he's the best coach I've ever had. But on the other hand, I was hoping he'd be selfish, too, and do what's best for him and his family."

Minus Webster, with Tony MacDonald and then Jim Rutherford handling the coaching, Windsor stumbled to the finish line 36-25-5, third in the Emms.

For the second straight spring, the Spitfires reached the semifinals, and for the second straight year, were bounced in six games. The North Bay Centennials were the suppliers of Windsor's exit in 1987, one year after the Guelph Platers sent the Spitfires packing.

"We were hardened from that experience," Spitfires assistant coach Dave Prpich said. "The more games we played, the better we got, because we grew together."

Look Who's Back

The Spitfires began the 1987-88 season with high hopes, and a familiar face back behind the bench. Tom Webster, forced to relinquish his NHL coaching job with the New York Rangers due to an inner-ear infection, returned to the club he'd coached before accepting the job on Broadway.

"My association with Compuware over the years, my close friendship with (Windsor GM) Jim Rutherford and (owner Peter) Karmanos make it easy for me to come back," Webster said.

The Spitfires brass welcomed Webster's return with open arms. "We are very happy to have as highly-qualified and as talented a coach as Tom back in the organization," Rutherford said. "We're sorry that the inner-ear problem made it impossible for him to continue his coaching duties with the Rangers, but we feel that their loss is the Spitfires' gain.

"We wanted him back the moment we heard he'd resigned."

Unable to fly due to his ear issues, Webster's contract included an escape clause which would allow him to leave should he regain his health and another NHL coaching job become available.

"The ear takes time to heal and that in itself is a big question," Webster said. "The doctors say in a year it could be healed."

Jabber Walks In

Already on top of the OHL with Peter Ing in goal, in December of 1987, the St. Louis Blues returned overage goalie Pat Jablonski to the Spitfires. They embraced his return, even though it meant dropping captain Paul Maurice from the roster.

During the 1986-87 campaign, Jablonski was third in the OHL with 22 victories, tied for first with three shutouts and posted a solid 3.30 goals-against average. Even though Ing had been playing well, the Spitfires were thrilled to get back such a solid, veteran goalie.

"(Spitfires GM) Jim (Rutherford) and I had talked about it and we just felt that we wanted to be sure at the position," Windsor coach Tom Webster said.

Spitfires Legend: Paul Maurice

The Windsor Spitfires were enjoying the best season in franchise history, but as the holiday season arrived, captain Paul Maurice found himself at a crossroads in his career. The veteran defenceman had been cast adrift after the return of goaltender Pat Jablonski left the club with one too many overage players.

Former Spitfires captain Paul Maurice coached the Carolina Hurricanes in the 2002 Stanley Cup final. (DH)

Windsor coach Tom Webster offered Maurice a position as an assistant coach on his staff, but Maurice asked for some time to consider his options, which also included a trade to another team to continue his playing career.

He headed home to Sault Ste. Marie, talked it over with his parents during the Christmas break and opted to accept the coaching position. "Once the shock wore off after that first week, it wasn't too difficult a decision, really," Maurice told the *Windsor Star*'s Dave Hall. "The key to it all was Tony MacDonald, and I never saw him or even spoke to him about it. I just remembered how he handled some difficult situations last year."

MacDonald, the club's director of player personnel, took over as coach from Webster during the 1986-87 season when Webster joined the New York Rangers and later stepped down, both times saying it was in the best interests of the club.

Paul Maurice launched his coaching career as an assistant with the 1987-88 OHL champion Spitfires. (DH)

"Twice Tony did what he thought was best for the team, even though the decisions may have been very tough for him," Maurice said. "Back in the summer, I told Tom and (GM) Jim (Rutherford) that I would help in any way I could this year, and I still have that commitment to live up to.

"So when Tom and Jim both said they thought it would be good for the organization to have me back to help out, I decided I would come back."

Webster welcomed Maurice back with open arms. "His knowledge, leadership and other qualities make Paul very valuable to us," said Webster, who made the transition from player to coach almost overnight himself. "It can be difficult. but Paul already has the respect of the players, so he won't have to win that, and I think he'll fit in right away.

"The players need a buffer sometimes between themselves and management and Paul will handle that role for us as well."

Maurice was impressed at how quickly his hockey knowledge was welcomed by the veteran Windsor staff. "Here I was, a kid fresh from playing the game, and whenever I had something to say, Tom showed me the same respect that he gave to (fellow assistant coach) Dave Prpich, who had years of experience in the coaching business," he recalled.

It turned out that Maurice was a natural behind the bench. He eventually got a head-coaching position with the Detroit Jr. Red Wings, taking them to the 1995 Memorial Cup, and became an NHL head coach with the Hartford Whalers at the age of 28. Maurice has also worked the bench for the Toronto Maple Leafs and is currently coach of the Carolina Hurricanes, a team he coached in the 2002 Stanley Cup final.

Paul Maurice Spitfires Stats

SEASON	GP	G	A	P	PIM
1984-85	38	0	3	3	47
1985-86	56	3	10	13	89
1986-87	63	4	15	19	87
1987-88	32	1	4	5	33

Record Setters

That the 1987-88 edition of the Windsor Spitfires was a special team was never in question. That they would prove to be one of the greatest teams in Spitfires history was firmly established shortly after the calendar turned from 1987 to 1988.

A club-record 16-game winning streak was launched the night of January 16, 1988 with a solid 6-1 victory at Windsor Arena over the London Knights. By the time they were done, the Spitfires clinched first place in their division and established numerous team and personal milestones, many that remain on the books to this day.

Ten of the 16 wins during the streak came on home ice. Three of the home-ice victories arrived via shutout – a 7-0 verdict January 28 over the Kingston Canadians, a 6-0 February 15 whitewash of the Kitchener Rangers and most resounding of all, a 13-0 February 8 victory of the Knights, one of three games during the streak in which Windsor registered double digits in the goals column.

Equally impressive was that all but five of the wins were decided by three or more goals and there was just a solitary one-goal game among the bunch. "We're playing well and we're getting efforts from different people through this stretch," Spitfires coach Tom Webster noted during the streak. "Before, we'd be getting either good goaltending, good defence or good scoring, but now everything is working well."

A 4-2 home-ice victory February 11 over the Guelph Platers was the ninth of the streak and Windsor's 37th win of the year, another new club record. The shutout of Kitchener was Windsor's 10th straight triumph, shattering the previous club mark of nine.

Even other hot teams proved no match for the mighty Spitfires. The Sault Ste. Marie Greyhounds arrived in Windsor February 20 riding a six-game winning streak, but fell 7-4, Windsor's 12th win in a row.

J.P. Gorley scored for the ninth straight game in that victory over the Soo. Launching a three-games-in-three-nights swing through northern Ontario, Jamie Allan's goal gave Windsor a 6-5 win at North Bay over the Centennials, the closest Windsor had come to succumbing since the streak started. The record run was finally halted March 4, with an 8-5 loss at London.

Cain is Able

Kelly Cain, the leading scorer on the 1987-88 OHL champion Windsor Spitfires with 133 points, looks back with fondness at a very special season in his hockey life. Cain was on one of the highest scoring lines in junior hockey history that season along with David Haas (107 points) and J.P. Gorley (77), but recalls more than just the goals and assists.

"I remember how well we all got along that season," Cain told the *Windsor Star*'s Dave Hall. "I think the chance to play with a group of guys who got along so well comes along just once in a lifetime.

"It was a great year, I can't believe all the things that happened. And it all happened because the Spitfires were winners."

Revving the Engine

His energetic play made Jim Revenberg a fan favourite at Windsor Arena. (WS)

No washing machine can get the job done without its agitator, a role that Jim Revenberg relished on the 1987-88 Spitfires.

The Spitfires won legions of fans of all ages during their run to the 1988 Memorial Cup. (WSHC)

"They were such a talented, mature team that I think they needed somebody like me to go crazy once in a while and wake them up," Revenberg told the *Windsor Star*.

Making the team was a daunting task, considering Revenberg didn't play organized hockey the year before. "I can remember asking for a tryout and (trainer Mark) Olesevich looked at me and said, 'Yeah, right, they'll have room for a walk-on,'" recalled Revenberg, son of former CFL player Gus Revenberg. "But I came to camp, and I was as surprised as anyone that I stuck around."

Revenberg finished with one goal and 206 penalty minutes in 66 games.

"Looking back, I was probably the luckiest guy who ever played for the Spitfires," Revenberg said. "I'd have to do some crazy stuff. I can remember running into (forward David) Haas in warm-ups just to get him wound up. I knew what my role was – get the crowd and my teammates pumped up.

"It was awesome playing in my home town for such a great team."

Spitfires Legend: Pat Jablonski

Pat Jablonski's biggest supporter was his big brother, Bobby.

'When I first started, they still had the wire fence behind the nets instead of the plexiglass," remembered Jablonski, who backstopped the Spitfires to the 1987-88 OHL title. "He'd stand behind the net and talk to me the whole game."

It was Bobby who first launched Pat's career as a netminder, taking him to the family basement of their Toledo, Ohio, home and suiting up his young sibling in pads and gloves, then propping him in front of the goal before taking aim.

Pat was two at the time. Bobby was nine. "I don't remember anything about it," Pat said, "but I must have liked it, because I stayed with it.

"Bobby was a forward, but he always wanted to be a goalie. Towards the end, when he got too sick to play out, he played goal."

Bobby Jablonski died of testicular cancer just prior to his 18th birthday. Pat was 11.

"By the time they found the cancer, it was too late," Pat said, his voice drifting. "There wasn't anything they could do."

Pat was playing in a tournament in Boston when his parents realized Bobby's time was near. They thought about calling him home, but waited. "They let me stay and I played out of my mind," Jablonski recalled of that last tournament game. "I stopped everything. I'd be lying on my back and stick my stick in the air and stop shots.

"I never played that well in my life."

Bobby died the day after Pat came home from Boston.

"He was my hero, my idol, the person I really looked up to," Pat said. "He was always there for me, working with me to get better."

Hockey was the destiny of each of the boys in the Jablonski household. All four of them – Bobby, Dean (a year older than Pat) and Pat's twin, Jeff, – were skating by the age of two.

That's not surprising, since Pat's dad, Greg, was a left winger with the International Hockey League's Toledo Hornets and his mom, Monica, skated with the Ice Follies.

"We tried other sports, like baseball and golf, but hockey was for sure," Pat said.

Road hockey games were endless. Ice rinks

were built with the first snow. And after dark, there were basement battles until bedtime.

Pat and Jeff both advanced up the hockey ladder. In 1988, Pat helped the Spitfires to the Memorial Cup final, and Jeff, who later played pro in the Detroit Red Wings' organization, helped Lake Superior State to the NCAA final. Pat also shares a unique achievement with his dad. Pat and Greg are one of only two father-son combinations to have both played for IHL Turner Cup championship teams.

Greg won with Toledo in 1963-64 and 1966-67 and Pat with Peoria in 1990-91. "Having our names on the cup together is pretty special," Pat said. "Those names, they're going to be there forever."

Pat played 128 NHL games for St. Louis, Phoenix, Montreal, Carolina and Tampa Bay, always reserving a special place in his memory for Bobby, the one in the family most responsible for Pat becoming a goalie.

"I still think about Bobby a lot, wonder about what he'd be doing today," Pat said. "That was the hardest thing I've ever had to deal with in my life."

Pat Jablonski Spitfires Stats

SEASON	GPI	GA	SO	GAA	W-L-T
1985-86	29	119	1	4.46	6-16-4
1986-87	41	128	3	3.30	22-14-2
1987-88	18	48	0	2.90	14-3-0

Feather In His Cap

Glen Featherstone was the sandpaper along the blue-line for the Windsor Spitfires, the guy who made you pay for every inch of the ice. Featherstone built a reputation in the Ontario Hockey League as a tough, aggressive defenceman, someone who asked no quarter and gave none.

He applied the same approach over the course of 384 NHL games with St. Louis, Boston, Calgary, the New York Rangers and Hartford, especially enjoying his time with the Bruins.

"It was just like playing in Windsor Arena again," Featherstone said. "The Garden in Boston was a better fit for my style of game."

Defenceman Glen Feathersone meets with fans who flocked to Windsor Arena to collect autographs and wish the Spitfires well in their 1988 Memorial Cup bid. (WS)

Featherstone gets philosophical when discussing the 1988 Memorial Cup, in which Windsor fell one victory short of the title. "In the course of a lifetime, a lot of things are going to happen, both good and bad," he said. "You enjoy the good times and work through the tough times."

Overall, he'll never forget his time in Windsor. "There's a lot of good memories," Featherstone said. "Windsor will always be a special place to me."

Perfect Playoff

The Windsor Spitfires completed an unprecedented run when they captured the 1987-88 Ontario Hockey League championship.

They were absolutely perfect. A 12-0 run through the post-season put Windsor in a class by itself. No team has ever equalled the performance.

That Windsor was able to maintain this perfect roll was made even more impressive by the

Spitfires' coach Tom Webster gets right in the middle of the celebration as he is carried by J.P. Gorley (22), Jamie Allan (17) and Kelly Cain (10) after Windsor was crowned the 1987-88 Ontario Hockey League champions. (WS)

17-day layoff the Spitfires endured between their first-round sweep of the Kitchener Rangers and the first game of their semifinal series against the Hamilton Steelhawks.

Such was the drag between game action that Windsor arranged for an exhibition tilt against a team of former National Hockey League stars such as Darryl Sittler, Bill Derlago and Steve Shutt that ended in a 7-7 tie.

Still, when the Spitfires took the ice at Windsor Arena for the opener against the Steelhawks, there was trepidation in the minds of both participants. "Any time you cage up 22 guys and don't let them do anything for 17 days and then turn them loose, you know they're going to come out fired up," Hamilton coach Bill LaForge said. "We just hope to weather the storm and then come back at them."

They nearly did. In fact, the night of April 12, 1988, before 2,251, the Steelhawks came the closest of any team to knocking the perfection out of the Spitfires.

With the clock ticking towards midnight, a superb solo rush by Windsor defenceman Paul Hampton at 6:32 of the second overtime period gave the Spitfires a 5-4 victory over the Steelhawks, ending a four-hour, 20-minute marathon.

Afterward, Hampton embraced Spitfires coach Tom Webster and shared his belief as to who was the real hero of the night. "I didn't win the game for us, you did," Hampton told Webster. "It was the coach's conditioning program which won the game for us."

"Tom did a great job of keeping us in game shape," centre Adam Graves said. "We owe this win to him."

Webster wasn't about to argue the point. "I'll tell you, am I ever glad I really skated the heck out of these guys during practice," said Webster, whose club hadn't played since March 25. "We worked hard on our physical conditioning, and it really showed in the overtime."

Early on, it didn't appear that the game would offer a major challenge to the Spitfires.

Windsor led 3-0 by the middle of the second period, and 4-1 late in the stanza, but three successive goals by Hamilton's Ken McRae forced overtime. "We got tired," Webster said. "We really got drained. We needed to get that second effort, and I'm pleased we could dig down and find it."

Spitfires captain Graves cited Windsor's character for helping to put them back on the path to victory. "Some people don't believe in second wind," Graves said. "But it's there – it exists. We really had our legs in the first two periods, but then in the third, they were gone.

"By the overtime, we had our legs back and I think Hamilton was tired. The only thing that kept the game going was their goalie (Mike Rosati). He was fabulous."

Webster could sense he was sending out a different club when the extra frames began. "There was a better feeling in the dressing room going out for the overtime than there was going out for the third period," Webster said. "I knew we were going to win, and the guys knew it, too."

The exuberance inside the dressing room was palpable, as was the sense of relief. "I can't remember ever playing in a game like this before," Graves said. "But then, I guess it doesn't really matter when you get the goal, as long as you win."

"I would have waited another three hours," Hampton grinned. "As long as I knew we were going to win."

Windsor took the next three from Hamilton, then steamrolled Peterborough in four games to earn the franchise's first trip to the Memorial Cup.

That Hat Pulls It Out

They'd won 35 of their last 36 games. In post-season play, they'd taken 12 straight in the OHL playoffs, followed by three in a row to reach the Memorial Cup final.

All that stood in the way of Windsor's first national junior crown were the defending Memorial Cup champion Medicine Hat Tigers.

When Windsor jumped to a quick 3-0 lead, there was delirium. In the end, though, there was only disappointment. Trevor Linden's late goal competed a Medicine Hat rally for a 7-6 victory.

Windsor had come up one win short of a title.

"For the longest time, I was crushed when we didn't win," Brad Hyatt, who led all OHL defenceman with 88 points that season, said. "At the time, it was the most important thing in my life outside of family. I knew I wasn't going to play in the NHL and have a chance to win a Stanley Cup so this was it for me.

"I couldn't talk about it for years because it was so disappointing to come so close and fail. We lost two games after Christmas that year and to lose that last one was the worst time of my life."

The passage of time has lightened the burden, and most choose to reflect on the happy times of that remarkable 1987-88 campaign. "I think that's the team I remember the most out of any of the teams I played on," Spitfires forward Darrin Shannon said. "We had such a great season, the friendships you develop when you win, they last forever. It was really an awesome experience and certainly something you will always remember for the rest of your life."

"I don't think a day goes by that I don't think of something funny or something great that happened while I was playing hockey here," recalled defenceman Paul Hampton. "I didn't play much hockey after my last year here in Windsor, so all my memories in hockey are from here and they're great memories. We were such a tight-knit team. All the guys got along really well. There weren't any cliques. It was just one solid effort from everybody."

Despite the setback, the Spitfires were still honoured by a rally in the city upon their return from Chicoutimi, Quebec, site of the 1988 Memorial Cup tournament.

The Brothers Shannon

Spitfires forward Darrin Shannon was the fourth player chosen in the 1988 NHL entry draft. (WS)

Darryl and Darrin Shannon were separated by a year in age and seldom on the ice. The Shannons played minor hockey together in Alliston, Ontario, and Darrin followed Darryl to the Spitfires in 1986. More than teammates, more than siblings, they were always each other's best friend. "He's someone I can trust, someone I can always go and talk to," Darryl said of his younger brother.

Both were key components on Windsor's 1987-88 OHL title squad, the first Spitfires team to play in the Memorial Cup tournament. And even though Windsor didn't win, the Shannons made history there. Darrin (left wing) and Darryl (defence) were both named to the all-tournament team, the only time brothers have ever been selected.

"Whenever we played together, we were always on successful teams," Darryl said.

In Windsor, Darryl was the steadying influence along a veteran blue-line, a second-round draft pick of the Toronto Maple Leafs in 1986. Darrin was the highly-touted NHL prospect, going fourth overall to the Pittsburgh Penguins in 1988.

"I played against Darryl a lot in practice," Darrin remembered.

After a trade, Darrin launched his NHL career in Buffalo, and Darryl played in the 1999 Stanley Cup final with the Sabres. Both played together in Winnipeg, and at different times, were part of the Leafs' organization.

"There's a lot of fond memories," Darryl said.

"Windsor's been a big part of my hockey upbringing," added Darrin.

Spitfires Legend: Peter DeBoer

Some like to refer to Windsor as the cradle of hockey coaches. Entering the 2010-11 NHL season, there are four former Spitfires coaching NHL teams – Claude Julien (Boston), Joel Quenneville (Chicago), Paul Maurice (Carolina) and Peter DeBoer (Florida) – as well as Windsor-born Ron Wilson, in charge of the Toronto Maple Leafs.

Maurice and DeBoer were teammates with the Spitfires from 1985-88, both playing in the 1988 Memorial Cup final.

A cerebral centre with the Spitfires, DeBoer led the club in scoring with 45 goals and 91 points in 1988-89 while captaining the team. Already, it was apparent that like Maurice, another thinking man's player, DeBoer was headed for a future in coaching. DeBoer worked as Maurice's assistant coach with the OHL champion Detroit Jr. Wings, who played in the 1995 Memorial Cup final.

"I knew right from the time when Pete and I were coaching in Detroit that Pete was a head coach," Maurice said. "You train yourself to think like that and it becomes part of your personality."

DeBoer took over as head coach of the Plymouth Whalers and later the Kitchener Rangers, leading them to the 2003 Memorial Cup. "It's a level of the game where you can make a real difference for these kids," he said of junior hockey.

In 2007, DeBoer became just the eighth coach to work 800 games behind an OHL bench. His phone began ringing with pro offers. Many times, he said, 'Thanks, but no thanks.'

In 2008, the Florida Panthers dialed him up. This time, DeBoer answered the call.

"Family was a big part of it," DeBoer said of his hesitation to go pro. "We had three kids in kind of a four-year period. This time, all three of my kids were in school full-time and were all in the grade-school system. Prior to that, the offers I had, I still had at least one or two at home.

"I just thought this was the window to take a shot at it, see how I liked it and if I was any good at it and see where it went from there."

He remains connected to the OHL. DeBoer and Adam Graves, also teammates on the 1987-88 Spitfires, purchased ownership interest in the Oshawa Generals. "I can remember riding the buses when Adam and I played with the Spits, but I never imagined owning a team with him," DeBoer said. "We both feel indebted to the OHL for our careers and feel this is a great way to stay involved with a league we both love."

Peter DeBoer Spitfires Stats

SEASON	GP	G	A	P	PIM
1985-86	55	3	6	9	20
1986-87	52	13	17	30	37
1987-88	54	23	18	41	41
1988-89	65	45	46	91	40

Heading To America

Barely sixth months removed from the first Memorial Cup appearance in franchise history, Windsor was rocked with some startling news about the Spitfires. In December of 1989, owner Peter Karmanos announced he was planning to seek an OHL expansion franchise for Detroit and would sell the Spitfires.

If Karmanos's bid was approved, he intended to sell the Spitfires to one of two local groups of investors with whom discussions had already been held. "There will definitely be a team here in Windsor," Spitfires general manager Terry McDonnell told the *Windsor Star*. "That will be part of the sale agreement."

Karmanos needed to find a buyer by January 16, 1989, the OHL deadline to accept bids for expansion teams. He only intended to sell if he was successful in acquiring a new team from the league.

"Pete's having a difficult time coming to grips with the idea of selling the Spitfires," Compuware director of hockey operations Jim Rutherford said. "He's become very attached to the city and he's still not completely comfortable with the idea. And that's why if it happens, it will have to be to someone we are totally satisfied with."

The January 16 deadline arrived and the Spitfires were sold to an unnamed local investor, with Compuware getting its expansion franchise for Detroit.

Eventually, longtime Spitfires fan and local businessman Vince Bassman was named as majority owner among a group of investors that had purchased the club. "When I heard the team was for sale, I decided to try and put together a group because I think it's important that the team remain in Windsor," Bassman told the *Windsor Star*. "It's good for the city in many ways. Along with many other teams, the Spitfires have put Windsor on the sports map and I wanted to see that continue."

Steve Riolo and Vic Gabriele were Bassman's partners, and they were officially approved as the new owners of the team at an OHL governors' meeting on February 27, 1989.

Rutherford offered the new owners a piece of advice on his way out the door. "Nobody's in junior hockey to make money, but you'd better be prepared to lose some," Rutherford said. "The last (Spitfires) owner (John McHale) wasn't, and the franchise nearly folded."

Spitfires Tidbits

- Windsor coach Tom Webster guided Canada's fortunes as head coach at the 1988-89 world junior championship in Anchorage, Alaska, where Canada finished in fourth place.

- Spitfires players J.D. Urbanic and Paul Maurice both married sisters that they met while playing in Windsor.

- Trevor Walsh played for the Spitfires in 1988-89, and later played four seasons in the Australian Hockey League with the Adelaide Avalanche, suiting up for Australia in the C Division of the IIHF world hockey championship in 2004 and 2005. He was the leading scorer in the 2005 tournament, collecting 6-6-12 totals.

- Brad Stepan, a Spitfires left-winger from 1986-87, is the father of Derek Stepan, who captained Team USA to a gold medal in the 2009-10 World Junior Championship.

- The 1988-89 Spitfires lineup included twin brothers Troy and Trent Gleason, cousins Dean and Tyler Pella and Jason Stos, who would be joined on the Windsor roster the following season by his twin brother Jon.

- Ron Jones played for Windsor in the 1988 Memorial Cup, two years after playing for the Western Hockey League's Portland Winter Hawks in the 1986 Memorial Cup.

- Jason Simon, a Spitfires left-winger in 1988-89, won the 2007-08 Allan Cup title as national senior hockey champions with the Brantford Blast.

Spitfires players Bill Bowler (left), Ed Jovanovski (centre) and Mike Martin (right) are recognized for their participation in the 1995 CHL Chrysler Cup by Spitfires owner Steve Riolo (left), GM Mike Awender (centre) and co-owner Vic Gabriele (right). (DH)

FOUR

The Riolo Years

THE NEW OWNERS OF THE WINDSOR SPITFIRES – Windsor's Vince Bassman, Steve Riolo, Ray Pittao and John Lot, and Vic Gabriele of Leamington – admitted that first and foremost, they were fans of the team.

"I'm like most other fans, I guess," Bassman told the *Windsor Star*'s Dave Hall. "You always dream about what you'd do if you owned the team. I guess we'll soon find out."

Bassman and his partners paid close to $550,000 cash for the franchise. Pittao put up 25 per cent of the money, while Riolo, Gabriele and Lot each contributed 23 per cent and Bassman chipped in the other six per cent. They guaranteed the team wouldn't leave town. "We've made that commitment to the hockey fans of Windsor," Bassman said. "We're here to stay. I don't know how else to put it."

Getting Involved

While Riolo and Gabriele considered themselves casual fans of the team, Bassman allowed that he was a full-fledged fanatic. "When I decided to get involved, I started looking around for people who had the same basic philosophy as I do," Bassman said. "Steve and Vic fitted into the picture perfectly. Both are committed to running a first-class operation. They both want to see it run in a business-like fashion and they both want to see the Spitfires retain their reputation as a solid organization."

Riolo was of the belief that owning the Spitfires would offer him some relief from the challenges of day-to-day business. "I've always found that a hockey game is a good place to go to relax after work," Riolo said. "And owning the team will make it even more relaxing. It's an investment and we're going to do our best to make it successful and profitable, but the bottom line isn't the money. It's being involved in something that a lot of people turn to for entertainment that excites me about this."

Gabriele even admitted the he didn't get to as many Spitfires games as he would like. "I guess I will now," Gabriele said. "None of us are involved to make a pile of money but that doesn't mean we're going to throw it away, either. If it's marketed properly and operated in a business-like fashion, I think the team can break even at the very least every season."

Motor City Smitty

The first order of business for Spitfires general manager Terry McDonnell and the new owners was to hire a coach. Tom Webster had left Windsor to take over as coach of the NHL's Los Angeles Kings.

They settled on a local hero – original Spitfire and former NHL tough guy Brad Smith. "We interviewed six or seven people," co-owner Vince Bassman said. "Some were OHL assistants, some were former pros and some were junior B or midget coaches. Eventually, we sat down and tried to decide who best fit the profile of the guy we wanted – it was Brad. His work ethic is unquestioned, his enthusiasm for the game is unmatched, and he's already proven himself willing to learn."

Brad Smith was the first to both play for and coach the Spitfires in the OHL. (DH)

The hiring of Smith, part of the 1975-76 Spitfires when they returned to major junior hockey, and a return to red, white and blue team colours from the brown and orange hues employed by Compuware, seemed to indicate the new Spitfires were looking to turn back the clock.

His playing career idled by a back injury, Smith, the ex-NHL tough guy lovingly known by his throng of supporters as Motor City Smitty, was only willing to take sentiment so far. "I think every player who plays for his hometown team dreams of returning one day as coach," Smith said. "But I didn't take this job because it was my dream – this is reality. And I didn't take this job because I needed it, but because I wanted it."

Spitfires Legend: Jason York

A sensational offensive performer in the junior ranks, Jason York completely reinvented his game as a professional and the change led to a lengthy NHL career.

York collected 93 points as captain of the Spitfires in 1990-91, the best numbers posted by a Windsor blue-liner since Joel Quenneville's club-record 103 points in 1977-78.

All that productivity changed when he stepped up to the highest level of hockey. "When you come to the NHL as a young defenceman, you're so focused on playing the game well without the puck, on playing solid defensively, offence sometimes becomes secondary," York said. "Once you gain some experience, you gain confidence. You're more willing to get involved in the play, to jump up into the rush."

Regardless, he found that his forte during 757 NHL games with Detroit, Anaheim, Ottawa, Nashville and Boston between 1993-2007 came in keeping the other team from scoring. "I'm not a flashy, offensive guy," York said late in his NHL career. "I just try and be solid every game."

He delivered 140-526-666 numbers in 1,299 NHL games, nothing to sneeze at, but hardly the pace at which he tallied up points with Windsor. "Jason is a well-rounded player," was how then-Anaheim GM Pierre Gauthier described York in 2001. "He can participate in the offence and get the puck out of our end. He's not an intimidating guy, but he is always near the top on his team with hits."

Selected 129th overall by the Red Wings in the 1990 NHL entry draft, York credited the many great players in the Detroit dressing room for helping him refine his game in a way that would enable his enduring NHL career. "I learned so much from guys like Paul Coffey," York said. "Just watching the work ethic employed by stars like Coffey and (Steve) Yzerman teaches you a lot about what it takes to be one of the best."

Originally acquired by the Spitfires in 1988 from the Hamilton Steelhawks, York was dealt to the Kitchener Rangers for players to be named later during the 1989-90 season and played for the Rangers that spring in the Memorial Cup final. One of those players to be named later turned out to be York. He was re-acquired by the Spitfires in the summer as an overage player and named captain of the team.

York was born in Nepean, Ontario, but his wife, Laurel, is from Windsor and they spend a significant amount of time in the city during the summer. Windsor became his home away from home.

(Left)
Jason York works over London's Dennis Purdie in front of the Windsor net. (DH)

(Above)
Windsor coach Brad Smith was always a fan favourite wherever he went. (WS)

Jason York Spitfires Stats

SEASON	GP	G	A	P	PIM
1988-89	65	19	44	63	105
1989-90	39	9	30	39	38
1990-91	66	13	80	93	40

Out For Twenty

The Spitfires were stunned Jan. 10, 1990, when coach Brad Smith was handed a 20-game suspension for his actions in a Dec, 28, 1989 game against the London Knights. The incident which led to Smith's suspension occurred three seconds into the third period of that game when four Spitfires dropped their gloves and jumped their London opponents. Smith admitted to instructing his players to get "physically involved" with the Knights, but denied telling them to fight. "We were getting pushed around in our own building and I was sick of it," Smith told the *Windsor Star*'s Dave Hall.

Five minutes after the brawl, Smith reportedly urged another of his players to go after a Knights' player, according to OHL commissioner Dave Branch, at which time referee Dave Lynch ejected the Spitfires' rookie coach. Branch indicated Smith's suspension was the result of an accumulation of episodes involving him and his team. "There were five other incidents this year which caused the league to issue warnings to Brad," Branch said. "One resulted in a $250 fine and another in a three-game suspension. I don't think you can attribute Brad's actions to inexperience – it's a matter of what's right and wrong."

In, Then Out

There was joy in Windsor when the Spitfires, who'd squandered a 3-1 series lead in their 1991 OHL first-round playoff series against the London Knights, then fell behind 2-0 in Game 7 at London, rallied for a 5-2 verdict and a second-round date with the Niagara Falls Thunder. But the joy was short-lived.

Windsor coach Brad Smith and assistant coach Dave Prpich were both suspended for the first two games of the series for their actions toward referee Don VanMassenhoven following Windsor's Game 6 loss to the Knights. "Smith and Prpich both waved towels in the direction of referee Don VanMassenhoven, Prpich gave the choke sign, they both used sticks as 'rifles' in a

Spitfires forwards Cory Stillman (19) and Todd Warriner (17) were both first-round selections in the 1992 NHL entry draft. (DH)

shooting motion, entered the ice surface after the game and verbally abused the referee," OHL commissioner Dave Branch said in announcing the suspensions.

With GM Wayne Maxner behind the bench, Windsor dropped the first two games, and were swept aside in four straight after Smith and Prpich returned to the job.

Singing Siblings

Just call them the singing Spitfires. Windsor defencemen Jamie and Peter Allison were part of a band with their sister Leann from a young age. "My uncle taught us to play," Jamie Allison said. "We'd play at family gatherings and eventually, we formed a band. We called it the Family Circle Band." They performed well enough to win the Canadian Open singing competition.

Peter toiled for the Spitfires from 1991-92, while younger brother Jamie, Windsor's top draft pick in 1991, played just one season as a Spitfire before a trade across the river to the Detroit Jr. Red Wings, but later enjoyed an NHL career of 851 games from 1997-2006 that included stops in Calgary, Florida, Chicago, Columbus, and Nashville, where he was able to combine both of his unique talents.

In 2004, he cut a country and western demo tape for RCA and performed at local night spots in the country capitol of the world. "They told me they're always looking for angles to promote," Allison said. "Well, I've got my angle. I really couldn't have asked for a better spot. You drive down Music Row and see all the big labels. It was pretty awe-inspiring."

Allison later returned to his on-ice passion and today works as an assistant coach with the OHL's Brampton Battalion. "It has been a thought to pursue music, but it is a tough decision because music is hard to get into," Allison said.

Two In One

Spitfires history was registered on the floor at the 1992 NHL entry draft when, for the first time in franchise history, two Spitfires heard their names called during the first round of the draft. In fact, both were selected among the top 10 choices.

First up was left-winger Todd Warriner, who was tabbed fourth overall by the Quebec Nordiques. Two picks later, centre Cory Stillman went sixth overall to the Calgary Flames.

One year earlier, Oshawa's Eric Lindros balked at going first overall to the Nordiques, but Warriner, who posted 40-41-81 totals for the Spitfires during the 1991-92 OHL season, had no qualms about Quebec. "It's always been my dream to play in the National Hockey League," Warriner told The Montreal Gazette. "I have no problems going anywhere. I'm just happy to get my chance. I can speak my share of French, so I don't feel as though (language) is going to be a problem."

Stillman was equally anxious about his NHL opportunity. "You want to make your mark, to establish yourself, so you don't go from prospect to suspect," he said.

Stillman, who collected 90 points in 53 games of an injury-plagued 1991-92 campaign, was of the opinion that he and Warriner made each other better. "We complement each other," Stillman told The Calgary Herald. "He's a goal scorer and I'm a playmaker. We're a one-two punch. He knew where I was on the ice and I knew where he was. Sometimes, he would get the glory and sometimes I would. It just depended on who was hot and who was not."

Spitfires Legend: Cory Stillman

Early in his NHL career, there were those ready to label Cory Stillman a bust.

Then he burst through with a vengeance. Stillman looked to be down to his last chance when he attended the Calgary Flames' 1997 training camp without a contract.

"It was a gamble, but there wasn't much else I could do," Stillman recalled. "It wasn't like I had teams beating down the door to sign me. There were going to be 75 players in camp, and I don't think they were going to miss me."

Stillman posted a 27-goal campaign in 1997-98, the first of seven 20-goal seasons he's enjoyed during his NHL career. "That was Cory's third year (as an NHLer) and it's often the case that the third year is when a player begins to emerge," remembered then-Calgary general manager Al Coates. "Maybe we expect too much from these kids too soon."

Stillman burst into prominence with the Spitfires, collecting 101 points as a rookie in 1990-91, earning OHL rookie-of-the-year honours. A year later, the Flames made him their first pick in the NHL entry draft.

Through the 2009-10 season, he'd played 960 NHL games with the Flames, St. Louis, Ottawa, Carolina, Tampa Bay and Florida, collecting 266-422-688 totals and winning Stanley Cups with the Lightning (2004) and Hurricanes (2006). Thanks to the 2005 NHL lockout, Stillman became the first player since Claude Lemieux (New Jersey 1995, Colorado 1996) to earn rings in consecutive seasons with different teams.

"He's an underrated player," said Peter Laviolette, Stillman's coach in Carolina.

Stillman acknowledged that the wait was worth it. "It's taken me longer to earn more respect," he said.

After leaving the Spitfires, Cory Stillman won Stanley Cups with Tampa Bay (2004) and Carolina (2006). (DH)

Instead of being written off, Stillman has written an impressive story of success.

"Sometimes, I think we're a little hasty when you hear hockey people ready to write some player off who's 23 or 24," Coates said. "Cory is proof that if you're patient and willing to wait a couple of seasons, you can be rewarded."

Cory Stillman Spitfires Stats

SEASON	GP	G	A	P	PIM
1990-91	64	31	70	101	31
1991-92	53	29	61	90	59

Todd's Tale

The first OHL player selected in the 1992 NHL entry draft when he went fourth overall to the Quebec Nordiques, superstardom was envisioned for Spitfires left-winger Todd Warriner.

It never materialized. Warriner's talent didn't show at the NHL level, and he became a journeyman player who played 453 games with six different teams, never scoring more than 12 times in a single season. He was traded by Quebec to the Toronto Maple Leafs before playing an NHL game. "It's just part of the game," Warriner said of the moving around. "Everywhere I've been, I've just tried to work hard, give it my best and learn something."

It never materialized for Warriner. His talent didn't show at the NHL level, and he became a journeyman player who skated in 453 games with six different teams, never scoring more than 12 times in a single season. Quebec traded his rights to the Toronto Maple Leafs before Warriner played in the NHL. "It's just part of the game," Warriner said of the moving around. "Everywhere I've been, I've just tried to work hard, give it my best and learn something."

Warriner spent two seasons with the Spitfires, netting 36 goals as a rookie and 41 during his draft season of 1991-92, but plummeted to 13 in 23 games in 1992-93 prior to a trade to Kitchener. "I can't really explain it," Warriner said of the fall off. "Whether I got stale or what, but I wasn't coming to the rink prepared and I wasn't happy."

He played for the Canadian Olympic team that won a silver medal at the 1994 Winter Games in Lillehammer, Norway, making Warriner the first Spitfire to capture an Olympic medal. "The Olympics are that much bigger, and when you play countries in Europe you feel it," Warriner said. "Canada is well-respected and there's a lot of pride on the line."

He also netted the first goal in Air Canada Centre history while playing for the Leafs in a 3-2 overtime win over the Montreal Canadiens on Feb. 20, 1999. In typical Warriner fashion, he forgot to retrieve the milestone puck. "It didn't occur to me to get the puck until I got to the bench and by that time it was gone," Warriner said.

Changes At The Top

A disappointing 19-42-5 slate during the 1992-93 season led to the dismissal of GM Wayne Maxner and saw the Spitfires finish last in the Emms Division and miss the playoffs, leading to sweeping changes within the club's organizational structure. On May 7, 1993, team co-owners Steve Riolo and Vic Gabriele bought out their former partners Ray Pittao, John Lot and Vince Bassman. Under the new arrangement, Riolo remained team president, while Gabriele would serve as governor, a position formerly held by Bassman.

"The other three partners wanted to sell their shares of the hockey team," Riolo told the *Windsor Star*'s Mary Caton. "Vic and I made a commitment when we bought the team a few years ago to keep it in Windsor and we wanted to stay in hockey."

A Toronto-based group including Brad Robins and former NHL defenceman Jerome Dupont had reportedly made a bid to buy the Spitfires and move the franchise to the Toronto area. "There was interest outside the city from people who wanted to buy the club," Gabriele said.

"If the (outside) offer had been $2 million, then we would have sold," Riolo said. "But it was an affordable situation, so Vic and I decided to step in. We've got a new lease with the city now and we feel we can turn this club around."

Special Ed

The one bonus from the dismal 1992-93 season was that Windsor garnered a high pick in the OHL Priority Selection Draft and utilized it to take Ed Jovanovski with the second overall choice. Jovanovski was a local product of the Windsor Minor Hockey Association and a popular pick with fans.

"It was definitely a bonus, staying at home with mom and dad, having them cook for you, sleeping in your own bed," Jovanovski said. "I honestly think it was the best thing that ever happened to me, staying home, playing for Windsor. We had good teams and there's a lot of memories."

Spitfires Legend: Ed Jovanovski

Generally, they're the first words out of Ed Jovanovski's mouth when any of his NHL teams have visited Joe Louis Arena and he spies a familiar face from his hometown of Windsor.

"How'd the Spitfires do last night?" he'll ask.

Jovanovski, who didn't play organized hockey until the age of 11, was deemed the first

Becoming the first Spitfire to be selected first overall in the NHL entry draft when he was taken by the Florida Panthers to launch the 1994 draft, Spitfires defenceman Ed Jovanvoski was known as much for his offensive skill as he was for his physical presence. (DH)

overall choice in the 1994 NHL entry draft by the Florida Panthers. In 1996, still a teenager, he played in the Stanley Cup final.

"He watched my games and eventually decided to give it a try," said Deni Jovanovski, Ed's older brother. He began playing three years before Ed. "I don't know why he waited so long. Whenever he played road hockey, he was always a dominant star."

As Jovanovski was with the Spitfires. As he was almost from the outset in the NHL.

The Stanley Cup finals. The World Cup of Hockey. The first pick in the NHL entry draft. A world junior championship.

By the age of 20, Jovanovski had already assembled quite an impressive resumé. A resumé that only grew. He added an Olympic gold medal with Canada in 2002, while developing into one of hockey's most complete defencemen, a daunting physical presence with the requisite skills to quarterback a power play.

"He plays with a lot of authority," said Marc Crawford, Jovanovski's coach in Vancouver, where Jovanovski enjoyed a 17-goal season in 2001-02. "He skates with authority, moves the puck with authority, jumps into the play with authority, and hits with authority."

Every team he's played for, Jovanovski has instantly made better. "Eddie on any team is going to help a lot," said Phoenix Coyotes captain and current Jovanovski teammate Shane Doan. "He jumps into the play and makes things happen. When he's going, he makes things a lot easier for the forwards. We're fortunate to have him."

As much as he cherishes his NHL achievements, it's clear that playing for his country has given Jovanovski tremendous pride. "It's what it means to be a Canadian hockey player," he said. "And it's what makes it so special when you succeed."

Ed's father, a professional soccer player in his native Macedonia, understands this. "It wasn't just something he did for himself, it was for the whole country," Joe said of his son's gold medals. "It's pretty emotional, thrilling, a special moment," added Ed, who's also pulled on a Canadian sweater in the world championships.

All en route to establishing himself among the all-time greats to come out of Windsor, and from the Spitfires.

"My old buddy Joel Quenneville won't like this, because he always said he was the best defenceman ever to come from Windsor, but I think Jovo's overtaken him now," Crawford said.

Windsor-born Ed Jovanvoski didn't play organized hockey until he was 11, but quickly fought his way to the top. (DH)

The best defenceman in Windsor. One of the best defencemen in the NHL. And one of Canada's best defencemen.

Ed Jovanovski Spitfires Stats

SEASON	GP	G	A	P	PIM
1993-94	62	15	36	51	221
1994-95	50	23	42	65	198

Tale Of The Tape

Seen any good movies lately? Gary Agnew shrugged at the thought.

"No, but I think there's a lot of people who just saw a really bad one," the coach of the Kingston Frontenacs said from the safety of the visitors' dressing room at Windsor Arena shortly after a December 8, 1994 Ontario Hockey League game against the Spitfires, a game that forever will be known as the tale of the tape.

As fans entered the rink that night, each was presented with a video entitled, "The Not So Great Moments in Sports." A few hours later, those same fans used them to create a not-so-great moment of their own.

Kingston was comfortably on its way to a 6-3 win and the clock was winding down when an altercation broke out between Windsor's Vladimir Kretchine and Chris Van Dyk and Kingston's Marc Moro.

Frontenacs' forward Brett Lindros, seeing that his teammate was outnumbered, doubled back and delivered a glove facial of uppercuts toward Van Dyk. Eventually the officials dispersed the combatants, but that's when the real trouble began.

First, one movie bounced off the ice surface. Then another.

Finally, a cascade of videos rained down from the seats, in a bizarre episode of Roeper and Ebert meet World Wrestling Entertainment.

Only this wasn't scripted. Just scary.

"That's dangerous," Agnew said. "I don't know what goes through people's minds that makes them do something like that. It's just not right."

Lindros, the object of these erstwhile movie critics' ire, was even more disdainful of the video-launching performance. "It showed a total lack of class," he said. "If I see one of my teammates in a two-on-one situation like that, I'm going to help him out."

The younger brother of Eric Lindros was

equally disappointed by the unscheduled movie release. "I can understand the frustration of the fans, but that's no excuse for throwing stuff at us," Lindros said.

"They threw pucks at our heads," added teammate Colin Chaulk.

"And Snapple bottles," offered another player.

"And tire irons," said a third, who had obviously watched Slap Shot one too many times.

There weren't any tire irons aimed iceward. But that didn't make what happened any less excusable. "Unless its Nerf balls, I don't know that they should be giving fans anything when they come in the doors," Agnew said.

"I've never seen anything like that," Windsor coach Mike Kelly said.

If there was a silver lining in this black cloud of a night, at least the Frontenacs had something to watch on the bus on the way home. "Before the game, they gave us a copy to put in the VCR," Agnew said. "Now, everybody on the team has got one."

Raining Rodents

To this day, those who were at Windsor Arena on that fateful evening maintain a steadfast curiosity.

Was it an accident? Was foul play involved? Or was it simply a case of the little guy not being able to take it anymore?

The Spitfires were on their way to an impressive 4-1 decision over the first-place Sault Ste. Marie Greyhounds in a fight-filled Ontario Hockey League game when something plummeted to the ice surface.

Behind the Spitfires bench, assistant coach Dave Prpich caught the falling object out of the corner of his eye. "It landed just inside the blue-line, in front of our bench," Prpich said. "At first, I thought it was one of the fans throwing something on the ice."

This something wasn't a spectator-aimed missile, it was a squirrel that apparently had lost its balance while scurrying across the steel girders atop the ice. The furry visitor bounced once, then lay motionless until an arena worker arrived and carried the tiny rodent away to its final resting place on the business end of a shovel.

Falling rodents were just part of what made the Barn a unique place to watch a game and that certainly wasn't the only night that interlopers from the animal kingdom affected play. Former Spitfire Jason Spezza was foiled on a breakaway during a 2001 game when he lost the puck after being buzzed by a sparrow.

Back when he toiled for the Niagara Falls Thunder, former NHL goaltender Manny Legace was tending the net at the notorious rush end of the rink, where the locals made life a living hell for visiting goalies until protective mesh was installed to alleviate the dangers of flying pucks.

Before that time arrived, goalies like Legace were targets of missiles from fans almost as often as they were of pucks fired by Windsor players. "One night during a stoppage in play, I was cleaning the snow from my crease and I saw something come flying down in front of me," Legace said. "I thought it was just a Coke and I was going out to sweep it into my net, when I noticed that it was moving. It was a rat and it was still alive, so I decided to leave it there for the officials to deal with."

Rats were frequent companions back in the days when the senior Windsor Bulldogs were the main tenants of Windsor Arena. Returning in the wee hours from a road trip, players dreaded being the unfortunate soul who had to enter the dark rink first and turn on the lights. "The worst was when you'd come back on a Friday night," former Bulldogs player Jack Costello remembered. "They had bingo there back then and they hadn't cleaned up the debris yet. When you came into the rink, you could hear the tiny footsteps of the rats running all through the place."

There were other elements capable of making a dent in the proceedings, often when Sault Ste. Marie visited. A September, 1984 Windsor-Sault Ste. Marie game was postponed by fog. On March 4, 1982, the Greyhounds were forced to push a stalled Zamboni from the ice surface.

They weren't the only team that suffered, though. London Knights defenceman Brian Seljan suffered an electric shock after touching a metal shower handle after a March 21, 2001 game

Bill Bowler is the only player in Spitfires history to record three consecutive 100-point seasons. He reigns as the Spitfires' all-time scoring leader. (DH)

at the Barn. A February 21, 2002 Ottawa-Windsor game was cancelled by a power failure. On November 10, 2002, a Plymouth-Windsor game was held up for 82 minutes when a pane of glass broke and no replacement was available.

"When things like that would happen, we'd just look at each other and say, 'That's Windsor Arena,'" former Spitfires coach Tom Webster said.

Bowling Over Barnes

When Blair Barnes came to town to witness in person his Windsor Spitfires career points record of 296 as it fell by the wayside, the most astonishing thing to him was that the record remained in his name.

"I hate to see it go," Barnes said. "But to be honest, I thought that it had been broken before now because of all the players who have gone through here. Ernie (Godden) went through here. I figured it was gone, so I didn't think about it.

"It should have been broken by now."

The night of February 10, 1994, it finally was, thanks to a wrecking ball by the name of Bill Bowler.

Barnes, a Spitfire from 1977-80, attended a February 8, 1994 Spitfires game at Windsor Arena against the Owen Sound Platers as guest of the team. Barnes dropped the puck for the ceremonial opening faceoff and was recognized for his achievement by a crowd of 2,552.

Bowler entered the fray with 294 points to his credit in a Spitfires uniform and he didn't take long to tie Barnes, collecting assists on a pair of goals by Adam Young, the second coming just 22 seconds into the second period. But the elusive record-breaking point could not be had in a 7-6 loss to the Platers.

Darryl Lavoie tried to give his second goal of the night to Bowler, who had skated in front of his point shot, but never touched it. "It wasn't my goal or I would have taken it," Bowler said of the gesture by Lavoie. "If it's for the record I better make sure it's mine – besides, too many people were watching."

Bowler had five excellent opportunities to break the record during the balance of the game, but Platers goalie Jamie Storr thwarted four of them and Dan West fired a goal-mouth pass from Bowler wide on the other.

"I was hoping tonight would be the night," Bowler said. "I wanted to do it because Blair was here and my parents came down but there's always tomorrow – well Thursday."

The Sault Ste. Marie Greyhounds were the visitors that night and there would be no agonizing wait for Bowler. Bowler drew the second assist on a Craig Lutes goal just 54 seconds into the game for his record 297th point. The crowd of 2,459 gave him a standing ovation as he pumped a gloved hand in the air and was mobbed by his teammates near the penalty box.

Bowler went on to collect four points in a 5-4 loss to the Greyhounds on a goal and three assists and left the man he replaced at the top of the heap quite impressed.

"He's an aggressive player," Barnes said of Bowler. "He had some good shots, but I was more impressed with a few of the passes he made. He's got a unique style offensively and I saw him make some great defensive plays where he came back to pick up a man."

Billy Clubs Another Record

A quick flip through the Windsor Spitfires' record book will lead a person to recognize that Bill Bowler was one special player for the team. He's represented on virtually every page and a couple of those milestones were achieved during the second week of February in 1995.

Bowler's impressive run actually started in late January. His four-assist performance in a 7-0 win over the London Knights January 28, 1995 gave Bowler 100 points for the season. In the process, Bowler became the only Spitfire to record 100 points in three seasons.

"It's something I'm proud of and it's a milestone," Bowler said. "You start each year hoping to get 100 points because you pride yourself on being a scorer. I'm very happy with it."

In his farewell Ontario Hockey League season, Bowler still has his eyes fixed on a few other records. Two of them would fall his way February 9, 1995 at Windsor Arena.

As the Spitfires prepared to take the ice for a showdown with the Sault Ste. Marie Greyhounds, Bowler was poised become the best set-up man in OHL history. He entered the contest with 303 career assists and a share of the league record with former Ottawa 67 Brett Seguin.

One assist and he'd have the record to himself. With two assists, he'd also break former Spitfire Brent Jarrett's season assist record of 88, set in 1979-80. "I did have a goal at the start of the season to be the all-time assist leader and I'm close," said Bowler, who had 24 goals, 87 assists and 111 points on the season.

Spitfires coach Mike Kelly knew his star player was a lock to make his mark. "I think it's safe to say Bill Bowler will get the record," Kelly said. "Even if it isn't tonight, you know he'll get an assist at some point the rest of the way."

While Bowler had chased several records that year, Kelly said it never became a distraction in the dressing room. "In the room, everyone cares about each other and they care about Bill Bowler," he said. "There's no animosity and the only thing they want to know is how they can help."

Actually, it was Bowler who was the most adept at offering helping hands. And in a 10-3 rout of the Greyhounds before 4,133 at the Barn, he was quick to deliver on his record promise.

Bowler finished the night with two goals and four assists, easily surpassing both standards he was pursuing, but his performance was overshadowed by a brawl that started in the penalty box and later spilled into the stands.

Sault Ste. Marie's Brad Baber and Matt O'Dette jumped to the Windsor side of the penalty box in the second period. There to meet them on the other side were Adam Young, Ed Jovanovski and D.J. Smith – all of whom ranked among the league's top 10 in penalty minutes. The Greyhounds' Joe VanVolsen, who cleared the penalty box glass to join in the melee, got

Windsor's Bill Bowler fights off London's Jason Allison for possession of the puck. (DH)

No one set them up like Bill Bowler, who collected an OHL-record 318 assists during his Spitfires career. (DH)

involved with fans in the hallway while leaving the ice, but the biggest loser of all was scorekeeper Borden Hildenbrand, who suffered an eight-stitch gash to his leg from a flying skate.

"Jovanovski, Younger and I got into a brawl in the penalty box," Smith said. "First one guy jumped in, then another and it was on."

Spitfires Legend: Bill Bowler

During his Spitfire days, it was difficult to miss Bill Bowler. Unless you were an NHL scout, that is. Despite finishing his OHL career as Windsor's all-time scoring leader and displaying a dazzling ability to distribute the puck and see the ice, the five-foot-nine Bowler was considered undersized by NHL standards and was never drafted.

He spent five years toiling in the International Hockey League before garnering his first contract from an NHL club, with the Columbus Blue Jackets in 2000. Bowler played nine games for the Blue Jackets during the 2000-01 season, the only NHL action of his pro career.

"I was never drafted and spent six years in the minors before getting my NHL shot," Bowler said. "For a lot of successful people, it didn't come instantly. Sometimes, it takes a little persistence and a little patience."

The big man will get every chance to show he can't. The little man may never be offered the opportunity to show he can.

"They can knock you all they want, but if they don't give you a chance, how do they know you can't do it at that level?" Bowler said. "When you're a young guy, you think if you do your job, it will pay off. As you get older, you learn about the game behind the scenes.

"There's a lot that goes on, why some guys get a chance and some guys don't."

Bowler left the game prematurely at the age of 29 due to injury.

"I was forced to retire," Bowler said. In training camp with Nashville in 2002, he tore the abdominal muscle off the bone, requiring surgery. He signed with Boston the next season, but failed his physical. Bowler made one last-ditch comeback effort, winning a German League title with Krefeld in 2002-03.

"It was a great experience, but I was in a lot of pain," Bowler said. "I wasn't anywhere near the player I used to be. I knew I was at the end."

Eventually, Bowler would go into coaching, working with the Spitfires for two seasons as an assistant coach. He and D.J. Smith ran the bench as co-assistant coaches during the 2005-06 season.

"He's someone with that rare combination of ultra skill and tough competitiveness," said Chris McSorley, who coached Bowler with Las Vegas of the IHL. "Bill is the kind of guy who is willing to take responsibility on the ice."

Bill Bowler Spitfires Stats

SEASON	GP	G	A	P	PIM
1991-92	66	25	63	88	28
1992-93	57	44	77	121	41
1993-94	66	47	76	123	39
1994-95	61	33	102	135	63

Spitfires forward unit of Bill Bowler, Dave Roche and Tim Findlay dominated the OHL during the 1994-95 season. (DH)

Assembling A Line

They had game. All they needed was a name.

The Spitfires forward unit of Bill Bowler, Dave Roche and Tim Findlay dominated the OHL during the 1994-95 season, leading to a contest to name the trio. Among 330 entrants, the Assembly Line was chosen as the winner. "I think it suits our team, with our city being so automotive," Bowler said. "It's a Motor-City type of thing."

Veteran overage centre Bowler was the one who made the line go, collecting an OHL-leading 102 assists among his 135 points that season.

Right-winger Findlay, the rookie of the unit who contributed 34-42-76 numbers, turned down a scholarship to play NCAA hockey at Illinois-Chicago to join the Spitfires. "Right when I got there, it hit me that I didn't want to do this for the next four years," Findlay said of his visit to the school. "It felt foreign to me. It hit me as a whole different world down there. As soon as I got home, I told my folks I didn't think that going to school in the States was going to be the right thing for me to do."

Acquired from Peterborough to complete the trio, left-winger Roche produced 55-59-114 totals. "He's the prototype of the power forward every team is looking for," said Ed Johnston of the Pittsburgh Penguins, the NHL team that drafted Roche. "He's a big physical player and he has great hands."

Roche, who moved up to play on a line with Pittsburgh captain Mario Lemieux the following season, acknowledged the role his linemates played in his NHL arrival. "One thing I have to do is give credit to Billy (Bowler) and Timmy (Findlay) because we all worked hard together," Roche said.

Detroit Shakedown

It was supposed to be a rout, a quick shuttling aside of the Spitfires by the first-place Detroit Whalers, who'd finished 38 points ahead of Windsor in the OHL regular-season standings during the 1995-96 season.

On the ice, their first-round playoff series certainly started out that way. The Whalers,

Former Spitfires winger Matt Cooke helped the Pittsburgh Penguins win the 2008-09 Stanley Cup. (DH)

coached by former Spitfire Peter DeBoer, raced to a 3-0 lead on the virtue of 5-3, 5-2, and 6-4 victories.

Undaunted, the Spitfires maintained belief that they weren't done. "Hey, they were the ones who are ranked ninth in Canada and we're not ranked anywhere," Spitfires captain Mike Martin said. "So, as far as that goes, there's no pressure on us."

Down 3-0, Windsor pulled out its red special-occasion sweaters, worn just once during the regular season for a home loss to Owen Sound, and backstopped by goalie Terry Joss, immediately spawned a three-game winning streak, forcing Game 7 while building momentum and confidence.

"We were the underdogs, but we basically played three straight Game 7s," remembered D.J. Smith, a defenceman with that Spitfires club.

In the end, the clock struck midnight on this Cinderella story. Plymouth routed Windsor 9-2 in Game 7 at Oak Park Arena.

Spitfires Legend: Matt Cooke

Matt Cooke has never forgotten his Windsor roots, perhaps because his game and his character are so firmly rooted in Windsor's blue-collar, work-ethic values.

"He's the kind of player that you want to have on your team," explained Jordan Staal, Cooke's frequent linemate with the Pittsburgh Penguins. "He creates such energy, tries to get some big hits and get the guys going. He drives the net hard, he makes plays and tries to score some goals. He got all those factors."

Added Penguins forward Maxime Talbot, "You'd rather have Matt Cooke on your team than the other team."

The Spitfires were fortunate enough to suit the gritty Cooke for three seasons, including a 45-goal, 95-point campaign in 1996-97, launching an NHL career with Vancouver, Washington, and Pittsburgh that so far has seen him skate in 738 games and pot 114 goals.

"He's a guy who pressures other teams," Penguins coach Dan Bylsma said. "He's in your face, drives the net, creates room for the people around him."

Marc Crawford, Cooke's first NHL coach with the Canucks, compared Cooke's game to that of a four-time Stanley Cup winner. "He's very similar to Kris Draper," Crawford said, pointing to Detroit's spunky Grind Line centre when the Wings won titles in 1997, 1998, 2002 and 2008, and a onetime Spitfires draft pick. "Their No. 1 asset is their speed and they utilize that speed to bring energy to the game."

Ed Jovanovski missed teaming with Cooke in Windsor by one season, but later suited up alongside him in Vancouver. "He's always making something happen out there," Jovanovski said of Cooke. "He's in on the forecheck at 100 miles an hour, making the big hit, forcing the key turnover. Those are the kinds of guys who win you games in the playoffs."

Cooke won a Stanley Cup with Pittsburgh in 2008-09, helping the Penguins rally from a 2-0 series deficit for the triumph, drawing inspiration from his old team after watching the Spitfires lose the first two games of the Memorial Cup, then sweep four games to take the title.

"I know they were in a tough situation, but they battled through," Cooke said of the Spitfires. "I'm happy for Windsor. I know (Spitfires coach) Bobby (Boughner) and (Spitfires assistant coach) D.J. (Smith), when I played there, he was our captain. I'm just so excited for them and happy that they could pull it out."

Matt Cooke Spitfires Stats

SEASON	GP	G	A	P	PIM
1995-96	61	8	11	19	102
1996-97	65	45	50	95	146
1997-98	23	14	19	33	50

He Shoots, He Scores

Ron Vogel made Spitfires history that's yet to be equalled the night of January 9, 1998, at the Sarnia Sports and Entertainment Centre. With Windsor leading 3-2 and the Sarnia Sting net vacated for an extra attacker, Vogel ventured from his net to corral a dump-in. He gave the impression he was going to bank the puck off the boards. When the Sting players moved over, he lifted it down the ice.

It skidded the length of the rink and into the net, making Vogel the first goalie in Spitfires history to register a goal. "It barely made it," Vogel said. "(Teammate Jeff Martin) had to blow it over the line. I just wanted us to get an insurance goal. I didn't care how it went in. It was actually kind of a stupid play on my part. We were only up one goal at the time."

Vogel finished the night with 39 saves and was named first star of the 4-2 Spitfires victory.

Sarno Wins Scoring Title

There wasn't much to celebrate about the 1997-98 edition of the Spitfires. They finished the Ontario Hockey League season out of the playoffs at 19-42-5 under the direction of coach/general manager Tony Curtale.

Thankfully, Peter Sarno gave people reason to come to Windsor Arena. In what may have been the most unheralded scoring title triumph in OHL history, Sarno became the first Spitfire to wear the crown since the club rejoined the league in 1975-76 and the first overall winner from Windsor since Earl (Dutch) Reibel in 1949-50.

That Sarno won it while wearing street clothes only served to add to the surrealism of the scenario. A three-point effort during a 13-4 loss to the Erie Otters at Windsor Arena March 5, 1998 virtually guaranteed that Sarno would be scoring champion.

With three games left in the season, the Windsor centre, who'd been named the Ontario Hockey League's rookie of the year following an 83-point campaign in 1996-97, held a 24-point lead in the scoring race over Sudbury's Jeremy Adduono. Sarno's league-leading point total was 121 points. Adduono sat at 97 points.

"I guess I'll relax when it's over with," Sarno said. After that game and with the league scoring title wrapped up, Sarno decided to call it a season and rest his injured wrist.

Peter Sarno, Corey Locke and Marcel Dionne are the only players to win back-to-back OHL scoring titles. (DH)

Spitfires teammates Jamie Wentzell (24) and Peter Sarno (centre) celebrate a goal. (DH)

"From what I know, I'm probably going to be called up, and I didn't want to risk it," said Sarno, an Edmonton Oilers draft pick who, as it turned out, was headed for the American Hockey League's Hamilton Bulldogs after the conclusion of the OHL season for the AHL playoffs. "I don't have a contract, but they have me signed to an insurance policy in case I get hurt," added Sarno, who was thought to have ligament damage in his wrist.

While he was excited to become the club's first OHL scoring champ, Sarno heard the catcalls from the Windsor Arena faithful on more than one occasion due to his league-leading minus-41 rating. "I hate it and I get ridiculed all the time about it," he said. "They look at the points then look over (to the plus/minus) and wonder what's wrong."

Sarno said that was the area he wanted most to concentrate on improving prior to the 1998-99 season. "I realize now there's more to hockey than points," Sarno said. "That's just the one part I'm excelling at."

As events unfolded, Sarno would work on that aspect of his game in a new arena. He was dealt to the Sarnia Sting in the off-season. With Sarnia, Sarno won another scoring title, collecting 130 points in 68 games. He was the first player in the league to garner back-to-back scoring crowns since Marcel Dionne did it with St. Catharines in 1969-70 and 1970-71.

Kugel Banned

The afternoon of Sunday, October 25, 1998 was billed as Family Day at Windsor Arena but, by the end of the day, family values had taken quite a beating. So did Owen Sound Platers forward Jiri Golicic, courtesy of Spitfires tough guy Jeff Kugel.

It would be the last punch Kugel ever threw in an Ontario Hockey League game.

A 7-2 Spitfires victory featured 14 fighting majors during the final frame, including a line brawl at 4:18 during which Owen Sound's Adam Mair and then Kugel left their benches to join the altercation. Kugel punched Golicic to the ice, then chased the Platers' Chris Minard halfway around the rink before officials gained control and got him off the ice.

"Everyone tried to stop me, but there was no holding me back," Kugel said. "I knew I had to go out there and stick up for my teammates." Kugel was assessed a gross misconduct for his actions, Mair got a game misconduct and Owen Sound's Sean Avery picked up a match penalty for a baseball-swing slash at Windsor's Mark Ridout.

Owen Sound coach Dave Siciliano blamed linesmen Glenn Anderson and Steve Stasiuk for the bench-leaving incident. "(Golicic) isn't a fighter and he's getting beat up," Siciliano said. "The linesmen had it broken up, then they let (Ridout) go back and beat on him some more. Our guy (Mair) had no choice. He had to go."

The six-foot-six, 250-pound Kugel talked about turning Windsor Arena into a scary place again. "Teams used to be afraid to come in here and we want to put that fear back in them again," he said.

Windsor coach Tony Curtale praised his club's performance. "Our guy didn't leave the bench first, our guys didn't swing their sticks," he said.

Siciliano questioned whether Kugel – who had one goal and 84 penalty minutes in 44 OHL games – should be in the league and apparently, OHL commissioner Dave Branch shared Sicilano's vision.

Branch acted quickly and harshly to ensure that Kugel wouldn't get another opportunity to wreak havoc on the ice. The next day, he suspended Kugel indefinitely and November 2, 1998, following a hearing at the league's office, assessed Kugel a lifetime ban from the OHL and a 25-game suspension from all major junior hockey.

Kugel was the sixth player and the first Spitfire to be banished from the league for life.

Stayzer's OT Heroics

The Spitfires battled from a long way back to get the opportunity, so perhaps the lengthy wait for a final outcome wasn't all that arduous.

Especially considering the result went their way.

The Spitfires experienced that pure, instantaneous explosion of emotion that comes with a victory in sudden-death overtime on the night of March 20, 1999. But this one was even more exciting than usual.

Blair Stayzer's goal at 1:14 of the second overtime period lifted the Spitfires into a playoff spot and ended a see-saw battle with the Kitchener Rangers that began long before their fateful meeting at Windsor Arena.

"That was a fabulous feeling," remembered Dave Prpich, the Spitfires coach in that game. "A lot of guys on that team were not emotional, and that genuine outpouring of emotion is what sports is all about. As soon as he scores, you jump the bench and hug whoever you can find to hug."

Stayzer's second goal of the game ended the four-and-a-half hour marathon and gave the Spitfires a 2-1 win over the Rangers in the first Ontario Hockey League tiebreaking game since 1970. In that game, the Oshawa Generals defeated the Hamilton Red Wings 5-4.

Both Windsor and Kitchener finished the season with 52 points, ahead of only the expansion Brampton Battalion (19 points).

Naturally, Stayzer viewed the goal as his most significant tally. "I can't think of another goal in my career," said Stayzer, who scored his first goals in a month in the sudden-death win. "That has to be the biggest goal I've scored by far."

The Rangers came within an inch of ending the affair seconds earlier. Breaking three-on-two, Kitchener's Richard Kazda had his shot turned aside by Windsor goalie Ron Vogel.

The Spitfires quickly transitioned the play toward the Rangers end and Robin Boucher fed Stayzer on the fly as he wheeled around the Kitchener defence and beat goalie Reg Bourcier with Windsor's 62nd shot of the game.

"Rick Pracey (the Spits goalie consultant at the time) said the weakest part was his glove side," Stayzer said. "That's where I was going."

Stayzer had little chance to enjoy the moment. As the crowd of 2,337 rose to its feet, Stayzer turned with his arms raised and was immediately buried on the ice, becoming the bottom slice of an extra-thick hero sandwich. "I think (Luc) Rioux hammered me first and I just hit the ground," Stayzer said.

Holding a commanding 62-35 edge in shots, the Spitfires were remarkably calm throughout against an opponent that wouldn't go away. "We pretty much joked about things between periods," said captain Jeff Martin, who had four excellent chances to score but was blanked. "Mostly it was ripping guys who had chances to score. What did I have, 25 shots?"

Stayzer took a little ribbing too. He had two chances to win it in the first overtime, but shot wide on one and scored on the other opportunity, only to have it waved off by referee Bill Prisniak.

Stayzer eventually got his chance to smile and celebrate with his teammates, who'd completed a long comeback from a five-point deficit behind Kitchener January 30 to secure the eighth and final playoff spot in the OHL's Western Conference.

At the other end of the ice, the Rangers – who'd lost 2-1 to the Guelph Storm in their final regular-season game to force the sudden-death game – stood stunned by the outcome. Fully five

Former Spitfires goalie Michael Leighton backstopped the Philadelphia Flyers to the 2010 Stanley Cup final. (DH)

minutes after the Spitfires left the surface, several members of the Rangers remained on the ice, struggling to accept the reality that their season was over.

"It's a pretty disappointing end to my OHL career," Kitchener captain Darren Mortier said. "We had 20 guys battle all year and I just don't think there's anything to be said afterward."

As it turned out, Windsor didn't have much left to celebrate afterward, either. The top-seeded Plymouth Whalers, who finished 54 points ahead of the Spitfires in the standings, swept the first-round playoff series between the two teams.

Spitfires Legend: Michael Leighton

It started as a tribute, and quickly grew into a memory lane, filling three walls of the family home in LaSalle.

The Michael Leighton hockey sweater collection.

"We've got pretty much all my jerseys," said Leighton, the former Spitfire who backstopped the Philadelphia Flyers to the 2010 Stanley Cup final. "We have them up on the wall, and the wall's pretty full. There's not much room for more jerseys."

There's his Spitfires sweater, his Ontario Hockey League and American Hockey League all-star sweaters, as well as one from each of his National Hockey League stops.

"All three walls along the one room have all of his jerseys," Jennifer Leighton said of her husband's array of goalie garments. "Between NHL and all of his AHL teams, I'm not sure how many are down there, but there's quite a few."

If you're keeping score at home, since graduating from the Spitfires in 2001, Leighton has made seven NHL stops – Chicago, Buffalo, Anaheim, Nashville, Montreal, Carolina and Philadelphia. Add in five AHL teams and the roadmap becomes quite populated with destinations.

He's the only goalie who keeps track of GAA and GPS.

From the outside, it seems so easy. The dream life. First-class hotels. Charter flights. Fine dining.

The NHL.

What more could a guy want?

The reality is that far more professional athletes live the life of Leighton than the life of Riley.

"It's hard to think of anything long-term, because of the way things have gone in the past, but it's also hard not to dream about what it would be like to be stable somewhere for a few years," Jennifer said. "People like to think our life is very exciting and luxurious and whatnot, but it's very stressful. We're constantly on the move. There's a handful of players that are lucky enough to be stable and get long-term contracts, but the majority of the players don't have that stability.

Every Stanley Cup run proves to be a proving ground for an unlikely hero.

In the spring of 2010, Leighton filled that bill for Philly. He paid his dues. Now he's paying dividends.

Another overnight sensation who was years in the making.

Michael Leighton Spitfires Stats

SEASON	GPI	GA	SO	GAA	W-L-T-OTL
1998-99	28	112	0	4.84	4-15-2-2
1999-00	42	118	1	3.12	17-17-2-0
2000-01	54	138	2	2.73	32-11-6-2

Michael Leighton led Windsor to a first-round playoff series win over Sarnia in 2000, capturing Game 7 on the road in overtime. (DH)

Kelly Arrives, Webster Returns

Tom Webster hugged his granddaughter and smiled.

"This is why I came back," he said through his unwavering grin.

Across the hall, Steve Riolo's mouth was also agape in a festival of enamel.

There hadn't been many days in recent memory when the Spitfires and their supporters had had reason to smile. May 19, 1999 was one of those days.

With the return of Webster as coach and the addition of Mike Kelly as general manager, the Spitfires organization gave itself the chance to step up among the elite of Ontario Hockey League clubs.

"I asked my wife, 'Can we afford these two people?'" Spitfires owner Riolo said, describing his new dream team as, "the best GM and coach in junior A hockey."

Webster won Stanley and Memorial Cups as a player and as a coach and guided the Spits to their only Memorial Cup appearance in 1988. Kelly also went to a Memorial Cup as GM of the Guelph Storm.

"These are family men with strong character," Riolo said. Family lured Webster back. His son and daughter both lived in Windsor. Brent Webster joined his dad's staff as an assistant coach.

Kelly, a former teacher, thrived on working with junior-aged players, applying a simple philosophy when dealing with teenagers. "I treat

Windsor centre Fedor Fedorov is the younger brother of 1993-94 Hart Trophy winner Sergei Fedorov. (DH)

them the same as I would my own son," he said. "I want a team based on the principles of work ethic and responsibility."

Webster shared that view. "You want to give these kids a solid foundation to grow from, to continue on with their life," Webster said, citing the example of Mike Wolak, a player he coached with Windsor's 1988 Memorial Cup squad, who became a doctor. "The kind of commitment it took him to make it through medical school started here."

Riolo just wanted to be able to make a commitment to becoming a fan who just happens to also pay the bills. "I want to step back. I want to come to the game, sit in my box and look out and see 3-4-5 thousand fans, having fun at the game," Riolo said.

The Other Brother

The Windsor Spitfires were playing an early-season game at London during the 1999-2000 campaign when a radio reporter spied a familiar name on the club's roster.

"Fedorov," said the fellow. "Is he a brother?"

"No, he's from that other Fedorov family that lives in Bloomfield Hills," answered a sarcastic voice.

Spitfires centre Fedor Fedorov, was indeed the younger brother of Detroit Red Wings centre Sergei Fedorov. And when you're the younger sibling of the 1993-94 Hart Trophy winner, everyone knows your name before you have the chance to make one for yourself.

It also meant there was a price on his head. "Every guy in the league is taking a run at me because of the name on the back of my sweater," Fedorov said.

His older brother beamed with pride whenever Fedor's name was mentioned. "He wants to be his own man," Sergei Fedorov said of his little brother.

"It's like with Mark Howe," added Windsor coach Tom Webster. "He was Gordie Howe's son, but he wanted people to know him first as Mark Howe and you know what, he did a pretty good job of it. Fedor is doing all the things necessary to be himself. He's doing a great job of being Fedor Fedorov."

Regardless, Fedor never shied away from following in his brother's footsteps. "People who know me, who know hockey, know that I'm Fedor," Fedorov said. "Sergei, I'm very proud to be his brother. I can't change that and I wouldn't want to. I'm actually lucky to have a role model like that."

He scored seven goals in 60 games with Windsor that season, but potted 33 in 2000-01 following a trade to the Sudbury Wolves. "This is a tough league, but everyone tells me you have to play here to make it to the NHL," Fedorov said of the OHL.

He ended up playing 18 NHL games with Vancouver and the New York Rangers, and Fedor spent the 2009-10 season with Magnitogorsk Metallurg of Russia's Kontinental Hockey League, where his teammates included his older brother.

Spezza trade

Of the many deals in Spitfires history, none shook the city the way the club's November 15, 2000 deal with the Mississauga IceDogs did. In one fell swoop, one blockbuster of a move, Windsor acquired the best player in major junior hockey.

The Spitfires got centre Jason Spezza. In return, the IceDogs received forwards Tyler Eady, Ryan Courtney, and Mike James, defenceman Steve Rawski, and a second-round draft pick.

"I've only seen two 15-year-olds who were better," one NHL scout said of Spezza during his OHL rookie season. "Bobby Orr and Wayne Gretzky."

"His skill level for a young guy with his size and physical status, it's impressive," London coach Gary Agnew said of Spezza. "You don't see too many guys who are able to handle the puck and see the ice the way he does."

Windsor coach Tom Webster, a teammate of Gordie Howe and Bobby Orr, and later Wayne Gretzky's coach, saw similar greatness in Spezza's uncanny ability. "He's the type of athlete who is in a position to break a game open for you every time he takes to the ice," Webster said.

Spitfires centre Jason Spezza was the second player chosen in the 2001 NHL entry draft, taken by the Ottawa Senators. (DH)

Spitfires Legend: Jason Spezza

Many hockey fans admire the work of Jason Spezza. Spezza simply admires a work of hockey. "I'm a big NHL fan," Spezza said.

Since he was 14, experts projected Spezza as the next phenom to take the NHL by storm.

If he listened, it never showed. "You'd think he'd be a cocky guy, you know, 'I've got the world by the hand,' but he's real down to earth," Windsor teammate Steve Ott said.

Roommates at the 2001 world junior championships in Russia, Ott got a crash course in Spezza's passion for the game. "We just talked hockey, hockey, hockey," Ott recalled. "We both love the game so much."

For Spezza, that meant being glued to the set whenever the NHL was on television. The mornings were devoted to careful study of the previous night's summaries. "I'm looking at the standings every day," he said.

When he's on the ice, people are generally glued to Spezza's every move.

"He's got great offensive skills," said Tom Webster, who coached Spezza in Windsor. "He handles the puck well, has great vision and he can shoot. He's always asking questions and the things he can't do are all teachable."

Like Mario Lemieux and Wayne Gretzky and other great ones who came before him, Spezza also had his share of detractors. "I think I've always been picked on," Spezza said, shrugging off the oft-heard criticisms of his game. "It doesn't bother me. I knew there were going to be a lot greater expectations placed upon me.

Windsor's Jason Spezza played for Canada in three world junior tournaments. (DH)

"People think I can win games single-handedly, but that doesn't happen in hockey. Even when Gretzky was with the dynasty in Edmonton, they had a lot of great players, not just one good one."

The Ottawa Senators, who took Spezza with the second pick of the 2001 NHL entry draft and have seen him produce 475 points in 464 NHL games, appreciate what he brings to the table.

"He wants to get better," said Montreal Canadiens coach Jacques Martin, Spezza's first NHL coach with the Senators. "He wants to be the best player he can be. That's all you can ask of an athlete."

Don't be fooled into thinking it's a destination reached by accident.

"They love being out there," Webster said of the great players. "That's where they're the happiest. You look at a guy like Tiger Woods. He's the best golfer in the world, but what's he usually doing? Practicing to get better.

"They are continually looking for ways to improve, methods of doing things differently, to continue their success. It's not a conscious choice. It's the way they live. It's not work for them. It's their passion."

Jason Spezza Spitfires Stats

SEASON	GP	G	A	P	PIM
1999-00	41	36	50	86	32
2000-01	27	19	26	45	15

Ott's Frenetic 50-Goal Finish

Two attractions drew 4,000 to Windsor Arena the night of March 22, 2001.

In the main event, a 4-2 victory by the Spitfires over the Sarnia Sting in the final game of the Ontario Hockey League season, the team clinched the third seed in the OHL Western Conference playoffs and a first-round playoff date with the Owen Sound Platers. On the undercard, there was the most fascinating sprint to a 50-goal season perhaps in all of hockey history.

Spitfires left-winger Steve Ott was the player on the cusp of the magical milestone, entering the contest with 49 goals, but it was the fashion in which he arrived at this focal point that had everyone in the game talking.

Sitting with 40 goals on the season and four games left to play, Ott began his odyssey with a hat-trick March 11 in a 9-2 rout of the Sault Ste. Marie Greyhounds. He followed up with another three-goal effort in a 5-2 decision March 15 over the London Knights. A third consecutive hat-trick March 19 in a 4-2 doubling of the Plymouth Whalers earned Ott OHL player-of-the-week honours and left even the usually-talkative Spitfire dumbfounded when asked if he'd ever scored three hat-tricks in a row.

"Maybe in the driveway," Ott said, laughing. "But not in a meaningful game like this one."

League officials were unable to determine whether Ott's run was a league record. "I can't imagine it's happened too often, but it's not a statistic that was ever kept," OHL spokesman Aaron Bell said.

As he readied for the regular-season finale, Ott sought to keep his eyes on the real prize. "Now that I'm this close, I'd love to get there because so few have," Ott said. "But we can't lose sight of our goal, which is to finish as high as we can. Individual numbers are great but they can't come at the expense of team goals."

As it turned out, both of Ott's wishes would come true, and in spectacular fashion. With less than six minutes to play and the score tied 2-2, referee Pat Smola signaled for a penalty shot after Sarnia's Kenny Jung covered the puck in the goal crease.

Windsor coach Tom Webster selected Ott to take the shot. With the entire crowd on its feet, Ott raced in and lifted a backhander past Sting goalie Robert Gherson and there was instant pandemonium.

"I've never felt like that before," Ott said. "I've never heard this place so loud. It was amazing. It was great to get the 50th, but it was even greater to get it when the entire team needed it."

With his goal, Ott joined Tim Findlay, Jason Cirone, Dave Roche, Kelly Cain, David Haas, Gerry Leroux, Blair Barnes and Ernie Godden in the franchise's 50-goal club.

Steve Ott scored 10 goals in the last four games of the 2000-01 season, including three hat-tricks, to reach the 50-goal plateau. (DH)

Spitfires Legend: Steve Ott

It's fair to say that there's little down time in Steve Ott's world. "My quiet time is reading to my daughter (Layna Grace)," Ott said. "That kind of lulls me right out, playing with her. The rest of the time is pretty much full throttle."

When he arrived as their second pick of the 2000 OHL Priority Selection Draft from the junior B Leamington Flyers, the Spitfires knew immediately that Ott was a unique individual and player. "I've never seen a kid so determined to succeed," Windsor GM Mike Kelly said. "He never rationalizes anything. He never compromises anything. And he has above-average skill."

Perhaps that determination was derived from a life lived in transit, often being the new kid in class. An armed forces brat, Ott was born in P.E.I. and learned to skate in Gypsumville, Manitoba, a town so small it takes longer to find it on the map than it does to drive through it.

He played his first organized hockey in Winnipeg and spent his formative years in Toronto, before settling in Stoney Point just prior to adolescence.

"I've been almost everywhere," Ott said.

On the ice, his game isn't nearly as complicated. "Going hard to the net, finishing checks," Ott explains. "Being myself out there. I call it kamikaze style."

It's a style that's allowed Ott, 28, to play 410 NHL games with the Dallas Stars, who selected him 25th overall in the 2000 entry draft.

Former Spitfires forward Steve Ott ranks among hockey's most annoying agitators. (DH)

Dallas coach Marc Crawford, no shrinking violet himself as a player, brightens considerably when he talks about Ott, drawing parallels between his game and that of Stars captain Brenden Morrow, a six-time 20-goal scorer.

"He's really become a very good player," Crawford said. "He puts puck in the right places. He understands what the other team is trying to accomplish. He's also got that antagonistic gene, which is good. You need all sorts of energy to get through not only a game, but a season, and he brings a lot of that energy."

It's a character trait his teammates have always admired.

"A guy like Otter brings skill and he's got that edge where he can be an agitator," former Dallas centre Stu Barnes said. "I think that's why guys like and respect the way he plays, because he goes out and plays a hard, clean game. You can be an agitator that way – skating hard, finishing your checks, being tough on the puck and winning those battles. That's as difficult to play against as anything."

Ott wouldn't have it any other way. Though Ott's job description may seem simple, his is a demanding position to fill. But it's a skill a team will always require.

"I don't think I'm an enforcer one bit, but guys like myself sticking up for guys, more of a role guy, those guys are going to be around forever," Ott said.

Steve Ott Spitfires Stats

SEASON	GP	G	A	P	PIM
1999-00	66	23	39	62	131
2000-01	55	50	37	87	164
2001-02	53	43	45	88	178

Final Four Showing

Windsor's best playoff run in 14 years ended with a five-game Western Conference final series loss to the Erie Otters, but the Spitfires' season didn't conclude without hope for the future.

"Deep down, we really felt we were going to come back," Spitfires captain Craig Mahon said. "We gave it the best we could."

With 16 players eligible to return for the 2002-03 season, the Spitfires were hoping to take that next step. "This year, we took a big step forward," Spitfires defenceman Tim Gleason said. "Next year, I think we'll be better. We should have a lot of guys returning and we should know better what to expect."

Mired in last place in the conference January 4, the Spitfires regrouped to moved into the sixth playoff spot, and followed with upsets of Sault Ste. Marie and Guelph before falling to the eventual OHL champion Otters. "This was a year to build on," said Mahon, an overager whose career was ending. "They'll be a very solid hockey club next year."

The Ottawa Senators claimed two Spitfires in the first round of the 2001 NHL entry draft – centre Jason Spezza (second) and defenceman Tim Gleason (23rd). (DH)

"The sad part is you end on a losing note, but think about the playoff run," added Spitfires head coach Tom Webster. "I'm proud of this hockey team and how far they've come. To go as far as we did is gratifying."

Backstopping the run was overage goaltender Cory Campbell. Acquired from Belleville, whom he'd taken to the Memorial Cup in 1999, Campbell was voted club MVP for the regular season and playoffs. "I think the praise goes to the goaltending," Spitfires forward Steve Ott said. "He's been consistent like that since Christmas and that's a key factor."

Windsor hadn't advanced this far in the playoffs since 1988, when the Spitfires won their first OHL championship and went all the way to the Memorial Cup final before losing 7-6 to the Medicine Hat Tigers.

The Spitfires traded Jason Spezza to Belleville in 2002 to acquire reigning OHL scoring champion Kyle Wellwood, a native of nearby Oldcastle. (DH)

Spitfires Legend: Kyle Wellwood

When reigning OHL scoring champion Kyle Wellwood was acquired by the Spitfires from the Belleville Bulls for Jason Spezza at the 2002 trade deadline, it was a huge deal, and the catalyst for a Windsor run to the OHL final four.

"He's amazing," Windsor right-winger Phil Gibson said of Wellwood. "He gets into one of those tight spots where two or three guys are right on top of him and you think, 'He's toast.' You look back a split second later and somehow, he's out of there."

An introspective sort who can often be found passing the time with a good book while others engage in card games, Wellwood makes up for what he lacks in foot speed with incredibly imaginative vision.

"I usually hang back and watch the play and wait for my chances," Wellwood said.

Opponents were awed by Wellwood's elusiveness, both with and without the puck. "He's so shifty, you can't give him any space," added defenceman Carlo Colaiacovo, an NHL teammate of Wellwood's with the Toronto Maple Leafs. "You have to try and hit him as much as possible."

Easier said than done. "I don't know that there's anybody in the game who can move laterally as quickly as he does," said Windsor GM Mike Kelly, who engineered the deal.

Wellwood won fans throughout the league with his cerebral skills. "The little things he can do with the puck, his vision, the way he sees the ice so well, those are things I tried to pick up on, factors that can make me a better player," Erie Otters forward Brad Boyes said.

"He's my dad's guy," offered Dallas Stars coach Marc Crawford, whose father Floyd was the head scout for the Bulls, the team which originally drafted Wellwood. "He has great vision. He sees the ice so well. He's a heck of a hockey player."

Wellwood, a local product from Oldcastle who wore sweater No. 97 with the Spitfires because his grandfather Harold Wellwood's favourite players were Detroit Red Wings legends Gordie Howe and Ted Lindsay, was selected in the 2001 NHL entry draft by the rival Leafs. "Just like that, everyone switched sides to their arch-nemesis," Wellwood said. "Even my grandpa changed sides. Seventy years as a Red Wings fan and now he's pulling for the Leafs."

Wellwood found performing in hockey-mad Toronto to be somewhat of a challenge. "Playing hockey in that city, it was a big adjustment, especially with the team doing badly," Wellwood admitted. "You can't go anywhere without being recognized.

"Everybody wants to talk about the team with you and they've all got their ideas on what changes we need to make to get better. It felt like I was living in a soap opera."

Wellwood moved to the Vancouver Canucks in 2008 and scored 32 goals for them over two seasons.

Kyle Wellwood Spitfires Stats

SEASON	GP	G	A	P	PIM
2001-02	26	14	21	35	0
2002-03	57	41	59	100	0

Up In Flames

Expected to contend during the 2002-03 season, Windsor's season was quickly lost in the embers of undisciplined play and personal agendas, a factor which ultimately led to the departure of coach Tom Webster.

A few weeks before the end came, Webster was reminiscing about the 1987-88 Spitfires OHL championship club that he'd guided to within one win of the Memorial Cup. "If there were problems in the room, I never heard about them," Webster recalled. "(Adam) Graves and (Paul) Maurice took care of the problem before it ever got to me.

"Now, I'm always putting out fires."

In the end, Webster ultimately flamed out. Citing health reasons, Webster, 54, tendered his resignation February 27, 2003.

"I could see his health was suffering," Windsor GM Mike Kelly said. "I could see how frustrated he was."

The final straw came during practice two days before Webster's resignation, which was marred by a physical confrontation between Webster and left-winger Mike James. At his wit's end, Webster slashed and later cross-checked James, who had messed up a drill. Assistant coaches and players combined to restrain Webster.

"I think it showed just how much the stress was draining on him," Spitfires captain Tim Gleason said.

Kelly replaced Webster behind the bench. "Tom didn't feel he handled it very well," Kelly said. "It was totally out of character for him."

Top: Windsor's Kyle Wellwood beats St. Michael's goalie Andy Chiodo on a breakaway. Bottom: Spitfires centre Kyle Wellwood played the entire 2002-03 OHL season without being assessed a single penalty minute. (DH)

Craig Kennedy (303), Craig Mahon (300) and John Scott Dickson (306) are the only players to suit up for 300 games as Spitfires. (DH)

The 300 Club

Two of them shared the same given name. All of them were teammates. And each played at least 300 games in a Spitfires uniform.

Craig Kennedy. Craig Mahon. John Scott Dickson. In the history of the Spitfires franchise, this trio are the only players to play that many games in a Windsor uniform.

"It shows you're durable," said Dave Prpich, who coached all three players. "You have to average 60 games over five years, and that's not easy."

Left-winger Dickson played a club-record 306 games between 2000-05. Right-winger Kennedy finished with 303 games in a career that spanned from 1999-2004, and defenceman Mahon finished with 300 games in a career that went from 1997-2002.

"Not too many guys do it," Dickson said.

Mahon and Kennedy both served as captain of the club. "I remember when I was 16, I said I never wanted to be a five-year man," Kennedy said. "I've seen it all in this league and I know for young guys it's a struggle mentally when you're used to playing 40 games in bantam."

Mahon is the only player in franchise history to captain the Spitfires over three seasons. "I had numerous players say that he's the best leader they've ever been involved with," said Mike Kelly who served as coach and GM of the Spitfires during Mahon's tenure. "Sometimes, within the confines of this arena with the fans, he was much maligned, but he had a world of respect in that dressing room."

Spitfires Legend: Tim Gleason

Sixteen steps. That's the walking distance from the Detroit Little Caesar's dressing room to the visitor's NHL dressing room at Joe Louis Arena.

In minor hockey with Little Caesar's, Tim Gleason walked down that corridor many times. Every so often, he'd steal a look at where the big guys suited up, envisioning the day he'd be in there.

"When you're a kid, you think about stuff like that, but it never seems real," Gleason admitted.

A native of Clawson, Mich., it was Gleason's intention to play NCAA hockey when the Spitfires selected him with the first pick of the 2000 OHL draft. "We had to convince him that this was the right organization for him, that the right people were in charge, that it was going to be the right place from him to develop," Windsor coach Tom Webster said. "All we asked was that he give us a chance."

Gleason opted to do so, and he never looked back. "It's part of growing up, of being responsible," Gleason said of the decision he made to come to Windsor. "That starts with my parents, for sure. They show you a lot, teach you a lot, but it's up to you to remember it when you get older."

Captain of the Spitfires during the 2002-03 season, he brought that same maturity to the ice surface. "My job is on the offensive at the other end, but defence is most important," Gleason explained. "I take care of my own zone first and then jump into the play."

Selected 23rd overall by the Ottawa Senators in the same 2001 NHL entry draft which saw Ottawa take Windsor centre Jason Spezza second overall, Gleason was dealt to the Los Angeles Kings before ever playing in an NHL game. He made his debut with the Kings in 2003.

Acquired by Carolina in 2006, Gleason was a huge reason why the Hurricanes reached the Stanley Cup Eastern Conference final in 2009. "We have always had a lot of time for Tim Gleason and what he does," Hurricanes coach and former Spitfires defenceman and captain Paul Maurice said. "When I came in, he had a real bad ankle injury and just played through it, and by the end of the year and in the playoffs, he was outstanding for us.

Defenceman Tim Gleason of Clawson, Michigan was Windsor's top pick in the 2000 OHL Priority Selection Draft. (DH)

Spitfires captain Tim Gleason goes down to block a shot in front of goalie Ryan Aschaber. (DH)

"He's so good for our team and such a good man and leader, and I think that's what's happening. He is now evolved into the leader and vocal guy on our back end. He's physical, he'll fight. He plays hard minutes against the other team's best players."

Gleason added another feather to his cap last season, and it was silver lined. He was part of the USA squad that won the silver medal at the 2010 Vancouver Winter Olympic Games.

Tim Gleason Spitfires Stats

SEASON	GP	G	A	P	PIM
1999-00	55	5	13	18	101
2000-01	47	8	28	36	124
2001-02	67	17	42	59	109
2002-03	45	7	31	38	75

Larger Than Life

Cam Janssen learned lessons in dedication from his parents. Amy Janssen, a nurse practitioner, and husband Dennis, a construction worker, surrendered their dream home in Eureka – an upscale suburb about 50 km from St. Louis – to enable their son to pursue his dream.

"A big, beautiful house, out in the woods," Janssen said, a look of longing dancing in his eyes. As Janssen progressed steadily up the hockey ladder, so did the accompanying costs.

"The travelling every weekend, the food, the hotels, it was very expensive," Janssen said. "We couldn't handle it anymore, so we moved out, got a smaller house. They downsized in houses to finance my hockey career. They've spent so much money on me over the years, but I will repay them."

Cam Janssen fought 79 times in a Spitfires uniform. (DH)

That day arrived, and to say right-winger Janssen fought his way to the NHL would be an understatement. According to hockeyfights.com, Janssen dropped the gloves 79 times during his Spitfires career from 2001-04, making him a fan favourite. He's fought 80 times as an NHLer with the New Jersey Devils, the team that selected him in the 2002 NHL entry draft, and the St. Louis Blues, his current team.

"He loves to play, loves life and is hungry to learn," said Tom Webster who coached Janssen in Windsor. "He constantly wants to improve. If there's a challenge there, he accepts it."

Some would find playing for their hometown team to be among those challenges. Suiting up for the Blues, Janssen savours every minute. "Playing in the NHL is one thing, but to be playing for your hometown team, it's unreal," Janssen said.

"It's unbelievable. I have my house there that I've had since I broke into the league. I live next to my parents. It's great to go home and have your whole family there supporting you. In this kind of business, you're up and down so much and it's just good to have that kind of support."

Yes, he's repaid his parents, bought them a beautiful, new dream house for helping make his dreams come true. Janssen has also closely followed the fortunes of the reigning Memorial Cup champion Spitfires since he left town.

"Right when I leave, they start getting good," he laughed. "I'm always telling the guys that playing in Windsor was just a blast. It was the funnest time of my life. That's where I started. (Former Windsor GM) Mike Kelly really took me, developed me as a player and got me to the NHL. Now I'm here, supporting my family, doing good and feeling good."

Miracle Comeback

Led by the strong will of Steve Downie, Windsor rallied from a 3-0 series deficit to defeat Sault Ste. Marie in the opening round of the 2005 OHL playoffs. (DH)

Down 3-0 in the 2005 OHL playoff opening-round series against the Sault Ste. Marie Greyhounds, the Spitfires needed a miracle, and a hero.

They found both in Steve Downie.

In Game 4, Downie netted the overtime winner in a 4-3 Windsor victory. John Scott Dickson's tally, set up by Downie, won Game 5 in overtime by a 6-5 count. Celebrating his 18th birthday, Downie netted the winner in Game 6, a 4-3 Windsor verdict.

"They're feeling the pressure," Downie said. "I know I would be if I was in their place."

Even the Greyhounds were acknowledging Downie's impact on the turnaround in the series. "The biggest reason that team is in the series is No. 7," Greyhounds head coach Craig Hartsburg said of Downie. "There's no question he's outplayed some of our best players when the game is on the line."

The teams worked double overtime in Game 7, Windsor finally winning it 3-2 on Dickson's goal 33 seconds into the fifth period, again on a feed from Downie. "I just put it at the net and it went in," Dickson said. "I don't know what to think. I'm so happy."

It was just the second time in OHL playoff history that a team had rallied from a 3-0 series deficit – Ottawa did it against Oshawa in 1988 – and the first time a team had done it by winning Game 7 on the road.

"We made history," said Windsor goalie Kyle Knechtel, who stopped 49 shots in the Game 7 triumph. "It's awesome."

Windsor's joy was short-lived. The Spitfires were swept by London, the eventual Memorial Cup champions, in the second round.

Their Backbone

Dave Prpich went to the Memorial Cup as an assistant coach with the Spitfires in 1988, so to label his final season with the team as his finest hour with the club would probably be stretching a point.

As head coach of the club, though, he made his farewell tour with the team one worth remembering, helping the Spitfires rally from a 3-0 series deficit to beat the Sault Ste. Marie Greyhounds in the opening round of the 2005 OHL playoffs.

It wasn't the first time Prpich had stepped in to dig the club out of a deep hole. A loyal soldier who worked for nothing more than an honourarium and the use of a car, Prpich always answered this team's call in their time of need.

Were there a Rolaids Relief Man award presented in the Ontario Hockey League, Prpich would have been the annual recipient. Whenever there was disarray within the Spitfires organization, Prpich stepped in to stop the bleeding. When storm clouds gathered over Windsor, Prpich was this team's version of Ghostbusters.

He was the one they always called.

Seven times, Dave Prpich stepped in to serve as interim head coach of the Spitfires. (DH)

Seven times, he filled in as Windsor's interim coach. He was the man always willing to fall on the grenade, to take one for the team.

"I played for a lot of great coaches over the years – John Muckler, Al MacNeil, John Brophy, just to name a few – but I'll tell you, none of them have got anything on Dave," said former Spitfires coach Brad Smith, who worked with Prpich on his staff.

In 2004-05, Prpich was the glue that held the team together through several firestorms that could have easily given the Spitfires all the ammunition they needed to self-destruct.

He took over when Mike Kelly stepped down as coach, babying the club through a horrible losing streak when the season could have easily been derailed, as everyone with power inside the organization, including owner Steve Riolo, took turns publicly bashing their effort.

It was Prpich who arranged to bring Detroit Red Wings associate coach Barry Smith over to run practices and he was also the driving force behind the mid-season addition of former Spitfires' captain D.J. Smith to the coaching staff.

When Kelly was let go as general manager late in the season, Prpich carried the club through the uncertainty, helping the team keep its focus.

Ultimately, though, his best work came with Windsor down 3-0 in its 2005 opening-round playoff series against the Sault Ste. Marie Greyhounds. Every opportunity was there for the Spitfires to make a meek exit from the post season. Instead, buoyed by their coach's belief, they manufactured a rally never before seen at this level, coming back to win, taking Game 7 on the road.

"That last year, I probably had as much fun going to the rink as any team I'd been with," Prpich said. "I tried to make the game fun again. Remember, these are teenagers, and when we were that age, the thing we wanted to do most was have fun."

Today, Prpich works as a consultant with the Kitchener Rangers, and has helped that team to a pair of Memorial Cup tournaments.

Cal O'Reilly dished out 81 assists with the Spitfires during the 2005-06 season. (DH)

Spitfires Legend: Cal O'Reilly

If there were only one cookie left, Cal O'Reilly would happily pass the plate to the next person. Were he to board the bus and find only a solitary seat available, he'd gladly step aside so someone else could rest their weary bones.

He's just that kind of guy. Always has been, but that's not news to fans of the Spitfires.

He was Windsor's passing fancy, a playmaker whose 81 assists during the 2005-06 season were good enough for fifth on the club's all-time single-season list.

"I've always been a passer, it's in my genes," said O'Reilly, who collected 149 assists in three seasons with the club.

"Cal has the ability to find his teammates," said Bill Bowler, Windsor's assistant coach in 2005-06. "He really has vision out there. He's always aware of where the other players are, which is a great trait to have. Guys love playing with a guy like that."

Bowler could speak with some authority on the subject, since the 102 assists he collected during the 1994-95 season stands as Windsor's club mark for helpers.

The life of O'Reilly involved a lifetime of dishing it off. Sharing is bred into his bones.

"That's the way I grew up," O'Reilly said. "That's the way my parents raised me.

"That's the way I like to be."

These days, O'Reilly offers a helping hand to the Nashville Predators. He's produced 11 assists for them in 42 NHL games played since 2008.

Cal O'Reilly Spitfires Stats

SEASON	GP	G	A	P	PIM
2003-04	61	3	18	21	2
2004-05	68	23	50	73	16
2005-06	68	18	81	99	8

Aliu-Downie

In terms of memorable moments that have occurred during the Spitfires' long and illustrious history, not many were as dramatic in the changes it brought about. And no other moment was witnessed by as few people as this one.

No one anticipated that history would be made when the Spitfires took the ice for a September 28, 2005 practice at the old Barn. But one cross-check and two fistic bouts later, the direction of the franchise would forever be changed.

According to witnesses at the practice, the Spitfires had just finished a drill when veteran Spitfire Steve Downie and rookie Aliu exchanged words, Downie criticizing Aliu's efforts during the drill. Downie raced off the bench and made a beeline for Aliu, the club's 2005 top draft pick and cross-checked Aliu in the face.

Two spirited fights between the two players ensued. "Steve's strong willed and Akim is strong willed and they went at it," Spitfires coach-GM Moe Mantha said. "I won't have this. We're supposed to be a team."

As the real cause for the altercation came to light, it quickly became apparent that these Spitfires were anything but a team. An Ontario Hockey League investigation revealed that Downie's assault of Aliu was the result of bad blood between the two stemming from when Aliu had refused to partake in a hazing ritual on the team bus returning from a September 9 preseason game in London in which rookies were ordered by veterans to strip and cram themselves into the bus bathroom.

Both players were suspended by the team, although the league ordered Aliu's suspension rescinded, while handing Downie a five-game sitdown. But the worst was yet to come. Downie left Windsor, demanding a trade and was ultimately sent to Peterborough. Aliu returned to action, but left the team later in the season and was dealt to Sudbury.

After a prolonged OHL investigation, commissioner Dave Branch suspended Mantha for the season as GM and for 40 games as coach, while fining the club $35,000.

Mantha never coached the team again. He was fired November 25, 2005 by team owner Steve Riolo, who questioned Mantha's integrity in a press release. Mantha immediately hired Toronto lawyer Brian Greenspan and within five days, Riolo had retracted his statements and reached a settlement with Mantha.

Down 3-0 to the Sault Ste. Marie Greyhounds in their 2005 OHL opening-round playoff series, Steve Downie (7) willed the Spitfires to victory, literally and figuratively clearing the Greyhounds out of the way. (DH)

Two For One

Windsor's 2005-06 season resembled a script from a bad B-movie, but the work the Spitfires got behind the bench was A-plus.

Sitting 2-9 and dealing with the 40-game suspension of coach-GM Moe Mantha following a hazing scandal, the Spitfires were left in the hands of co-assistant coaches D.J. Smith and Bill Bowler, neither of whom had ever served as a head coach in the major junior ranks.

Consider what these rookie coaches were left to deal with that season:

The Spitfires' best player (Steve Downie) quit the team and was traded to Peterborough. Akim Aliu, the club's top draft pick, quit the team and was traded to Sudbury.

Coach-GM Mantha was suspended by the OHL and later fired by owner Steve Riolo. The team went through two trainers and four equipment managers.

"The amount of change and turnover that has gone on since the start of the season is phenomenal," Bowler said.

Yet under Smith and Bowler's tutelage, this club steadily turned it around and finished third in the OHL's West Division at 32-29-3-4, posting a club-record 15-game home-ice winning streak.

"I think we both believed that we could get the job done," Bowler said.

The team quickly believed in them too. "They might not be as experienced as the other coaches, but they know hockey," Windsor goalie Anthony Guadagnolo said. "I've learned so much about the game from them."

Both Smith and Bowler were recent NHLers and that seemed to register with their team. "There's not that much difference in age, about 10 years, between us and the players," Smith said. "We've also both recently played in the NHL and I think that matters with the players, too."

After losing to the Plymouth Whalers in a seven-game opening-round playoff series, the first-year coaches deflected the kudos toward their embattled players.

"Considering what these young men have gone through and what they accomplished, I honestly give these guys a lot of credit for the way they've handled things and the way they've performed," Bowler said.

End Of The Line

No one was involved with the Windsor Spitfires longer than Steve Riolo, part of the ownership group from 1990-2006. In 1997, he bought out partner Vic Gabriele and became sole owner of the team.

During his 18 years running the show, Windsor went through 18 coaching changes and a half dozen general managers, enjoyed just seven winning seasons, won eight of 22 playoffs series and missed the playoffs three times.

"Eighteen years and no championship, not even getting to the fourth round (the league final) is a disappointment," said Riolo, whose teams compiled a record of 501 wins, 582 losses, 80 ties, 28 overtime losses and four shootout losses.

The Riolo era ended February 14, 2006, when sale of the team to Bob Boughner, Warren Rychel and Peter Dobrich was announced. Only three weeks earlier, Riolo had denied rumours of an impending sale. "The team is not for sale," he said. "It won't be sold."

Riolo loved the Spitfires and wanted to win badly. The city owed a debt of gratitude to Riolo, who stepped up in 1990 to help keep the team in Windsor.

"It's been 18 years of good memories," Riolo said. "They are three good owners, especially Bob Boughner, who is the main guy. I feel very good and if they ever need help, I'll be there to help and support.

"I don't regret any moment. I have a lot of good memories and feel honoured to have owned a franchise of this calibre."

On April 6, 2006, the OHL board of governors voted to officially accept Boughner, Rychel and Dobrich as the new owners of the franchise. "I think it's been a very good day," OHL commissioner David Branch said after the vote.

Riolo suggested several local groups had approached him to sell. He also indicated there were offers to buy and move the club outside the city to Niagara Falls and New York, but said it was important to him to keep the team in Windsor.

"That's one of the main reasons I chose to sell to these three guys," Riolo said. "I know they will keep the team in Windsor and we want the team to stay in Windsor."

Spitfires Tidbits

- Ryan O'Neill, a Spitfires forward from 1991-93, today works as an Ontario Hockey League linesman.

- Playing for the Canadian team in the 1999 United Hockey League All-Star Game, former Spitfire Shawn Heins won the hardest shot competition with a blast of 106 miles per hour, the heaviest shot ever recorded in professional hockey.

- Mike Martin (1995-96) and Jeff Martin (1998-99) are the only brothers to have served as captains of the Spitfires.

- Michael Rupp, a Spitfires forward in 1997-98, scored the Stanley Cup-winning goal for the New Jersey Devils in Game 7 of the 2003 final series against Anaheim. It's the only playoff goal he's scored during his NHL career.

- Spitfires centre Kyle Wellwood played the entire 2002-03 OHL season without garnering a single penalty minute.

- Tom Jefferson, a Spitfires forward in 2004-05, was the younger brother of former NHL forward Mike Danton, who served five years in prison after he was convicted of a plot to kill his former agent David Frost.

- David Bowman, a Spitfires defenceman from 2000-04, won the 2001 Minto Cup Canadian Junior A Lacrosse championship playing for the St. Catharines Athletics.

The fall of 2006 marked the dawning of a new era for the Windsor Spitfires. While the players stand at attention for the national anthem, coach Bob Boughner, one of three new co-owners of the team, is visible behind the bench. (DH)

FIVE

Winning Ways

THERE WERE THOSE IN THE HOCKEY WORLD who could always see the potential for the Spitfires to become one of the elite hockey programs in the Canadian Hockey League.

"It could be the next London," one Ontario Hockey League general manager noted.

That comment came shortly after London won its first Memorial Cup title while playing in front of more than 9,000 fans a night in a new rink, and just months before Bob Boughner, Warren Rychel and Peter Dobrich announced their purchase of the Spitfires on February 13, 2006 from Steve Riolo.

It didn't take long for the new ownership group to deliver on that potential and create a franchise that has become the envy of many in both the Ontario Hockey League and CHL. "I don't think there's a better program in junior hockey," former NHLer Don Barber told the *Windsor Star* after his son Riley Barber was drafted by the Spitfires. "These guys show a passion and everyone wants to be there."

The formal announcement between the two parties capped more than two years of negotiations. "There's been a lot of anxiety," Boughner said. "We've been so close sometimes and other times, it seemed like it was so far away."

It was a strange agreement that saw Riolo's ownership phased out and the new owners slowly settling in. "It's been a long, drawn-out process," Dobrich said.

Even when an agreement was announced, Riolo didn't simply turn the keys over to the new owners. When the purchase was made public, it was noted that Riolo would maintain control of the franchise for the final 14 games of the 2005-06 regular season and whatever number of playoff games followed, which turned out to be one round.

Ownership of the team would be turned over seven days after the season was complete. That came April 14, more than two months after the initial announcement.

While Riolo would get a few more weeks with the team, the new ownership was allowed to start putting its stamp on the franchise. Dobrich immediately began working on the business side for ticket sales and fans quickly gave their vote of approval to the sale. Within two months, season ticket applications were up nearly 13 per cent.

Rychel also dove in and took control of the team's scouting staff to begin preparing for the new ownership's first draft, which was less than three months away. "It will be my draft with the current scouting staff," said Rychel, who played more than 406 NHL games over eight seasons and won a Stanley Cup. "After that, we'll evaluate every position."

It became clearer each day that this new group was going to be very hands-on and that wasn't going to change once the sale was finalized. The OHL's board of governors overwhelmingly supported the sale in a move commissioner David Branch called, "a very good day."

By that time, the new ownership group was plowing ahead with a new vision. Rychel had left his job as a pro scout with the NHL's Phoenix Coyotes. "It's been five good years, but there's work to do done here," said Rychel, who would take on the title of vice-president and general manager of the Spitfires.

The new look of the Windsor Spitfires: trainer Joey Garland, goaltending coach Bill Dark, coach and co-owner Bob Boughner, assistant coach D.J. Smith, co-owner Peter Dobrich, co-owner and GM Warren Rychel, associate coach Bob Jones. (DH)

Dobrich took over as the team's governor and most realized that it was only a matter of time before Boughner, who was still playing in the NHL, joined in day-to-day operations. The team's majority owner, Boughner made the move in June once his 10th NHL season was complete.

On the day the veteran defenceman announced his retirement after 630 NHL games, he was installed as president and head coach of the Spitfires. "Ending my career and coaching really became one decision," said Boughner, the 27th person to coach the club since it joined the OHL in 1975-76. "Having this (team) made it a lot easier. It hasn't really struck me yet that my career is over. I'm sure it will in time, but right now I'm more excited about the Spitfires.

"I remember going to Spits games as a kid and sitting up in the corner. I've been a Spits fan since I was five years old. Getting here, in this capacity, is overwhelming."

The Plan

The new ownership of Bob Boughner, Warren Rychel and Peter Dobrich did not get caught up in basing success of their acquisition simply by the number of games the team would win or lose.

With Boughner as head coach and Rychel as general manager, the two would be responsible for the on-ice product, but the club's new owners had a bigger vision for the team. "We want to treat this almost like a little NHL franchise," Boughner said. "We want first class from when you walk into the arena, to how we run things inside our dressing room and our offices."

A final attempt by outgoing owner Steve Riolo to bring in veterans for one last shot at post-season glory left the incoming ownership with holes on the roster and lost draft picks as well. "There was a whole age group missing from the team when we took over," Boughner said. "We've had to retool and that can't happen overnight."

Assuming control of a club that had failed to win a single division title and finished under .500 in 10 of the 18 years under the previous ownership, the talk of rebuilding wasn't something easy to present to fans. "There's going to be some long nights," Boughner said. "You can say we're rebuilding and we're going to be young, but that doesn't lower the expectations."

Rebuilding the roster would take time, but there were other ways to convince fans there was a brighter future ahead. One of the first moves was to reach to the past, as the Spitfires agreed to terms with CKLW AM 800 to carry the club's games after a three-year absence from the 50,000-watt station. "We see this as long-term," CKLW program director Keith Chinnery said.

The club and CKLW had parted ways following the 2002-03 season. The Spitfires went two years without broadcasting games before partnering with CKUE 95.1 FM, but Boughner preferred the stronger signal reach of CKLW and the station's history with the club. "AM is traditionally sports," Boughner said.

Boughner said he spoke to fans, who wanted the move back to AM 800, and the owners continued to improve the team's stature in the community with the creation of the Windsor Spitfires Foundation. The goal for the foundation was to provide financial aid to local charitable causes. Just weeks after its establishment, the foundation was able to cover the cost for 12 local kids to play minor hockey whose parents were unable to afford it.

The small gestures helped rebuild the team's status in the community even with its first-year struggles on the ice. "You walk through the rink and people are shaking your hand, telling you what a good job you're doing and we're 18th or 19th in the league," Boughner said. "You can't say enough about that."

Season-ticket sales rose 40 per cent from the previous years and the business community followed suit with advertising and corporate sales increasing 30 per cent. "We're overwhelmed by the support," Boughner said.

The Foundation

Warren Rychel was a 13th-round draft pick in the Ontario Hockey League and while he does boast a Stanley Cup title, he was never drafted into the National Hockey League.

So, in some ways, it seemed a little strange that three months after becoming a part owner of the Windsor Spitfires, Rychel was banking on his first OHL draft as general manager to be the turning point for the franchise. "It's going to lay the foundation for the next three years," Rychel said. "What I wanted to start with was to establish a good base and then mature in a year. By the second year, they'll be significant and by the third year, on top of their game."

Looking back, Rychel's words almost seem clairvoyant, with Windsor's 2006 draft producing seven players that would play on a regular basis in the league. Four went on to be drafted in the NHL, another would sign a free-agent NHL deal and five would end their junior career in Windsor with a pair of Memorial Cup rings. "We could not have done what we've done the last four years without that draft," Spitfires head coach Bob Boughner said. "That's a credit to Warren and his (scouting) staff."

Rychel felt confident that with him and Boughner having a background in the NHL, the organization was well equipped to show young players how to win. "When you're selecting 18-year-olds (in the NHL), you have a better idea (of the talent level)," said Rychel, who had been a pro scout for the NHL's Phoenix Coyotes. "But, with these (15- and 16-year-old drafted) kids, it's how they adapt and what you do after you get them.

"You can add pieces sometimes (through trade), but you have to develop your own."

Rychel did everything in his power to ensure the odds for success were more in his favour when the time came for his draft.

Greg Nemisz (64) and Adam Henrique (14) were the first two players ever drafted by the Spitfires' new ownership group. (DH)

Windsor had the seventh pick in the first round and its own pick in the second round, but Rychel made trades with Saginaw and Oshawa to secure extra picks in the second. "We're getting four of the top 29 picks and that's great for us," Rychel said.

Power forward Greg Nemisz would become the new ownership's first-ever selection. Centre Adam Henrique, whom Rychel considered taking in the first round, would still be on the board at No. 24. Forward T.J. Battani was selected at No. 27. Although he was traded his first season with the team, he went on to play four years in the league and won an OHL title with Kitchener in 2008. The first defenceman taken by Rychel was Mark Cundari, who went at No. 29.

But when the club held a prospect camp a few weeks later, Boughner wasn't sold on the picks. "(Boughner) came to mini-camp with a coffee in his hand and asked, 'Where's the first rounder?'" Rychel said. "I said, 'He's the big guy in the red jersey.' Boughner said, 'No way.' He was still a bit gangly and we almost got into a fist fight. He asked me to get him a defenceman and the first one I got (Cundari) is five-foot-eight, but he's the best shutdown guy in the league now."

While the ownership was new, there was still a sales job to deliver for the club, which was coming off a highly-publicized hazing incident the previous season. "I didn't know much about the organization, just the stuff that happened the year before," Nemisz said. "I got TSN, so I knew about the (Akim) Aliu and (Steve) Downie incident."

Rychel's sales pitch to players, parents and agents was enough to convince everyone to give them a chance. "They said they were rebuilding and I'd get a chance to play," Henrique said. "Everything was new and we'd be the first guys in here and they'd build the team around us."

It would be a difficult inaugural season, with the club leaning heavily on youth. "That first year was a long year," Henrique said. "There were some rough games."

As Rychel had promised, it would be the job of Boughner, his coaching staff and the rest of the organization to teach them how to be winners. "It was tough that first half year," Nemisz said. "I wasn't physically ready. I think our practices the first year were two hours and 15 minutes a day. We were working on systems and skating hard."

The club only got younger as the season progressed, with Rychel committing to a youth movement. After a flurry of deals at the deadline, the Spitfires recalled fourth-round pick Eric Wellwood, whose brother Kyle Wellwood had played for the Spitfires and been a star in the league, along with goaltender Matt Hackett, for the rest of the season. "We just wanted to get younger quicker," Rychel said.

The inexperience showed most nights, but it's a group that learned the right and wrong way of doing things.

"We all made each other better," Cundari said. "It's doing the little things right to win a championship." Hackett was traded the following season in a deal that eventually landed Windsor Justin Shugg and Dale Mitchell, while 11th-round pick Adam Wallace became the sixth member of the draft class to crack the lineup.

"It turned out well and into one hell of a team," Cundari said. The Calgary Flames would take Nemisz in the first round of the 2008 NHL entry draft. Henrique would go to the New Jersey Devils in the third round. Cundari wasn't drafted, but earned a free-agent tryout with the St. Louis Blues and actually became the first player from the group to sign an NHL contract.

A year later, Wellwood was selected by the Philadelphia Flyers while Hackett, who had been dealt to Plymouth, was drafted by the Minnesota Wild. "I knew they would turn into good players with the environment and coaching here, but you never think you'll get five NHL contracts," Rychel said. "They're just great kids."

A group that only grew closer during their time with the Spitfires as they dealt with tragedy – the sudden death of captain Mickey Renaud in 2008 – as well as triumph – winning back-to-back Memorial Cups. "We're all so close and we'll be lifelong friends," Wellwood said.

In many ways, the group feels as fortunate for the friendships off the ice as for the success on the ice. "We're lucky to have gotten into the situation we did," said Nemisz, who made Canada's world junior roster in his final season along with Henrique. "We're best friends, we hang out all the time and we'll continue to be best friends."

The group left a mark on a once-sagging franchise that fans will never forget. In their final three seasons of junior, they compiled a regular-season record of 148 37 8 11 mark (a .772 winning percentage), a 32-7 mark while winning back-to-back league titles, as well as eight straight wins at the Memorial Cup that made Windsor just the eighth team to win back-to-back titles.

"There's a team picture hanging in the training room with the (2006 drafted players) around the Memorial Cup," Rychel said. "That's one of my favourite pictures. That was a hell of a draft. I don't know if you could duplicate it in 20 years."

Growing Pains

The puck is framed and still hangs on the office wall of Spitfires president Bob Boughner. The calendar had turned to October with the season more than three weeks old before the first-year head coach and his new ownership group finally had the taste of an OHL victory.

Eric Wellwood, Mark Cundari, Adam Wallace, Greg Nemisz and Adam Henrique were all part of the first draft class of Windsor's new ownership group in 2006. (WSHC)

Mickey Renaud tipped home Mike Weber's point shot with 16.6 seconds left in regulation and it stood as the winner as the Spitfires scored their first win of the season with a 2-1 decision over the Rangers in Kitchener.

Equipment manager Mike Hildenbrandt scampered onto the ice when the final buzzer sounded to make sure the souvenir didn't get away. "I'm proud of the guys," Boughner said. "This is going right next to the puck I scored my first NHL goal."

The season was eight games old before the Spitfires tasted that first win in front of the home crowd, with more than a half-dozen rookies dotting the roster on a nightly basis early in the campaign. "We had to add everywhere," Rychel said. "I wanted to integrate (youth) right away."

The veterans continued to trickle out of town, with homegrown talent like Jonathan Sciacca sent away and youngsters like Windsor native Harry Young coming in and eventually figuring in future success. "They're a young team, but a team that's going to be good in the future," the then 16-year-old Young said after arriving from Guelph.

Each youthful addition brought more growing pains, and Rychel admitted he knew life would be easier by simply bringing in older players that could help produce wins now. "You think about going down the left side of the road, but you have to stay the course," Rychel said. "If we have a hole, we'll fill it, but it has to make sense for our future. We'll look at anything that will improve our club for the future. No stone will be left unturned."

Each move was made with an eye towards the 2007-08 season and beyond. "In the past, I think there was a lot of patchwork done to bring in three or four players and make the playoffs," Boughner said. "I don't know if there was a real plan in place.

"We don't want to go through this (rebuilding every year). We want to (draft) our own kids and develop them and bring them along. It will be short-term pain for long-term gain and I think everyone knows it."

Even the older players traded away by the Spitfires could see the logic in the plan and understood it made perfect sense in junior hockey, where a career lasts between three and four seasons. "They're doing a good thing," said Cory McGillis, who was a first-round pick by Windsor in 2004, but traded at the deadline to Barrie that first season. "They could have taken a short cut (that first year), but they're sticking to the plan."

Rychel kept trading right up until the Jan. 10 deadline, and that included his two biggest commodities in goaltender Anthony Guadagnolo and defenceman Weber. "Sometimes it's hard for people to understand, 'Why are you trading the best goalie in the league?' or 'Why are you trading your best defenceman?'" Rychel said. "But they only have 30 games left in their OHL career. We could possibly get back a guy who will play 200 games and be an NHL draftee down the road."

Guadagnolo's deal landed future NHL first-round pick Josh Bailey, while Weber brought high draft picks to be used to rebuild. "These deals will only benefit us in the future," Rychel said. "We weren't going to make a lateral movement. It was done for the future."

When the dust settled after the deadline, Windsor was easily the youngest team in the OHL with five 16-year-olds, just one overage player and a pair of 19-year-olds. "We feel that we've brought in some talent, but it's young and it's going to take time to develop," Boughner said. "We have a pretty good foundation here now."

With as many as 13 rookies in the lineup, the Spitfires would stagger to the finish line, gaining just five wins over their final 33 games, as the club missed the playoffs for the first time in nine years.

In 68 regular-season games, the Spitfires would wind up with just 18 wins on the season, tied for the third-fewest in the franchise's 32-year modern-era history. The club's 43 losses were the most since the team lost 46 in 1983-84 and fourth-worst in franchise history. The 43 points were tied for the fourth lowest in club history.

The stretch run would prove especially painful. After the trade deadline, the youthful Spitfires would go just 5-23-1-4 over their final 33 games to close out the season. "The numbers are tough to look at," Boughner said. "It was something that had to be done and something the kids and the coaches had to go through."

The players were already looking forward to being a year older and wiser, whether it was a rookie, or a veteran like Bradley Snetsinger, who quickly signed on after the season to play an overage year. "This is a great organization and I want to be part of it (next year)," said Snetsinger, who led the team with 29 goals and 62 points. "I think we'll be a good team."

Windsor Spitfires Worst Records

SEASON	GP	W	L	T	OTL/SOL	P
1975-76	66	12	50	4	0	28
1983-84	70	19	50	1	0	39
1989-90	66	17	41	8	0	42
2006-07	68	18	43	2	5	43
1992-93	66	19	42	5	0	43
1997-98	66	19	42	5	0	43

Spitfires Legends: Taylor Hall and Ryan Ellis

Taylor Hall and Ryan Ellis never looked like rookies. Hall was only 15 when he debuted for the Spitfires in 2007 after being taken second overall in May's Ontario Hockey League draft.

At five-foot-nine, many considered the 16-year-old Ellis too small to be an effective defenceman in the league, and he slid to Windsor in the second round. "The talent is sick," Spitfires general manager Warren Rychel said after securing both in the draft.

Neither player was sheltered or eased into an already young Windsor lineup, with the club opting to let their talents rise to the highest possible level on the ice. "They're not worried about age," Hall said. "Boughie (head coach Bob Boughner) and the coaching staff have said that if you contribute, you'll get the ice time."

Hall had a pair of goals in his first OHL game and was named the game's third star. Ellis ran the team's power play from Day 1 and showed the cat-like reflexes of a third baseman in tracking down would-be clearing attempts by the opposition to keep the puck in the opposition's zone.

"(Hall and Ellis) are special players," Spitfires captain Mickey Renaud said. "They're poised beyond their years."

Not surprisingly, a unique bond developed between the two. Ellis would spend practice lofting pucks high in the rafters and down ice that Hall would chase down. It's a play that would lead to several breakaways in league games.

As warm-ups wrapped up prior to games, Hall would practice one last breakaway move before scooping up pucks. Before the two left the ice, Ellis would be waiting at the gate for a high five that became a nightly ritual.

"These two are the cornerstone of our franchise for the next few years," Boughner said.

Hall's 45 goals would set a new rookie club record, breaking the old mark of 41 set by Charlie Skjodt in 1975-76, and wound up second among league rookie scorers with 84 points in 63 games. "He's a franchise-type player," Rychel said.

The Edmonton Oilers made Windsor's Taylor Hall the first player chosen in the 2010 NHL entry draft. (DH)

Taylor Hall's 45 goals in 2007-08 were a Spitfires rookie record. (DH)

"Hall is one of the best players I've ever scouted."

With a cannon shot from the point, Ellis was making every OHL team regret passing on him in the draft. He finished his first season fourth among rookie scoring, registering 63 points in 63 games, which tied him for third in scoring among league defencemen. "If you did the draft over, I wouldn't be surprised if they went one-two," Boughner said.

Unfortunately, the OHL only allows each team to nominate one player for rookie of the year. Hall was a landslide winner and also became the team's first-ever Canadian Hockey League rookie-of-the-year winner, but couldn't figure out why his teammate got no recognition.

"I was wondering why (Ellis) didn't get any votes," Hall said after having the process explained to him. "I thought we'd go one-two."

While Hall's season was solid, he felt what Ellis had done was even more impressive. "I think it's harder for a rookie defenceman to step in," Hall said.

Ellis, who shared the Spitfire team rookie-of-the-year award with Hall, never begrudged his teammate any of the accolades that came his way. "He's definitely a great player," Ellis said. "He's the total package."

While he wasn't eligible for the league's top rookie award, Ellis's keen mind would be acknowledged by the league. He was named the Bobby Smith Trophy winner as scholastic player-of-the-year.

Ellis, who passed on a scholarship offer to Ohio State University to join the Spitfires, carried an 81 per cent average in school and became the club's first winner of the award since Darrin Shannon in 1987-88. "Ryan worked extremely hard from the start and his accomplishments at school ran hand-in-hand with his success on the ice," Rychel said.

In three seasons with the club, the duo would play a big role in the team's resurgence that started with a club record 51-point turnaround in 2007-08, and back-to-back Memorial Cup titles in 2008-09 and 2009-10. "It's not a secret that a lot of our team revolves around those two guys on our power play and even strength," Boughner said.

They paired to help Ontario win gold at the World Under-17 Hockey Challenge in their rookie season. After the Spitfires were eliminated from the playoffs that year, they joined Canada's under-18 team and won gold at the world championship.

While naturally blessed with an abundance of talent, what set the two apart from others was never being satisfied with the success of the day. "I don't think you can look at last year and be satisfied," Hall said. "You always want to get better and improve. A big key is staying motivated."

Ellis followed up his rookie campaign by making Canada's national junior team as a 17-year-old, while Hall failed to make the cut and was sent back to junior. Ellis helped Canada

win gold with seven points in six games. He would lead all OHL defencemen in scoring with 22 goals and 89 points in 57 games to finish seventh overall in the league, and his plus/minus rating was second in the league at plus 52.

Those were numbers that would earn him the Max Kaminsky Trophy at the OHL's outstanding defenceman. Darryl Shannon, in 1987-88, was the only other Spitfire to win the award.

With his height no longer an issue, the Nashville Predators jumped at the chance to grab Ellis with the 11th pick in the first round of the 2009 NHL Draft. "We think he's going to be a special player compared to a (power-play) specialist," Predators assistant general manager Paul Fenton said. "Some say he's small, but we don't.

"He's pretty dynamic and a great student of the game. He's a special talent in so many different areas. He's a good defenceman because he uses his senses and angles to take pucks away from bigger guys."

Because of a later birthday, Hall would not be eligible for the NHL Draft until 2010, but Ellis knew his teammate's motivation wouldn't lag. "Me and Hallsy, we know what we want to do," Ellis said.

Hall was MVP of the 2009 OHL playoffs and the Memorial Cup, where he hesitated in taking the Stafford Smythe Memorial Trophy. "I didn't know what to do with it," Hall said with a smile. "I wanted to lift the Memorial Cup."

Projected by many to be the first pick overall in the 2010 NHL Draft, Hall entered the 2009-10 campaign determined to show everyone that his game could go to an even higher level. "I've been waiting for this for a long time and it's finally here," he said. "There are a lot of good players out there and some people don't want me to go No. 1, but I'm just going to work as hard as I can."

His focus wasn't just on the draft. He wanted redemption for getting cut at the previous World Junior Hockey Championship and he would return to earn a spot on the silver-medal winning Canadian side. He was also focused on another championship in Windsor. "If we end up with another Memorial Cup, I don't care if I (get drafted) one, two or three," Hall said. "I just want to win a championship."

Ryan Ellis has won world under-18 and world junior gold medals, two OHL championships and two Memorial Cups with Windsor. (DH)

Spitfires defenceman Ryan Ellis is the complete package – offensively skilled, defensively responsible and a big-time bodychecker. (DH)

He showed his commitment to the team late in the season by passing on individual glory. After a three-point game put him ahead of Tyler Seguin for the OHL scoring title, Hall opted to rest the last two games of the regular season to be ready for the playoffs, instead of trying to maintain the advantage.

Seguin would get a single point in his final game to tie Hall for the scoring title. He became the first Spitfire in more than a decade to win the scoring title and finished with 40 goals and 106 points in 57 games, which was six fewer than Seguin played.

"I wanted the rest and I'm kind of happy about that, because after three days of rest, I feel really good," said Hall, whose team would hold Seguin pointless in a second-round playoff sweep of the Whalers.

For the second straight playoff campaign, Hall led the OHL in scoring and went on to win his second-straight Memorial Cup and again capture the tournament's MVP award.

In June, his year-long battle with Seguin was also settled when the Edmonton Oilers made the Alberta native the No. 1 pick at the NHL Draft. "You might never see a guy come through the doors in Windsor again like him," Boughner said.

Taylor Hall Spitfires Stats

SEASON	GP	G	A	P	PIM
2007-08	63	45	39	84	56
2008-09	63	38	52	90	60
2009-10	57	40	66	106	22

Ryan Ellis Spitfires Stats

SEASON	GP	G	A	P	PIM
2007-08	63	15	48	63	51
2008-09	57	22	67	89	57
2009-10	48	12	49	61	38

Fallen Hero

Mickey Renaud was chasing the Canadian dream.

Captain of his hometown Windsor Spitfires, Renaud was a big part of the club's hockey resurgence, and the 2007 NHL draft pick of the Calgary Flames looked sure of a future in pro hockey.

That dream came to an unimaginable end on February 18, 2008. Renaud was having breakfast at his family home in Tecumseh with a few teammates when he collapsed.

The six-foot-three, 230-pound Renaud was rushed to hospital, but was unresponsive and pronounced dead at the age of 19.

"He was perfectly healthy the last time I saw him," said Spitfires defenceman Elgin Reid, who sat with Renaud the day before as the team returned home from a road trip to Owen Sound. "It's such a horrible, tragic event."

It would be months before his family would learn that Mickey had died from a rare heart condition known as hypertrophic cardiomyopathy.

"He was such a quality, quality young man and he had all the ingredients to fulfill his dream and that was to play for our organization," said Calgary pro scout and former Spitfires head coach Tom Webster, who worked with Renaud almost weekly.

"He's got the same kind of qualities as (former Spitfire and NHL star) Adam Graves. As much as he cared about his goals, he was also worried about the next guy. Those are rare qualities and that's definitely from his parents (Mark and Jane)."

Hundreds of people waited hours in line to pay their respects to Renaud and his family at the funeral home. More than 1,200 would gather at St. Anne Catholic Church for his funeral four days later.

"It just goes to show the hockey community in Windsor cares," hockey icon Don Cherry said. "You don't get that feeling here in Toronto."

Talk to anyone who dealt with Renaud on a daily basis and you quickly learned he wasn't just another hockey player. "Every time I was around the guy, he put a smile on your face," Reid said. "He touched so many people."

Spitfires captain Mickey Renaud died tragically Feb. 18, 2008 from a rare heart condition. (DH)

The Spitfires were in the midst of a club-record 51-point turnaround in the standings and while Renaud didn't lead the team in scoring, he was the leader in many other aspects.

"We were close, you know that, and that's been said often," Reid said. "We can thank Mickey for that. He was the glue that held the relationships."

It's one of the reasons the Spitfires tabbed the third-year centre to be captain.

"There's not many players who come through that dressing room that share the qualities of Mickey," Spitfires president and head coach Bob Boughner said. "Mickey will be our captain forever in spirit and memory."

(Left) Mickey Renaud followed his father Mark into the Spitfires lineup. Mark Renaud was a Spitfires defenceman in 1975-76. (DH)

(Right) The Calgary Flames selected Spitfires captain Mickey Renaud in the 2007 NHL entry draft. (DH)

It was 11 days before the Spitfires would play another game, but the layoff made it no easier for players to move forward. "Hockey just seems like a secondary thought right now," Reid said. "It's tough to think about going on without Mickey, but we know we have to some time."

Regardless of the number of games that followed for each player, the moment was never forgotten. "We all want to move on to different things, mostly to play in the NHL," Spitfires goaltender Andrew Engelage said. "But this is one place we'll always remember."

A crowd of 4,228, many wearing red, jammed Windsor Arena for that first game back where the club honoured Renaud. "It's great to see how much everyone cared about Mickey," said his older brother Remy Renaud, who attended the game representing his family. "This shows he will not just be missed by family, but by the entire Windsor community."

Players, many who had gotten tattoos to remember Renaud, hit the ice for the pre-game warmup wearing a red jersey with Renaud and No. 18 on the back, and a captain's C on the front. The visiting Belleville Bulls wore warm-ups jerseys that featured a W for Windsor on the shoulder and Renaud's name and No. 18 on the back.

The club showed 16 minutes of video tributes to Renaud and the players held a pre-game ceremony where they put their warmup jersey on a table before they were removed from ice.

When the team captains were called for the

ceremonial first faceoff, Windsor sent no one out.

In the days and months following his death, the players never forgot Renaud. His dressing-room stall became a shrine at Windsor Arena and was later moved to the lobby at the WFCU Centre. Players bought a lantern that was lit every time they entered the dressing room at home and on the road.

Renaud's memory spread across hockey lines. The Detroit Red Wings held a moment of silence along with every team in the Canadian Hockey League. All 19 other OHL teams played a video tribute for Renaud while every league player wore a No. 18 sticker on their helmet.

The No. 18 was painted behind each net at Windsor Arena, while team jersey and warmup suits all had memorial patches to honour Renaud.

That spring, at the NHL draft in Ottawa, Josh Bailey and Greg Nemisz were both selected in the first round and the Spitfire teammates dedicated their selection in Renaud's honour. "There's not a day that goes by that I don't think about him," Bailey said. "I want to dedicate this to Mickey and his family. I know he would have been here and I know he's looking down."

The following season, the club opened the campaign by retiring Renaud's number and revealed a 10-foot banner with a four-foot high photo of Renaud.

City of Windsor Mayor Eddie Francis brought the crowd of 4,366 to its feet by announcing the road leading to the club's new home at the WFCU Centre would be named Mickey Renaud Way.

"It'll be a reminder for generations to come," Francis said.

The Calgary Flames announced a bursary in his name for older brother Remy and younger sister Penny.

Renaud's family was on hand and his father Mark, a one-time Spitfire defenceman, spoke passionately.

"Mickey is certainly here with us tonight," he said. "He lives in our hearts, in the hearts of his family and friends, teammates, coaches and his fans; everyone whose life was touched by his.

"He was a great hockey player and so much more. He was an outstanding young man and a wonderful son and brother. We are blessed to have known you Mickey and are so very proud of you."

Renaud's name would not fade and often came up that season in conversation. When the club won the OHL title, athletic therapist Joey Garland ran to the dressing room to get Renaud's jersey for the team photo.

That jersey was brought out again a few weeks later when the club clinched the franchise's first Memorial Cup title in Rimouski, Que., where the Spitfires rallied after losing the first two games to earn the title with four successive wins. "Maybe Mickey was watching over us and wanted to teach us a lesson," Spitfires forward Taylor Hall said.

Mark and Jane Renaud are on hand at the final Spitfires game at Windsor Arena to accept the banner of their son Mickey that hung from the rafters in the rink. (DH)

A shrine to Mickey Renaud's career on display at the WFCU Centre assures that the former Spitfires captain will always be remembered by Windsor fans. (DH)

The Sun County Minor Hockey Association, where Renaud grew up playing, established an award in his honour. The OHL also introduced a new league award that would be given out yearly to the league's top captain, while the team introduced a scholarship in his memory.

"It's very, very nice," his dad said. "It's a wonderful way for Mickey to be remembered for the person he was and the captain he was."

Mickey Renaud
Born: Oct. 5, 1988
Died: Feb. 18, 2008

Mickey Renaud Spitfires Stats

SEASON	GP	G	A	P	PIM
2005-06	68	8	18	26	70
2006-07	68	22	32	54	76
2007-08	56	21	20	41	73

New Logo

While the Spitfires wanted to embrace its past, the new owners also wanted the club to take on a fresh on-ice look for the future.

At the end of their first season, the club introduced a vintage third jersey to be worn during the 2007-08 season on Friday and Sunday home games. The jersey embraced the original Spitfires franchise, which operated in Windsor from 1946-53. The cream-coloured sweater featured a navy-blue W with the word *Spitfires* running through the letter.

"I think it looks sharp," Spitfires president and head coach Bob Boughner said.

The biggest change was to come the following season, when the club introduced a new jersey look that would debut in December after the Spitfires moved into the WFCU Centre. The logo of a plane descending in a square with a rounded top and bottom would be set aside.

"It was old, it was stale," Boughner said. "We

The new Spitfires logo, introduced following the 2007-08 season. (RG)

wanted to (change it) right away, but it was too much, too fast." All three owners agreed the old logo had to go.

"Tombstone is the way everyone referred to it," Spitfires governor Peter Dobrich said.

The club would replace it with a plane caricature with a shark-like mouth and flames shooting from the wing guns set on a shield background with the word *Spitfires* underneath.

"It jumps off the jersey and comes to life," Dobrich said.

The club looked at nearly 15 different logos before making a decision. "The logo's kid-friendly and it's serious," Spitfires vice-president and general manager Warren Rychel said. "There's a fine line. You don't want a cartoon. You want something serious."

It marked the seventh different logo in franchise history. The original logo, which the club used for its vintage jersey, was used from 1946-53.

When the club was playing junior A hockey, a blue circle logo with *Windsor Spitfires* set inside a blue maple leaf was used from 1971-75.

When the Spitfires joined the OHA Junior A Series, which would later become the OHL, a dominant red theme was added to a white maple leaf that read *Windsor Spitfires*. It was used from 1975-83.

When the hockey club was bought by Compuware in 1984, the successful minor hockey program in suburban Detroit, they shifted the look to the brown, orange and white colours it was known for, with the crest being the picture of a plane. That was used from 1984-89.

When Compuware sold the team, the logo shifted to the old red, white and blue with the descending plane. Former owner Steve Riolo introduced a third jersey in 2002 that featured the Ambassador Bridge and added green highlights to the red and white in honour of Riolo's Italian heritage.

The latest jersey had many of the features worn by the NHL's Washington Capitals and was launched just in time for the club's first Memorial Cup drive. "It's a microcosm of a new era," Spitfires forward Taylor Hall said. "This is an exciting time. It's a new brand of hockey."

The Spitfires and Guelph Storm face off to begin the final OHL game at Windsor Arena on Dec. 4, 2008. (DH)

Bye-Bye Barn

Windsor Arena had outlived its usefulness long before the Windsor Spitfires played their final game at the Old Barn in 2008.

Sure, it was instrumental in the Spitfires returning to junior hockey in 1975-76, but even that wasn't easy. "The first time we applied (to the league in 1974), they turned us down because the rink wasn't long enough," said Fred Sorrell, who was one of the four owners of the team at that time. "It was an old building that had its day even when we had it over 30 years ago."

Opened in 1925, it had served as a home to the NHL's Detroit Red Wings at one time and launched dozens of players on their way to a pro career.

"To me, it's where I started and like an old church," NHL hall-of-famer Marcel Pronovost said. "It's something you're used to going to. You knew where it's at.

"It's like an old pair of shoes, but it's past its due," Pronovost said.

Its structural shape lent to the Old Barn nickname, but teams coming into the rink in the '70s and '80s had another name for it – the Madhouse on McDougall, which was the street it was located on.

While many players enjoyed emerging from a tunnel to the ice surface, teams at Windsor Arena had to walk with fans through the hallway to get to the ice and rabid fans weren't looking for autographs in those days.

"It was mayhem back there," said Spitfires president and head coach Bob Boughner, who made the trip back home for three years while playing for the Sault Ste. Marie Greyhounds. "There were a few times the police and security had to be called."

It got no easier on the ice. For years, there was low glass along the boards and no glass behind the bench. That allowed fans to deliver

Windsor's Richard Greenop and Guelph's Leigh Salters squared off in the final OHL fight at Windsor Arena. (DH)

verbal jabs from the start of the game to the end.

"If you couldn't get excited here, you couldn't get excited anywhere," said NHL scout Don Boyd, who coached in London, Sault Ste. Marie, Newmarket and Sarnia. "That was this building."

Tough on the visitors, it was an adrenaline rush for players in the hometown uniform. "I don't think there's a better atmosphere anywhere from the first period on," former Spitfire and Windsor native Ryan Baldwin said. "There's no arena that will pump you up like the Barn."

That energy only increased with the playoffs.

"(I liked that) people are right on top of you, the fans are so close to the action," said former Detroit Red Wings captain Steve Yzerman, who played in Peterborough. "Even just walking through the hallway, the people are right there.

"All new buildings, for the most part in hockey, are very similar. You don't appreciate the old ones until they're not there."

But it had its drawbacks, from a lack of parking, to cramped hallways and tight fits in the more than 4,000 seats.

"I went back (towards the end) for a game for the first time and it brought back all the horrible memories, with the cramped hallways and the inadequate bathroom facilities," Sorrell said.

The boiler room served as the working room for the visiting coach. One player was shocked in the visiting showers because of the wiring. Blackouts, Zamboni breakdowns, ice problems and broken glass that couldn't be sized for replacement all made the need for a new home necessary.

A crowd of 4,334 squeezed in for the final game on December 4, 2008 as the Spitfires beat Guelph 2-1. Everyone came with a story to share and looking to generate one last memory.

"Every time I go there, there's always a story," said Baldwin, who was in Guelph's lineup that night.

Conor O'Donnell flips a glove-side backhander past Guelph Storm goalie Thomas McCollum for a 2-1 Windsor victory and the last OHL goal scored at the rink in the Spitfires' final game at Windsor Arena. (DH)

For some, there was a new story almost weekly.

OHL supervisor of officials Sam Sisco started working at the rink in the 1950s. He would get $1 for pulling a warm barrel of water around the ice to resurface it before there was a Zamboni.

In later years, he served as a linesman and then called games as a referee. He brought a screwdriver the final night to remove his nameplate from the press box.

"Of course, I'll miss all the memories," Sisco said. "I went from being a rink rat to a linesman and then a referee at Windsor Arena. You don't lose those memories."

That's a fact most could agree on that final night, as the club held a special post-game ceremony to lower the eight banners that hung from the rafters and players handed over their game-worn jerseys through a raffle for season-ticket holders.

"It was pretty nice," said former Spitfire defenceman Joel Quenneville, who went on to play and coach in the NHL and had one of the eight banners in the rafters.

"You got to see the fans (here). There aren't too many buildings with memories like this."

Centre Of Attention

Cries for a new arena home for the Spitfires had been heard for years.

A deal always seemed to fall apart before it could be realized, but just months after taking ownership of the club, Bob Boughner, Warren Rychel and Peter Dobrich learned they would be getting a new home.

A new 6,500-seat venue with three additional ice pads would be built in east Windsor at a cost of $64.9 million.

"Growing up, I've heard all about them building a new rink," said Spitfires captain and Windsor native Harry Young. "This is going to be incredible to finally get out there."

The new rink, whose naming rights gave it the title WFCU Centre, helped make the Spitfires the hottest ticket in town. Season-ticket sales jumped from 1,600 just prior to the new ownership taking over to 2,800 before the 2008-09 season began and nearly 3,500 by the time the club hit the new rink.

The first game sold out in less than an hour. In less than three seasons, the club had to cap season tickets at 5,250 and the Spitfires were among the top three teams in the league in attendance.

"We've got some of the most passionate fans, but there hasn't been much to celebrate," Boughner said.

City of Windsor Mayor Eddie Francis took a hands-on approach with each and every detail of the 332-square-foot complex, which was built on 40 acres of land.

"I'm just proud we were able to get it done," Francis said in praising the work of city council.

As the pieces came together, those who saw it rise from the ground grew more and more impressed.

"Honestly, without exaggeration, it's got to be the top facility in the OHL," Boughner said. "London is big (seating 9,090), but it doesn't have the detail.

"The tiled concourses, width of the hallways and our (working) facilities are better than some NHL teams have."

Fans, who had to stack cars on side streets downtown to get to Windsor Arena, suddenly had 1,850 parking spots and room for overflow.

While Windsor Arena had one party box, the new rink featured 31 suites and fans looking to be pampered could grab one of 632 platinum seats, which offered in-seat concession service, or a spot at the in-rink restaurant.

"It's spectacular," OHL commissioner David Branch said. "The attention to detail, the way it's family friendly and it's a great venue to watch a game."

Windsor was one of several OHL centres to debut new rinks in recent years, but the design is what made the WFCU Centre stand out.

While other rinks had concession stands around the rink behind the seats, you had to leave the concourse and walk into the seating bowl for hockey. "That's what it's like in the NHL," Young said. "That's an NHL rink. The stands are just for fans and hockey."

In the ever-competitive world of junior hockey, the rink gave the Spitfires a whole new advantage for recruiting players. "It really helps to have a new rink," London general manager and co-owner Mark Hunter said. "It takes a lot to recruit kids, so I think it's important to a team. You need the whole package."

Underneath the stands, the Spitfires suddenly had business space that featured six offices, as well as a board room, on one side of the hall. The other side housed the hockey operations and a combination playground and home-away-from-home for players. "Everything you need as a player is provided," Boughner said.

The hockey side had two offices for coaches, as well as another room for the equipment manager. A side room had a changing area for players, with the actual dressing room adjacent to it. The carpeted dressing room features 24 stalls, along with a large plasma television.

Next to that is the athletic therapist's office along with a treatment area with two training tables. Beyond that is a workout gym with a treadmill, stairmaster, weights and stationary bikes. Behind the gym is a players' lounge area, which features another plasma television.

Six showers doubled what was at Windsor Arena and players also had access to a steam room, hot tub and cold tub. Washroom facilities were next to that. "They're in the lap of luxury," Boughner said. "This is better than a lot of NHL rooms."

Branch said the new facility would not only help the Spitfires in recruiting players, but the league as a whole. "This establishes Windsor as our league anchor on the Western (Conference) side," Branch said. "A facility likes this helps the profile of our league from a business standpoint, as well as recruitment."

Months before the team's first Memorial Cup title, Boughner was predicting big things for the club's new home.

"I think it's time, with our new facility, that we put Windsor back on the map," Boughner said.

Belleville goalie Mike Murphy foils Windsor's Justin Shugg, one of 34 saves he made in shutting out the Spitfires 4-0 in the first game played at the WFCU Centre on Dec. 11, 2008. (DH)

First Goal

Who would have bet on captain Harry Young to score the first-ever goal for the Windsor Spitfires at the WFCU Centre?

"No one did," said Young, a Windsor Minor Hockey Association grad.

A flu bug and world junior hockey tryouts ravaged Windsor's lineup in the opening game at the facility, a 4-0 loss to Belleville on December 11, 2008.

It would be two games into the club's new home before a Windsor player finally found the back of the net.

Coming into the game with just three goals in 175 league games, Young's point drive beat London Knights goalie Trevor Cann at 7:52 of the first period in what would turn into a 5-1 Windsor victory.

"Smitty said I was going to get one," Young said, referring to Windsor assistant coach D.J. Smith.

The puck now sits in a trophy case in the Windsor dressing room and marks Young's feat.

As for the game puck marking the first win at the WFCU Centre, it had to be retrieved by a club official after a London player flicked it into the crowd at the end of the game.

Captain Bailey Sets Sail

The Spitfires played the remainder of the 2007-08 season without a captain following the death of captain Mickey Renaud on Feb. 18. Harry Young would eventually assume the captaincy during the 2008-09 OHL campaign, but the honour wasn't bestowed on him immediately.

Prior to the start of that season, the Spitfires handed the captaincy to centre Josh Bailey. Young, Greg Nemisz and Adam Henrique were all handed an alternate captain's A. All four were away at NHL camps when the decision was made.

Spitfires head coach Bob Boughner praised Bailey for the way he assumed a leadership role after Renaud's death. "He was huge," Boughner said of Bailey. "He brought his teammates together and took his team on his shoulders."

The Spitfires collect their hardware following the 2007-08 OHL season. On hand are co-owner Peter Dobrich, Taylor Hall and his rookie-of-the-year award, Bob Boughner and his coach-of-the-year award, GM Warren Rychel and Ryan Ellis and his scholastic player-of-the-year award. (DH)

The NHL's New York Islanders took Bailey in the first round of the 2008 draft, and he never got to wear the C for the Spitfires. On Nov. 30, the Islanders finally made the decision not to return Bailey to Windsor, which had already played 26 league games waiting for his situation to be resolved.

At that point, the Spitfires named Young captain, which got Bailey's blessing. "He really deserves it," Bailey said. "He's such a great guy and a perfect guy to be captain."

In a 5-2 win over Peterborough on November 30, 2008, Young, who was drafted and signed by the NHL's New Jersey Devils, became the first Windsor player to wear a C since Renaud.

"I'll try to take what I can from Mickey," said Young, who wears a tattoo to honour Renaud's memory. "He was the ultimate leader. I'm proud to be wearing it."

Young held the captaincy when the club secured its first-ever Memorial Cup in 2009 in Rimouski, Quebec and again the following season when the club won a second Memorial Cup in Brandon, Manitoba, becoming the first captain of successive Memorial Cup winners.

"I wore a C growing up," said Windsor native Young. "I always had a letter of some sort. I'm the kind of guy who leads by example. (The C) won't change who I am. I'll keep doing the same thing."

Top coach

It was more than just God-given talent that enabled Windsor Spitfires president and head coach Bob Boughner to carve out a decade-long career as a National Hockey League defenceman.

"He willed himself into a 10-plus season pro career as an undersized defenceman," Moncton Wildcats head coach and vice-president of hockey operations Danny Flynn said.

Flynn coached Boughner nearly two decades ago when he played junior hockey in Sault Ste. Marie.

"He was a high-character kid and a great captain," Flynn said. "I knew he had all the ingredients to be a good coach."

"I'm a rookie coach and there's no doubt I'll make mistakes," Boughner said at the time. "But,

Bob Boughner (centre) works the Windsor bench along with assistant coach D.J. Smith (front) and associate coach Bob Jones (rear). (DH)

I'm completely confident I can do the job on the ice. I've played against or played in every system imaginable."

Names like Ted Nolan, Paul Maurice, Joel Quenneville and Barry Trotz helped shape the way Boughner looked at the game. "I've learned from some of the game's best coaches," Boughner said. "With such a young team (that first year), I really saw my role as a teacher."

It was a painful first season behind the bench, with Boughner's rebuilding-squad winning just 18 of 68 games.

"I remember the first game, it was an exhibition in Plymouth, and we were down 4-0 a couple of minutes into the game," Boughner said. "I looked at D.J. (Smith, his assistant coach) and said, 'It's not as easy as I thought.'"

Boughner felt it was important to jump in from Day 1 and not wait in the wings for a better opportunity. "I didn't want to bring someone else in for a while, and then be the guy to ride in on a white horse when things were good," Boughner said. "I wanted to develop as a coach with them."

When success arrived in the following years, veteran players would often point to that tough first season. "We learned so much that year," Spitfires forward Greg Nemisz said.

Players will tell you that Boughner could always strike the right balance when approaching the game.

"You could joke with the coaches," Spitfires defenceman Rob Kwiet said. "They'll get on you when you make a mistake, but they understood and helped. The coaches made it fun to come to the rink every day. All those days, even when you maybe didn't want to practice, you enjoyed it."

Everybody had their job and everybody had their role and that included his coaching staff. "He knows when to have fun, but you also know with him when it's time to work," Spitfires forward Justin Shugg said.

While many head coaches in the game like to micro-manage things, Boughner had no problem delegating authority. If something wasn't going to his liking, Boughner wouldn't hesitate to reach for the phone to get another coach's perspective.

"I've made a few calls," Boughner said. "It's not so much I'm looking for help, I just think a lot of coaches do it."

During his second season in 2007-08, the club produced a franchise record 51-point turnaround, going from 43 points to 94 points, and missed winning the division title by a single point.

With that performance, Boughner became the first Windsor coach ever named Ontario Hockey League and Canadian Hockey League coach of the year. Boughner beat out Kitchener's Peter DeBoer and Belleville's George Burnett, who each guided their team to new franchise highs for wins and points.

"I voted for (Boughner)," said DeBoer, a former Spitfire captain. "He has quickly established an identity for his team in Windsor in his mould – tough, hardworking and skilled. The kind of team that people in Windsor can identify with."

It wasn't just the on-ice success that made Boughner stand out. He became the face of the franchise in February when captain Mickey Renaud died from an unknown heart condition at the age of 19. "That was probably the toughest week we'll ever go through," Boughner said. "There was no manual, right or wrong."

For an encore in 2009-10, Boughner would lead the Spitfires to a club-record 57 wins and 115 points along with the club's first Memorial Cup title. At 38, Boughner would sweep both coaching awards again and become the first CHL coach to win the award in back-to-back seasons.

"He's very deserving of that award and I really credit him for the help he gave me," said Spitfires forward Taylor Hall, who the Edmonton Oilers would make the first pick overall in the NHL entry draft a year later. "He's a good friend and I really support him."

Presented the award in Rimouski, Que., where the club was battling for the Memorial Cup, Boughner took the opportunity to acknowledge associate coach Bob Jones and assistant coach D.J. Smith. He brought both on stage when he received the award.

"It should be called coaches of the year," Boughner said. "After last year, I thought I should have brought them up. We're friends first and co-workers second, but when we're coaching every decision is a three-man decision. You ask any coach about success and he'll tell you it's the people around them. They're great coaches in their own right."

As much as Boughner craved success, he never hesitated to credit everyone involved in achieving it. "You have to credit the players, and (general manager) Warren (Rychel) and his staff brought in some great players that make it easier," Boughner said.

Spitfires co-owner and GM Warren Rychel beams excitedly as he hoists the Memorial Cup. (DH)

Spitfires fans whoop it up at Windsor Arena. (DH)

He would coach Canada's under-18 hockey team to the Memorial of Ivan Hlinka Tournament title and return to lead Windsor to another Memorial Cup title in 2009-10, before moving on to the NHL as an assistant coach with the Columbus Blue Jackets.

In his place, Jones was promoted to his first OHL head coaching post after 15 years in the league as an assistant coach, while Smith became associate head coach.

"The team is in good hands," Boughner said.

Bob Boughner Spitfires Coaching Stats

SEASON	GP	W	L	OTL	SOL	PTS
2006-2007	68	18	43	2	5	43
2007-2008	68	41	15	7	5	94
2008-2009	68	57	10	0	1	115
2009-2010	68	50	12	1	5	106

Making History

Much was expected of a young and talented Windsor Spitfires' club coming off a franchise-record turnaround in 2007-08, even though it was a season that ended in tragedy, with the death of captain Mickey Renaud, and disappointment, following an opening-round playoff loss to the Sarnia Sting.

The 2008-09 season wasn't even underway and the Spitfires, who won just 18 games two seasons ago, were suddenly everyone's choice to win the club's first Ontario Hockey League title since 1987-88.

Windsor opened the season with high expectations, and the No. 1 ranking in the Canadian Hockey League and management wasn't going to shy away from the spotlight.

"It was nice (being ranked No. 1), but we made sure we stayed there," said Spitfires general manager Warren Rychel, whose club was the only CHL team to stay in the rankings all 27 weeks and

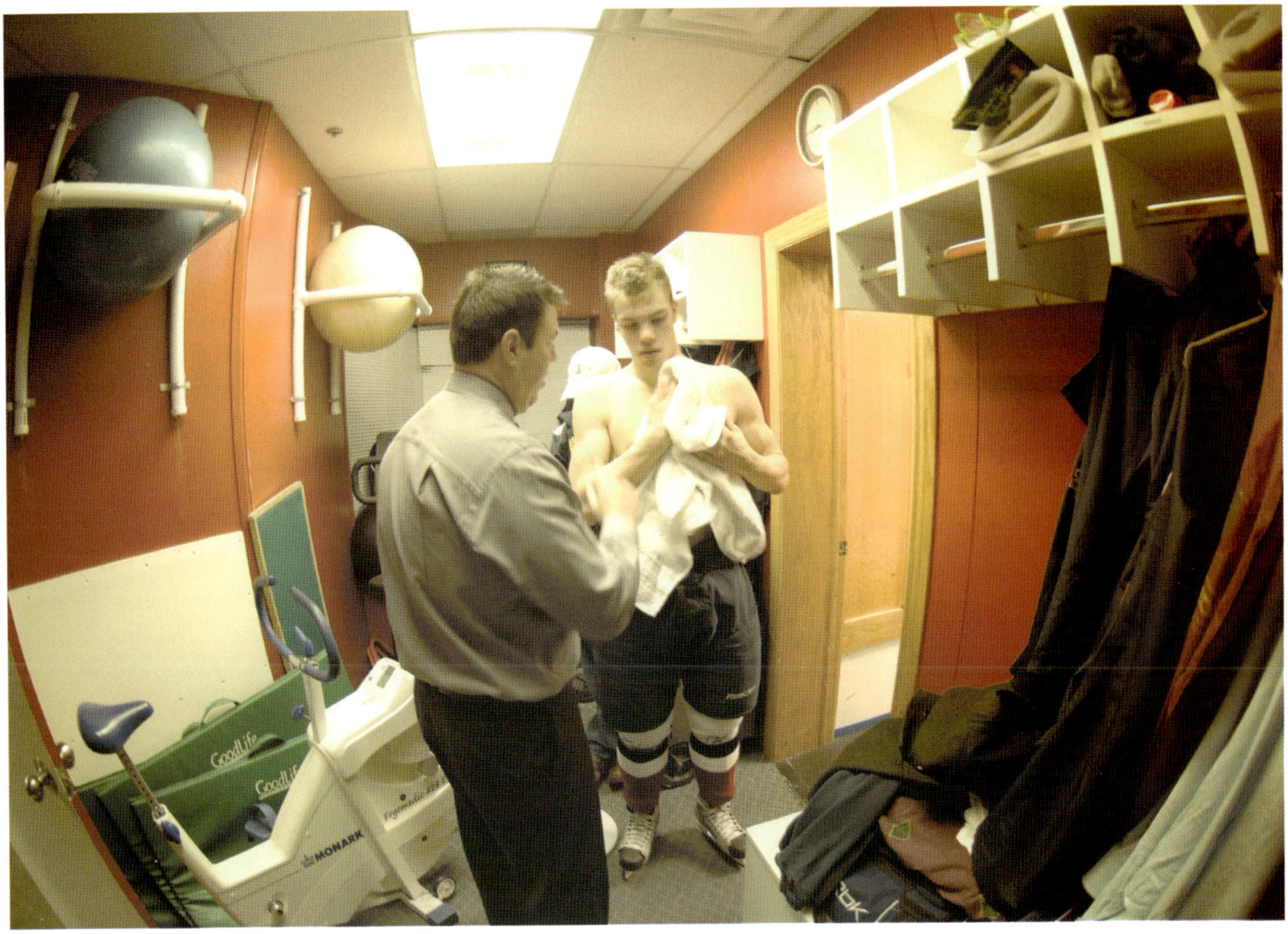

sit No. 1 for 20 of those weeks. "Every week I posted (the rankings when they were released on Wednesday) for everyone to see. We collectively raised the bar and wanted to stay there."

The club started the season with six straight wins and was 19-1 after 20 games. "It shows how good we are and that we deserve that No. 1 ranking," Spitfires second-year defenceman Ryan Ellis said.

There would be challenges along the way. The club started the season with seven players away at NHL camps. All were expected back, but by the end of November the New York Islanders opted to keep centre Josh Bailey for the remainder of the season. The Spitfires simply continued to adapt and roll on. "Everything seemed to fall in place, even through adversity," said Spitfire forward Greg Nemisz, who was an NHL first-round pick by Calgary the same day Bailey went in the first round to the Islanders.

With Bailey gone, Rychel began working with the Los Angeles Kings and would eventually bring European Import Draft pick Andrei Loktionov to Windsor. "Loktionov just slid in there and took (Bailey's) spot on the power play," Rychel said. The Russian centre, who played just one season in Windsor, responded with 24 goals and 66 points in 51 games and 33 points in 20 playoff games.

Windsor would also say goodbye to its home at aging Windsor Arena, where the club went to a team-record 12-0 to open the season. The new 6,500-seat WFCU Centre featured a larger ice surface where Windsor's talented young crew would be even more dangerous to opposing teams. "I had to adjust to the old Barn, but now I can play a full-out style," Spitfires forward Eric Wellwood said of the new rink.

With each win, management became more and more convinced that this team was capable of not only winning a league title, but the Memorial Cup. "We knew we were going for it," Spitfires head coach Bob Boughner said. "You don't get too many chances like this."

Associate coach Bob Jones and Taylor Hall talk strategy prior to a game. (DH)

The wins would continue to pile up. With 10 games left, the Spitfires earned their 51st win and 103rd point in an 8-2 win over Erie. That surpassed the club record of 50 wins and 102 points set in 1987-88. "I never look at numbers," Spitfires forward Richard Greenop said. "Maybe after the season, but you just want to come to the rink, stick to your game plan and don't let it get to your head."

The club would finish the campaign with 57 wins and 115 points. At the time, that was the second-best mark in league history behind the 59 wins and 120 points of the 2004-05 London Knights.

More important to the players was that it left Windsor with the best record in the league and home-ice advantage through the playoffs. "Being home for the playoffs, that's huge for us because the fans are so great," Nemisz said.

Experienced Hands

Windsor Spitfires head coach Bob Boughner and general manager Warren Rychel were not about to get caught up in regular-season success.

Although the Spitfires ran away from the pack during the regular season in 2008-09, the two veteran NHLers knew that post-season play would provide a different test for their young and talented squad. "We all know the playoffs are a whole different animal," Boughner said.

The club learned that the previous year when Windsor was the conference's third seed, but lost to a more veteran squad in sixth-seeded Sarnia. So, while the regular-season wins were piling up, Rychel moved to ensure the success would follow in the playoffs.

Windsor added grit by grabbing six-foot-three, 204-pound power forward Lane MacDermid from the Owen Sound Attack for second- and third-round draft picks. "When you're playing tough games against London and Guelph, he'll be a factor," Rychel said. "He makes us bigger and makes us tougher."

The son of Attack co-owner Paul MacDermid, who was a former Spitfire player, the big forward wasn't heartbroken by the deal. "It's a place where more NHL teams are going to see you," said the 19-year-old MacDermid, who was drafted by the NHL's Boston Bruins the following summer. "I'm happy to be here and to have a chance at a Memorial Cup is a once-in-a-lifetime thing."

Rychel tried some other moves to try and add to the depth of the club, with less success.

The club acquired veteran defenceman Patrick Moran from Guelph for a couple of draft picks, but the former second rounder could not crack the top six on the blue-line on a regular basis.

The club was in talks with Oshawa for top-rated prospect John Tavares, but the talented superstar would eventually wind up with rival London.

Rychel did trade talented young forward Andrew Yogan and a second-round draft pick to Erie for goaltender Brandon Maxwell. "I've coveted this player since the draft," said Rychel, who selected Jesse Blacker one pick after Erie took Maxwell 27th overall in 2007. "It's not a secret he wants to come to the OHL and we'll try to get him in a Windsor uniform."

Unable to secure his release that season from the United States National Team Development Program, instead, Rychel made Maxwell the centrepiece in a trade with the Kitchener Rangers.

Kitchener sent goaltender Josh Unice, overage defenceman Ben Shutron and centre Scott Timmins to the Spitfires. In return, the Rangers got Maxwell and overage forward Jake Lalonde, along with two second-round picks and a third-round pick. "We're absolutely ecstatic about this deal," Boughner said. "We knew we had some holes to fill and this strengthens us at every position."

All three had helped Kitchener win the OHL title a year earlier before falling in the Memorial Cup final to Spokane. "I think the three of us make Windsor better and a more dangerous team," said Timmins, a solid two-way centre who was fourth in league scoring when he came to Windsor. "I think we can make a (title) run."

The Spitfires tried to deal for the 20-year-old Shutron a year earlier before Kingston sent him to Kitchener. "I can put up some offence or I can be the shutdown guy," the six-foot, 195-pound Shutron said. "We're going to help the team, but we're just going to blend in. None of us has to come in and be the go-to guy."

Unice was an insurance policy for overage goalie Andrew Engelage. "(Windsor) looks a lot like the team I played for last year," Unice said. "They have scoring on every line, a power play that could be in the NHL and this is just a great opportunity to go to a team like this."

It left Rychel feeling confident that all possible steps had been put in place for the club to have a legitimate shot at an OHL title. "I think we improved every position and I think we're OK," Rychel said. "We're deep, we're tough, we can score and I think it's a team that will be hard to beat. We've worked extremely hard from the coaches to the scouts to myself and I think we have as good a chance as anyone."

Attacking the Attack

The league's top-rated offence was a juggernaut in the opening round of the playoffs against the Owen Sound Attack. Windsor outscored the Attack 26-13 in a four-game sweep and outshot the conference's eighth seed by a 235-112 margin, as the club won its first playoff series under the ownership of Boughner, Rychel and Peter Dobrich.

"It's something to be proud of," said Boughner, who was in his third season behind the bench. "It's a huge goal and now we can move on."

The only troubling part in the series was that goalie Andrew Engelage, who set a new league record with 46 wins, was pulled in both games in Owen Sound. Backup Josh Unice's relief effort allowed his teammates to rally for wins in both games.

"Usually, when you come in like that, you're coming into a hectic environment and you just want to calm the game down," Unice said. "If you can calm it down, usually everyone picks it up."

Whale Of A Series

In the longest series Windsor would have in the playoffs, the Plymouth Whalers won the opener, chasing Unice, who'd gotten the start, and were even after four games before the Spitfires won a suspension-riddled series in six games.

"It's a big relief," Spitfires centre Adam Henrique said. "It's been a battle the whole series."

The triumph put Windsor into the conference final for just the third time in 20 years and for the first time since 2002.

Engelage had regained his form by the end of the Plymouth series. He had 32 saves in the clinching game, including a left pad stop on Brett Bellemore in the final minute on a shot that would have tied the game. Henrique scooped up the rebound and ended it with an empty netter for a 4-2 win in Plymouth, and for his first playoff hat-trick. "We're all pumped to win this series," Engelage said. "I feel good to be in net and to win (the clinching) game."

Working Overtime

The record books weren't done with the Spitfires yet and the Western Conference final against the London Knights would go down in history.

With a long playoff history, the two had spent the season battling for both players through trade as well as for conference supremacy. "The rivalry speaks for itself," Spitfires defenceman Rob Kwiet said of the Knights, who posted a 49-16-1-2 record, but lost five-of-six meetings to Windsor. "The guys have no problem getting fired up for this one."

The star power on both sides was evident throughout. No team that had a two-goal lead in a game would win and all five games of the series would go to overtime, which was the first time that had happened in OHL history. "Every game someone had a lead and the other team battled back," Spitfires captain Harry Young said. "You were never safe."

In the end, Eric Wellwood's second overtime winner of the series in Game 5 sent the Spitfires to the league final. "Nothing compares to this," Wellwood said.

Dale Mitchell (front) and Taylor Hall celebrate a Windsor goal with their teammates on the Spitfires' bench. (DH)

(Above) Spitfires forward Eric Wellwood fires the puck past London goalie Trevor Cann while Andrei Loktionov looks on. (DH)

Marching Orders

The Brampton Battalion, who were in the league final for the first time in franchise history, would provide the final barrier to Windsor's title hopes.

After a 10-1 Windsor blowout in the first game, things tightened up, but the Spitfires would secure the title in five games, as Taylor Hall scored the overtime winner to clinch the series and earn playoff MVP honours. "That's the biggest goal of my life," the 17-year-old Hall said.

It was Windsor's second title in franchise history and the first one at home, with the 1988 title having been won on the road in Peterborough. "I think it means the same to everyone, but I'm proud I can do it in my hometown," forward Eric Wellwood said over the cheers of 6,582 at the WFCU Centre. "It was a goal and we set out at the start of the season to win it, but it's never easy."

Dale Mitchell's three goals in a span of just three minutes sparked Windsor's rally for a win over Rimouski in the Memorial Cup tie-breaker. (DH)

Adam Henrique (right), captain Harry Young and Taylor Hall are fired up after Henrique netted the overtime winner in the Memorial Cup semifinal against Drummondville. (DH)

A Comeback For The Ages

A league title would quickly become a distant memory as the club flew to Rimouski, Que. for the Memorial Cup, where everyone was proclaiming the Spitfires the tournament favourite.

"On paper, Windsor has a very good team," Drummondville Voltigeurs head coach Guy Boucher said. "They're on fire and have no weaknesses."

Adam Henrique dives into the glass to celebrate his OT tally that put Windsor in the 2009 Memorial Cup final. (DH)

Henrique is buried under an avalanche of jubilant teammates moments after netting the big goal. (DH)

Things did not play out according to plan early in the tournament, however. The Spitfires let a pair of one-goal leads slip away in a 3-2 overtime loss to Drummondville, and then fell 5-4 to the host Rimouski Oceanic to sit 0-2.

"You can't change the past, but you can change the future," Spitfires defenceman Mark Cundari said.

Windsor's final game of the round robin was against Kelowna, which had already earned a bye into the final with two wins. Offered the chance to end Windsor's season, the Rockets let a one-goal lead slip away as Windsor stayed alive with a 2-1 victory.

"It's a little better than any other win we've had," Windsor goalie Andrew Engelage said. "We're on the biggest stage and to finally get a win is huge."

With a spot in the tiebreaker, Windsor would make one final historical record for the season. "It was the year where everything went right," Hall said. "It was just meant to be."

No team had ever started the Memorial Cup tournament with two losses and won the event and no club had ever played its way

Spitfires defenceman Rob Kwiet snaps a shot on goal early in the Memorial Cup final. (DH)

Windsor teammates race to embrace Kwiet after his goal gave the Spitfires a 3-0 lead against Kelowna in the Memorial Cup final. (DH)

Windsor forward Greg Nemisz fights for position in front of the Kelowna net during the 2009 Memorial Cup final. (DH)

Nemisz celebrates a Windsor goal with his teammates. (DH)

Top: Spitfires teammates mob Taylor Hall shortly after he was named MVP of the 2009 Memorial Cup tournament. (DH)

Bottom: Windsor fans who made the trek to Rimouski proudly display their colours. (DH)

The Spitfires surround the Memorial Cup, while captain Harry Young and Ryan Ellis proudly display the No. 18 jersey of Mickey Renaud, their fallen leader. (DH)

MEMORIAL CUP CHAMPIONS COMMEMORATIVE PAGE

THE VOICE OF SOUTHWESTERN ONTARIO SINCE 1890

THE WINDSOR STAR

A DIVISION OF CANWEST PUBLISHING INC.

BREAKING NEWS AT WINDSORSTAR.COM

Believe! WE CAN

HISTORY!

Spitfires capture first Memorial Cup title

Sunday, May 24, 2009, Rimouski, Que.

The headline in this special commemorative edition published by *The Windsor Star* says it all. (WSHC)

through the tiebreaker to win it. The Spitfires started that improbable journey against Rimouski in the tiebreaker. The club trailed by two goals after two periods and second-year forward Justin Shugg had been knocked from the game and the tournament with a broken collarbone.

"I remember we were down 4-2 and you could hear how much pain Shugg was in," Rychel said. "You're thinking, 'Are we done? We can't go out like this.' It says a lot about our lineup. We came out (in the third period) and I don't think (Rimouski) knew what hit it."

Dale Mitchell scored three goals in a span of three minutes and 33 seconds to put Windsor in front for good in a 6-4 victory. "Who doesn't like to be the hero?" Mitchell said afterward. "I didn't want to go out a loser."

Overtime, which decided the first meeting between Windsor and Drummondville, would be needed again to settle matters in the semifinal. After building a 2-0 lead against the Quebec Major Junior Hockey League champs, the Spitfires eventually were forced to work the extra frame. Less than five minutes into the ses-

sion, Adam Henrique hammered home a rebound for a 3-2 win. He threw himself up against the glass and was immediately mobbed by teammates.

"You grow up watching this tournament and dreaming about it," Henrique said. "So, to go to overtime and score to get us to the final, it's the biggest goal of my life. I still can't believe it."

With renewed confidence in their game, the Spitfires were ready to complete the improbable comeback against Kelowna in the final. "I don't think anyone was going to stop us," Ellis said. "We came together."

Windsor's only other trip to the Memorial Cup ended with disappointment in the 1988 final, when the Spitfires lost 7-6 to the Medicine Hat Tigers, but the Spitfires quickly seized control of the 2009 final.

Windsor scored on its first three shots in the first eight minutes of the game and went on to a 4-1 victory to claim the 91st Memorial Cup and first in franchise history. It capped an incredible nine-day run where the club faced four straight elimination games, yet won them all to take the title.

"We never found an excuse to quit," Spitfires coach Bob Boughner said. "We took the hardest way you could to the Cup.

"I guess, you could say, there's a lot of destiny involved."

Spitfires goalie Andrew Engelage gets down low to see through traffic in front of his net, while Harry Young and Ryan Ellis stand on guard.
(DH)

Spitfires Legend: Andrew Engelage

Goalie Andrew Engelage never let the critics get to him. Passed over in his first trip through the Ontario Hockey League Draft, then Windsor Spitfires head scout John Bowler grabbed him in the 13th round the 2005 draft.

It would be another year, after the change in ownership, before new general manager Warren Rychel would finally give Engelage his break. Windsor already had goalies Anthony Guadagnolo and Jake Fischer, the latter having

Andrew Engelage does the splits to foil Kelowna's Mikael Backlund in the 2009 Memorial Cup final, while Andrei Loktionov races in to help out. (DH)

attended Canada's under-18 camp, in the fold, but Rychel opted to keep Engelage. "You always get surprises in camp," Rychel said. "Engelage is just too good a goalie to let go."

Being six-foot-five and 206 pounds made Engelage one of the biggest players at his position in the league, but also made him as big a target. "I know I can do it," Engelage said of being a No. 1 goalie in the league. "I know some people might not think it, and I want to prove it."

There would always be obstacles to overcome after Engelage became the No. 1 goalie with the 2006 trade of Guadagnolo to Owen Sound. When the club returned the following year, Engelage had many challengers for the top spot. Early in the 2007-08 season, Windsor dealt for Michal Neuvirth from Plymouth, and then acquired Jakub Kovar from Oshawa for Neuvirth.

That season, Engelage set a new club record for lowest goals-against average at 2.57, which broke Michael Leighton's mark of 2.73 set in 2000-01. Despite the success, it was Kovar who was named the No. 1 goalie when the Spitfires opened the playoffs in 2008. "It was a bit of a shot to the pride, but you have to battle through it," Engelage said.

Kovar opted to sign pro in his native Czech Republic over the summer and not return to Windsor and that opened the door for Engelage to return for an overage season.

Before camp, head coach Bob Boughner sat Engelage down to explain the situation. "I definitely owed him an explanation after last year," Boughner said. "I told him, 'This year, it's your job.' I don't want to deal for a goalie. The guys like him and respect him."

But days before the Canadian Hockey League rankings would make Windsor the preseason No. 1 team, The Hockey News named Windsor No. 2 and blamed goaltending concerns as the main reason.

The article was clipped and placed in Engelage's locker, where it served as a daily reminder. "It was good motivation for the guys and I know I have to prove myself and show I can be a top-flight goaltender," Engelage said.

When the OHL trade deadline arrived, the Spitfires did make a move for goaltending help. Josh Unice, who played in the Memorial Cup final a year earlier, was acquired from Kitchener, but only as insurance. Engelage's spot as No. 1 was secure.

Before the end of January, his 32-save effort helped Windsor beat Barrie 6-1. With it, Engelage earned his 33rd win of the season to break Leighton's club mark of 32 set in 2000-01.

"(The record) is nice, but it's the team in front of me," Engelage said. "The team helps out a lot."

Spitfires goalie Andrew Engelage set a CHL record in 2008-09 with 46 wins. (OHL)

He finally got a small taste of outside success when he was named the Western Conference's starting goalie for the OHL all-star game, which was played in Windsor. "I think it's starting to get there now where I'm getting a little more respect," Engelage said. "I'm just going to keep playing hockey the way I have been."

It wasn't always pretty or technically perfect, which is what brought out the critics, but it was effective. "Engy is the Rodney Dangerfield of goaltending," Spitfires goalie coach Bill Dark said. "Regardless of his accomplishments, he never gets the recognition that he is due. To his credit, he has turned this into a positive, using it as a motivating tool.

"He realizes he is controlling only what he can control like his work ethic, positive attitude, being a good team guy and his own preparation. He cannot control what others think of him."

With the season winding down, the Spitfires had wrapped up first place overall and had little to play for, but there was one last record. Engelage got the start in the final home game of the regular season and a 5-1 win over Plymouth earned the overage goalie his 46th win of the season. That broke the league record of 45 wins by a goalie, which was set by London's Steve Mason in 2006-07.

"I definitely see it as a team record," said Engelage, who won the Dave Pinkney Trophy for the OHL's lowest team goals-against average. "I've been there for these guys some nights and they've been there for me." He would finish the regular season with a remarkable 46-4-0-1 record and better his club mark with a 2.35 goals-against average.

"I owe a lot to my parents and to Bill Dark, who stuck with me for three years and was always behind me," Engelage said. "The wins are nice, but what I really like is I've only got five losses."

He would go 14-2-1 in the playoffs to help Windsor earn its second OHL title in franchise history before capping the season by going 4-1-1 to help the Spitfires claim their first Memorial Cup title.

"There's a lot of pressure (playing in a Memorial Cup final), but it's better to be in that situation than stay at home and watch it like I did last year," said Engelage, who was 64-7-2-1 on the season. "It's awesome to go out a winner."

Andrew Engelage Spitfires Stats

SEASON	GPI	GA	SO	GAA	W-L-OTL-SOL
2006-07	42	177	0	4.35	12-24-0-3
2007-08	40	100	2	2.57	20-10-4-4
2008-09	54	121	5	2.35	46-4-0-1

Coming Attractions

The doors had not even opened to the Windsor Spitfires' new home and already junior hockey events were committed for the WFCU Centre.

In a span of 12 months, the rink would host the 2009 Ontario Hockey League All-Star game, a Canada-Russia Super Series match and the 2010 CHL/NHL Top Prospects Game.

"Our league's desire is to support communities when they make a commitment like this," OHL commissioner David Branch said of the $64.9 million facility. "It's a star for our league."

It had been more than three decades since the league's all-star game visited Windsor. Wayne Gretzky played in the event, which was held at Windsor Arena in 1978.

"With a new arena, and an up-and-coming young team, we want to show we can put on a first-class event," Spitfires president and head coach Bob Boughner said.

Windsor's brass hoped to raise the bar on the standard for the event and added several extra features.

Local elementary schools were allowed free skating at the WFCU Centre, a family fun zone was set up and several OHL and NHL trophies were on display from the Hockey Hall of Fame.

"We're doing a lot of different things to interact with the community," Spitfires governor Peter Dobrich said.

The club made a big change to the skills competition, which is held before the game. The club added a post-skills competition concert and that was followed by an alumni game.

"I've had this on my schedule since August," said former Spitfires player and head coach Brad Smith, who is now director of player personnel for the NHL's Colorado Avalanche. "I wasn't going to miss this."

The Western Conference, which featured Spitfires Taylor Hall, Ryan Ellis, Andrew Engelage, Scott Timmins and Greg Nemisz, won the skills competition, but lost the All-Star game 11-6 to the Eastern Conference. A total of 11,779 fans flocked to the rink for the two-day event, which received rave reviews.

"It was the best ever and I mean that," Branch said. "What they did caused the OHL to go back and redo some of its bid guidelines. Kingston (which hosted the event in 2010) will use Windsor as a blueprint."

The Canadian Hockey League came back to Windsor for more the following season.

Over the summer, the Spitfires were awarded one of the two OHL games in the Canada-Russia Super Series, which both countries use as an evaluation test for their World Junior Hockey Championship rosters. "When the city built us this beautiful facility, we said we would try and bring events of this magnitude here," Boughner said.

Playing the gracious host, the Spitfires provided the Russian squad a rink suite to catch an OHL game.

"It's a good city and a very good arena," Russian forward Maxim Kitsyn said.

But again, the Spitfires wanted to turn the game into more than simply a one-day event.

"We're just trying to take an event and raise the bar a bit," Dobrich said. "We want to raise the bar each time (we do something) and put Windsor's stamp on it."

The club drew on the old Canada-Russia rivalry to turn the game into a two-day event. A VIP event was set up for fans with the Canada Cup trophy, which was contested five times from 1976 to 1991, brought in for fans to have their picture taken with. Funds raised from that event would go to local charities.

"You have the two biggest hockey countries in the world," said former NHLer Igor Larionov, who won the Canada Cup with Russia in 1984 and served as an honourary captain for the game. "It's pride for both countries and every time you see Canada and Russia at any level, there's excitement."

The Spitfires had four players in the game, with Hall, Nemisz, Ellis and Adam Henrique using their performances to eventually earn a spot on Canada's national junior team.

The match drew 6,353 to see the OHL squad win 5-2. Hall was named player-of-the-game for his team after scoring a goal and an assist. Henrique opened the scoring and Nemisz drew an assist.

Before the Spitfires could put even put the final touches on the November 23 OHL game against Russia, the CHL came calling for help.

Montreal was to host the CHL/NHL Top Prospects Game in January of 2010, but had to pull out. The CHL immediately turned to Windsor to host the game.

"They get it," Branch said. "To me, it characterizes the way this new group has done everything upon their arrival.

"It's just another example of what sets them apart as winners, both on and off the ice."

The two-day event January 19-20 would draw 11,611 fans to the WFCU Centre and hockey analyst Don Cherry, who coached one of the teams, was amazed at Windsor's support.

"We even had a sellout for the skills competition," said Cherry, who once played defence for the Spitfires. "We've never sold out the skills competition."

The game drew 6,193 with Hall, who was captain of Team Cherry and joined by Spitfire teammate Cam Fowler, setting up the game winner in a 4-2 win over Team Orr.

"He's shown he's the No. 1 player and he's done a great job of handling himself," Fowler said of Hall, who the Edmonton Oilers would make the No. 1 pick overall in the 2010 NHL Draft.

Repeating the Beating

The weight of expectations for the 2009-10 season was heavy for the Spitfires.

The club was coming off the first Memorial Cup title in the franchise's 34-year history and with a dozen veterans back in the lineup, anything short of a repeat performance was simply not acceptable. "If we hadn't won, the season would have been a failure," Spitfires captain Harry Young said.

Kamloops was the last team to win back-to-back Memorial Cups in 1994 and 1995 while no Ontario Hockey League team had won consecutive Memorial Cups since the Montreal Jr. Canadiens in 1969 and 1970. The last team to even secure two straight OHL titles was Sault Ste. Marie in 1991 and 1992.

"Two puts you in a category all your own," Spitfires head coach Bob Boughner said. "We'll have some obstacles. You've got a bull's-eye on your back. You have to be on every day."

It would be a season filled with hills and valleys as the Spitfires pursued a repeat performance. "With the team winning the (Memorial Cup), obviously the expectations are high," said highly-touted defenceman Cam Fowler, who joined the club from the United States National Team Development Program. "It's going to be a challenge."

In their minds, the Spitfires were focused on grabbing a second title. Deep down, each player knew the euphoria that came with a championship.

"We've done it once, so why let someone else have that feeling?" Spitfires forward Justin Shugg said.

On the ice, things were a little different. There wasn't the first-time feeling of being on top of the league that players savoured the previous season.

Windsor won six straight and 19-of-20 to start the 2008-09 season, but lost their first two in 2009-10 and had four losses in the first 10 games.

"At the start of the year, everyone was just looking to the playoffs and that may have taken a toll," Spitfires forward Eric Wellwood said. "We may have looked past some teams we shouldn't have."

Restlessness wasn't limited to the play on the ice. Weeks into the season, third-year defenceman Jesse Blacker, who was a second-round pick of the NHL's Toronto Maple Leafs, asked for a trade to a team that would give him a more prominent role. "We have a philosophy here that we won't let a player put his needs ahead of the team," Boughner said.

Blacker was eventually dealt to Owen Sound, while backup goalie Steve Gleeson, who left the team during training camp, was sent to Belleville.

While a couple wanted out, there were others welcomed into the fold. Forward Kenny Ryan, who was also a second-round pick of the Maple Leafs, walked away from a full-ride scholarship at Boston College to join the Spitfires.

"This is where I want to be," Ryan said. "With the coaching staff and the players they have, hopefully it can help me as a player."

Scott Timmins played in three straight Memorial Cups – with Kitchener in 2008 and Windsor in 2009 and 2010. (OHL)

Unexpected Returns

The Spitfires' offence got an unexpected boost and general manager Warren Rychel didn't have to lift a finger.

Two games into the 2009-10 season, the Spitfires would add overage centre Scott Timmins when the NHL's Florida Panthers ran out of contracts and could not sign him.

In early November, the NHL's Toronto Maple Leafs opted to send speedy winger Dale Mitchell back to junior hockey for an overage season.

"Mitchell and Timmins were big surprises," Rychel said. "Sometimes in life, you get some big surprises."

Timmins had 35 goals and 73 points in 66 games with Windsor and Kitchener the previous season and the Panthers took him in the sixth round of the draft. But the club's contract allotment was used up and the Panthers' only option was to send Timmins back to Windsor.

"He's going to sign an NHL contract," said Florida head coach Peter DeBoer, a former Spitfire who coached Timmins in Kitchener. "He'll play in the NHL, but the situation in Windsor, with the coaching and the experience, just made the decision easier."

A third-round pick of Toronto, Mitchell ran into a different squeeze with the Maple Leafs. A deep, veteran American Hockey League squad left Mitchell on the outs with the Toronto Marlies, and the Leafs did not want to send him to the East Coast Hockey League. The decision was made to return him to Windsor.

"It's something we didn't expect," Spitfires head coach Bob Boughner said. "It speaks well for the program that we can develop players for an NHL team when they send them back as overagers."

The additions only strengthened an already potent Windsor offence. "You can play fourth line on this team and you're still with great players," Mitchell said. "There's so much skill here and so much balance."

For the second straight season, the Spitfires led the league in offence. Timmins and Mitchell had their share, but both battled injuries during the regular season and lacked motivation at times.

"I came back and was kind of down on myself," the 20-year-old Timmins said. "(Not signing) was obviously in the back of my mind."

But the chance to win a second Memorial Cup provided plenty of motivation as the two looked to the playoffs. "It's not the year I expected," Mitchell said. "I felt I would play with the (AHL Toronto) Marlies, but coming back wasn't too upsetting.

Spitfires forwards Taylor Hall (foreground) and Adam Henrique both played for Canada in the 2010 world junior tournament. (OHL)

"My goal's another good playoff run and that's my focus. Now, you know you can go far. It's the best time of the year and it was probably the best three months of my life."

Both would provide leadership as much as skill and Windsor allowed each the opportunity to work on the smaller parts of the game that would help at the pro level.

The OHL's coaches acknowledged Timmins as the best defensive forward, the best penalty killer and the second best faceoff man in the conference. Solid accolades for a player that had also posted back-to-back 30-plus goal seasons.

"It's a nice honour," Timmins said of the OHL poll. "It's nice to get the respect for being one of the more notable guys on the defensive side."

Timmins was dominating in the faceoff circle in the playoffs and chipped in with 11 goals and 22 points in 19 games.

"I'm sure he didn't want to come back for an overage year, but he did all the little things well and that's why he's going to be an even better pro," Boughner said.

By the time the club's second Memorial Cup was secure, Timmins also had his contract with the Panthers. "I've been a spoiled player because I've played on some good teams the last few years," said Timmins, who had played in the 2008 Memorial Cup with Kitchener and the 2009 and 2010 Memorial Cups with Windsor.

World Juniors

An Ontario Hockey League title and Memorial Cup victory were not the only measures of just how good a squad the Spitfires had assembled. Ten of the world's top hockey countries gather each December to contest the World Junior Hockey Championship. It's a nearly one-month commitment for a player and for many teams in the Canadian Hockey League, a single player or two invited to camp is consider an accomplishment for the program.

In 2010, the Spitfires gave to the tournament like no other team.

"It speaks really well to how (head coach) Bob Boughner and (general manager) Warren Rychel have put together a quality program," Canadian head scout Al Murray said.

"They've shone at the Memorial Cup and in the OHL, a couple have been with our world under-18 (team) and (defenceman Ryan) Ellis was (with last year's world junior team)."

When Canada's 22-man roster was announced for the tournament, Ellis was back for a second year with the team and joined by Spit-

Greg Nemisz joined Spitfires teammates Ryan Ellis, Taylor Hall and Adam Henrique on Canada's 2010 world junior roster. (OHL)

fire teammates Greg Nemisz, Adam Henrique and Taylor Hall.

"Having the guys you know there helps your confidence," Hall said.

It marked the first time since 1996 that one junior team had four players named to the Canadian roster. "I know how good they are," Rychel said.

It wasn't just the Canadian squad that would strip stars from the Windsor roster.

Windsor-born defenceman Cam Fowler, whose family moved to the United States, was named to the American team. Spitfire teammate Kenny Ryan was a late addition to the U.S. camp, but failed to make the final cut.

"It's a little bittersweet," Fowler said. "You feel for the guys who worked as hard as you have."

Windsor would lose a sixth member of its team to the tournament when forward Richard Panik earned a spot with the Slovakian team.

"It's a testament to Windsor and it shows the quality of players we have," Fowler said.

Panik's goal for the tournament was simple. "It's going to be fun for me," Panik said. "I'm excited to go.

"I just want to play in the quarter-finals. I don't want to play (the relegation game)."

Despite a solid tournament where he had six goals and eight points in six games, Panik's home country was relegated.

As for Fowler, he got to see a whole different side of his Windsor teammates when the United States played Canada in the final game of the preliminary round. Canada would win 5-4 in a shootout to advance straight to the semi-finals.

"(That game) I blocked a shot from Ellis," Fowler said. "We were chirping back and forth the rest of the game. It was different being on the other side and seeing the intensity and fire in their eyes."

The Canadian Spitfires had grown up watching the tournament and knowing the expectations that came with playing for the team. "You're playing for Team Canada and everyone has their role," Henrique said. "There's no friends until we get back (to Windsor)."

Henrique was slowed by a shoulder injury in the tournament and finished with just one goal, but he dominated in the faceoff circle and led the tournament with a 79.4 per cent efficiency rating. "Faceoffs are one of the big parts of my game," Henrique said. "I wanted to be one of the best in the tournament."

Nemisz won gold with Canada at the World Under-18 Hockey Championship and that experience, along with winning an OHL championship and Memorial Cup, gave him new-found confidence. "No situation seems too big or too hard to handle," said Nemisz, who had a goal in the tournament. For Hall, the tournament was a chance at redemption after being cut the previous year. "I've never been cut," Hall said. "Last year, I was the young guy going out for the team and I thought I had to be someone special and play out of the normal circumstances."

He tied for third in tournament scoring with six goals and 12 points in six games, while Ellis tied with Panik for 15th in tournament scoring with eight points in six games.

The 2010 world juniors marked the second straight tournament for Windsor defenceman Ryan Ellis. (OHL)

"Last year, I didn't know what I was getting into," said Ellis, who was second among tournament defencemen in scoring. "I know they expect me to play a bigger role."

After losing to Canada in preliminary play, the Americans would work their way back through the quarter-final and into the final for a rematch with the Canadians. "It's a great rivalry and I'm sure a lot of people are looking forward to it," Henrique said.

Canada was seeking a record sixth consecutive gold medal and 20th all-time. Although the Canadians were 28-5-3 overall against the Americans, it was the U.S. that would take the tournament title with a 6-5 overtime win.

"Everyone else was in tears," Ellis said. "I was just more shell-shocked."

It gave Fowler bragging rights in the dressing room, but it's not what he was looking for as the two teams shook hands afterwards and he leaned over to whisper in Hall's ear.

"I told him he played his heart out and I was proud of him," said Fowler, who had two assists. "He told me I played a great game.

"I'm proud to call them my teammates."

Panik would be traded to Belleville shortly after the tournament, but Fowler, Hall, Ellis, Nemisz and Henrique would return to Windsor and eventually help the club win its second straight Memorial Cup.

Clinching Deals

The Spitfires learned a year earlier not to leave anything to chance.

Two big deals at the 2009 Ontario Hockey League trade deadline paved the way for the club's first-ever Memorial Cup title.

With the 2010 OHL trade deadline approaching, Spitfires general manager Warren Rychel was determined to make sure all the bases were covered again. "It's something we had to do," Rychel said.

A builder his first two years on the job, Rychel had to sell some of those assets in the next two seasons to help secure league and Memorial Cup titles in 2009 and 2010.

Windsor goalie Philipp Grubauer makes a glove save on Barrie's Alexander Burmistrov. Grubauer was acquired from Belleville at the 2010 OHL trade deadline. (WS)

In 2009, Rychel was able to accomplish that mostly with draft picks, but in 2010 Rychel had to deal young prospects he had scouted, drafted and recruited to Windsor.

"It's very tough to do," Rychel said.

A year earlier, he got three veterans with Memorial Cup experience from Kitchener and he used a similar strategy in a deal with the Belleville Bulls.

The Spitfires acquired Bulls defenceman Marc Cantin and forward Stephen Johnston, who had both played in the Memorial Cup in 2008. Windsor also got help in goal in Philipp Grubauer, who'd backstopped Germany to the World Junior B Division title.

"I think this solidifies us at every position," Rychel said. "We're deep at forward, we have a solid six-man crew on defence and two good goaltenders."

Cantin, who was the captain in Belleville, provided another shutdown defenceman for the club. "Every team in the OHL thinks Windsor is the team to beat and to be part of that is special," Cantin said.

After playing for a rebuilding Bulls team, Johnston was thrilled to get another shot at the Memorial Cup. "The Memorial Cup was the most fun I've had," Johnston said. "We were so close (losing in the semis) and I didn't think I'd get another chance because Belleville was so young. This is awesome, because Windsor's such a good team."

Grubauer was brought in to compete for the No. 1 job in net with Troy Passingham. "I hope to be the starting goalie, but you need that competition to push yourself," Grubauer said. "I'm so excited. It's a great arena and a great team."

Grubauer would win the No. 1 job in a battle with Passingham and posted a 20-1-1 mark in the OHL playoffs and Memorial Cup. "He's the reason we had any wins this season (in Belleville)," Johnston said.

The price was painful for Rychel. Rookie forward Austen Brassard, who was Windsor's first-round pick in 2009, was sent to Belleville along with Slovakian forward Richard Panik, whom Rychel lobbied for a year to get to Windsor, holdout goalie Steve Gleeson, and veteran defenceman Paul Bezzo, along with a second-round pick, third-round pick and seventh-round pick.

"This was a real tough one," Rychel said. "I think Austen is going to be a star. It's very tough to do, but something we had to do."

It would be no easier a few days later when Rychel made his final trade before the deadline.

He sent second-year forward Austin Watson, whom he recruited away from the University of Maine and the United States National Team Development Program, to Peterborough along with two second-round picks.

"(The) deal was a difficult one for us," Rychel said. "Watson has been great for our team both on and off the ice." In return, the Spitfires brought Peterborough captain Zack Kassian, a local boy from LaSalle, into the fold.

"Yeah, I paid a price, but there weren't other options out there like this," Rychel said. "He's back next year, he's a much better fighter and he's a hometown guy."

The six-foot-three, 215-pound Kassian was a first-round pick by the NHL's Buffalo Sabres. "When I was young, I went to my first (Spitfire) game and that's when I knew I wanted to play in the league," Kassian said. "I always wanted to put on that (Windsor) uniform."

The two deals made Windsor an older and more physical club as it looked to defend its OHL and Memorial Cup titles. "The one element we were missing is the sandpaper and the grit," Spitfires head coach Bob Boughner said. "Our experience from last year showed that to get as far as we did, you need the (Richard) Greenops and the (Lane) MacDermids to wear the other guys down."

Unlike Peterborough, Kassian just had to be a piece of the puzzle, and was anxious to chase a title he had heard about at home the year before. "They're a very talented team," Kassian said. "They've won a Memorial Cup and they're looking to make another run this year, and I'll do what I can to fit in."

Kassian gets 20

Zack Kassian's Spitfires debut didn't last long. And it would be a long wait before he played a second game in a Windsor uniform. Kassian was kicked out of his Spitfires debut for a hit on Barrie Colts forward Matt Kennedy, then handed a 20-game sit-down by the OHL as punishment for his actions.

"For sure, it started off pretty rough," Kassian said. "First game here, I get suspended for 20 games and all I can do is watch. It's never fun, but you've got to take the positives out of that. I came into the playoffs well rested.

"Obviously, you never want to sit for that many games, but when you do, you've just got to think of all the positives."

A right hand from Windsor's Zack Kassian knocks the helmet from the head of Kitchener's Dan Kelly during a fight. (WS)

Down The Stretch

The additions certainly made the Windsor lineup stronger, but it didn't change the day-to-day challenges.

All-Star Ryan Ellis, who was the OHL's outstanding defenceman the previous season, missed time with a bone bruise in his wrist. Scott Timmins suffered a concussion, Dale Mitchell missed time with a high ankle sprain while Greg

Nemisz was sidelined after his thigh was cut by a skate blade.

"There were issues," Rychel said. "The hardest part was fielding a full lineup, but when we did, you saw what happened."

The NHL/CHL Top Prospects Game was the last outside contest that Spitfires players would be asked to participate in prior to gearing up for the playoffs. When that event concluded, they were finally able to put more than three months of distractions aside and focus on putting the pieces together and preparing for a title defence with just 14 games left in the regular season.

"Since December we've had guys leaving," Young said. "It's good to get the boys back."

The regular season would not be as fruitful as the previous season as the Spitfires would finish second in the overall standings behind Barrie. The Spitfires had seven fewer wins and nine fewer points than the previous season, but the 106-point effort was still the second best in franchise history and the group was just as confident in their ability to repeat in the playoffs.

Eyes On The Prize

"We've got all the right pieces again," Windsor forward Dale Mitchell said on the eve of the 2010 OHL playoffs. "Our guys will be ready."

In the playoffs, the Spitfires found it much easier to focus with the ultimate prize of another league title and Memorial Cup closer every day. "We may have looked past some teams we shouldn't have (in the regular season), but now it's do or die," Windsor forward Eric Wellwood said. "We'll have a different mindset and there's no reason not to be up for every game."

The eighth-seeded Erie Otters proved no match in the first round of the Western Conference playoffs, with Windsor sweeping the best-of-seven series in four straight games.

For many veterans, it was accomplishing the task at hand, but it was a moment to savour for newcomer Zack Kassian. "I've been in this league for three years and never won a playoff series," Kassian said. "When the buzzer went, I jumped in the air because it's my first (playoff series) win."

In the second round against the Plymouth Whalers, many were predicting the same battle as the previous year, when the Whalers extended the Spitfires to a playoff-high six games. It never materialized. Windsor swept the series in four games and held Plymouth's Tyler Seguin, who shared the league scoring title with Hall, pointless.

"We've been challenged all year and there was certain talk about complacency, (NHL) contracts or a Memorial Cup hangover," Spitfires coach Bob Boughner said. "We always thought that when it was the real deal, we'd answer, and you can feel it."

A Miracle Comeback

Windsor's biggest obstacle to a second straight final appearance would come in the Western Conference final, where the Spitfires dropped the first three games of their best-of-seven series with the Kitchener Rangers and faced elimination in Kitchener in Game 4.

Late in the game, Windsor left-winger Taylor Hall stepped off the bench, took a perfect pass from teammate Scott Timmins and made the Rangers pay for a poor line change. He snapped a 5-5 tie in what turned into a 7-5 Windsor victory to stave off elimination. "We're just happy to get out with a win," Hall said.

A shutout victory at home would be followed by another nail biter in Game 6 in Kitchener that the Spitfires won to force a deciding game in Windsor.

"We didn't play well in the first three games (of this series), but once we got a win, we seemed to get our confidence back," Windsor forward Greg Nemisz said.

Only two teams in league history had rallied from a three-game deficit to win a series and both of those were in the first round, which included Windsor's 2005 rally against Sault Ste. Marie.

Windsor would become the first to do it in a conference final with a 4-1 win in the deciding game. "I've said all along this team can do anything it wants when it sets its mind to it," Young said.

Mark Cundari, Scott Timmins and Dale Mitchell celebrate a goal in Windsor's Game 7 triumph over Kitchener in the 2010 OHL Western Conference final. (OHL)

Windsor's Eric Wellwood flips a backhand past the outstretched hand of Kitchener goalie Brandon Maxwell. (OHL)

Taylor Hall, Cam Fowler, Ryan Ellis, Adam Henrique and Zack Kassian celebrate a goal against Barrie in the decisive fourth game of the 2010 OHL final. (OHL)

Final Answer

While the Barrie Colts had swept both games in the regular-season with Windsor, the Colts never knew what hit them in the league final.

Windsor won the first two games on the road despite having to play for the ninth time in 15 days.

"It's great to win two on the road, but it doesn't mean anything if you don't back it up by winning at home," Spitfires defenceman Mark Cundari said.

There was no letdown at home, as Windsor completed its third series sweep of the playoffs.

"It's quite a feat," forward Eric Wellwood said. "You have to go back to '92 (when Sault Ste. Marie won back-to-back) to see it."

There was plenty of bad blood during the series. Barrie fans were each given a box of macaroni prior to Game 1, and when Taylor Hall's overtime marker gave Windsor a 4-3 win, they showered the ice with the boxes of pasta. "I don't know why all those people were throwing away some good food," Hall said. "I guess they were a little bit mad, but I was kind of tempted to scoop up a couple of boxes for myself and eat them at my billet house."

During the OHL draft, held prior to Game 3 of the series, the Colts selected Kerby Rychel, son of Spitfires GM Warren Rychel, with their first-round pick. Rychel had indicated to other teams that he would select his son in the second round of the draft. "I was obviously a little shocked," Warren Rychel said. "It was a rough day for our family."

Near the end of Windsor's Game 3 victory, Barrie forward Darren Archibald took a run at Spitfires goalie Philipp Grubauer behind the Windsor net, crumpling Grubauer to the ice. "I don't like it," Barrie coach Marty Williamson said of Archibald's hit. "It isn't what we needed to do at that point."

After the sweep, Windsor's coaching staff refused to shake hands with the Barrie coaches. "What they did on draft day was disrespectful, reprehensible and immoral," said Windsor coach Bob Boughner, who felt Barrie's drafting of Rychel's son was a cheap attempt to disrupt the Spitfires. "They knew what they were doing. I know business is business. I understand that, but when you start involving families in what's supposed to be a happy day for Kerby and his family, that's a low blow."

Windsor's Zack Kassian goes to his backhand looking to beat Brandon Wheat Kings goalie Jacob De Serres. (OHL)

Sipping From A Second Cup

Cool and confident, the Spitfires brought a swagger to Brandon, Manitoba, looking to become just the eighth team in Memorial Cup history to win back-to-back titles.

"You could be looking at 11 guys off that roster that play in the NHL," one scout said.

Struggling a year earlier and having to win four straight elimination games to capture the club's first Memorial Cup title, the Spitfires rolled through the 2010 event in Brandon.

"I don't know if people down there (in Windsor) really understand how good that team is," Rogers Sportsnet play-by-play man Peter Loubardias said.

It started with a 9-3 pounding of the host team in the opening game. Brandon's Travis Hamonic sent Hall head first into the end boards in the first minute. The future first pick overall in the NHL entry draft bounced back without missing a shift and scored twice in the first period as Windsor opened a five-goal lead.

"It shows the kind of depth this team has," said defenceman Mark Cundari, who was one of 12 Spitfires to record at least a point. "Guys pitched in from all over."

The Spitfires clinched a spot in the final with a 6-2 win over the Western Hockey League champion Calgary Hitmen two days later.

"This is where we wanted to be last year," Windsor forward Justin Shugg said. "Having to win four games and have back-to-back games is hard."

With a spot in the final locked up, Kelowna had the chance to knock Windsor out of the Memorial Cup in 2009, but lost the final round-robin game to the Spitfires. Windsor came back to win four successive games to take the title with a win over Kelowna in the final.

Windsor didn't make the same mistake in 2010 against Moncton, and knocked the Quebec Major Junior Hockey League champs out with a 4-3 win in overtime.

"Kelowna didn't knock us out and look what happened," Windsor winger Dale Mitchell said.

With one game left, the Spitfires never lost their focus in the final against Brandon.

Windsor scored a 9-1 win over the home team that tied the tournament record for the most lopsided decision in a final. Toronto beat Quebec 9-1 in the 1973 final.

"I think this team, in my opinion, could be mentioned in the same breath as the greatest

Adam Henrique (14) and Tayor Hall (4) celebrate another Spitfires goal during Windsor's 9-1 rout of Brandon in the 2010 Memorial Cup final. The score tied the tournament record. The Toronto Marlboros beat the Quebec Remparts 9-1 in the 1973 Memorial Cup final. (OHL)

junior hockey teams Canada has had," said Windsor coach Bob Boughner, whose team outscored the opposition 28-9 in the tournament. Eight different players scored for Windsor and 13 had at least a point to become just the eighth team to win back-to-back Memorial Cups.

"This team will be remembered as one of the greatest, that's for sure," Cundari said. "After last year, we knew what we were going to do."

Top 10 point totals in franchise history

2008-09 – 115 points (68 games)
2009-10 – 106 points (68 games)
1987-88 – 102 points (66 games)
2007-08 – 94 points (68 games)
1994-95 – 85 points (66 games)
1977-78 – 80 points (68 games)
2000-01 – 80 points (68 games)
2002-03 – 80 points (68 games)
1986-87 – 77 points (66 games)
2001-02 – 77 points (68 games)

Top 10 win totals in franchise history

2008-09 – 57 wins (68 games)
1987-88 – 50 wins (66 games)
2009-10 – 50 wins (68 games)
1994-95 – 41 wins (66 games)
2007-08 – 41 wins (68 games)
2002-03 – 37 wins (68 games)
1986-87 – 36 wins (66 games)
1979-80 – 36 wins (68 games)
1977-78 – 36 wins (68 games)
1999-00 – 35 wins (68 games)

Spitfires Tidbits

- Kenny Ryan began the 2009-10 season playing for the NCAA champion Boston College Eagles and finished the season playing for the Memorial Cup champion Spitfires.

- Through the end of the 2009-10 season, forward Andrei Loktionov was the only member

Windsor's Philipp Grubauer (left), Craig Duininck (centre) and Adam Wallace (right) pose with the Memorial Cup. Looking for a change of luck, Duininck shaved off the right side of his beard when the Spitfires fell behind 3-0 to Kitchener in the OHL conference finals. After his close shave, Windsor won eight straight games. (OHL)

(Left)
Windsor's Taylor Hall lifts the Stafford Smythe Memorial Trophy as MVP of the Memorial Cup for the second straight tournament. (OHL)

(Right)
Windsor's Bob Boughner was the first coach to win back-to-back Memorial Cups since Don Hay with Kamloops in 1994-95. (OHL)

Former Spitfires defenceman Joel Quenneville (left), coach of the 2009-10 Stanley Cup champion Chicago Blackhawks and Eric Wellwood of the 2009-10 Memorial Cup champion Windsor Spitfires display their prizes at Windsor's Canada Day parade. (Donna Corston)

of either of Windsor's back-to-back Memorial Cup winners to have played an NHL regular-season game. He suited up for one game with the 2009-10 Los Angeles Kings.

- Besides current Spitfire Cam Fowler, the 2010 gold medal-winning United States team at the World Junior Championships included forward Derek Stepan, son of 1986-87 Spitfire Brad Stepan, and goalie Jack Campbell, a 2010 Dallas Stars first-round draft pick who signed to play for the Spitfires beginning with the 2010-11 season.

- Windsor's Harry Young is the only player to captain back-to-back Memorial Cup-winning teams.

- Three of the eight back-to-back Memorial Cup champions have had direct ties to Windsor. Besides the Spitfires (2009-10), the Medicine Hat Tigers (1987-88) beat the Spitfires 7-6 in the 1988 Memorial Cup final and the Cornwall Royals (1980-81) won the 1981 Memorial Cup final 5-2 over the Kitchener Rangers in a game played at Windsor Arena.

- Ryan Baldwin began the 2009-10 season playing for the Memorial Cup champion Spitfires and finished it playing for the Sutherland Cup OHA Jr. B champion LaSalle Vipers.

- Austin Watson, a member of Windsor's 2008-09 Memorial Cup team, is the oldest of 10 children.

- Windsor's 4-3 victory over the Saginaw Spirit on Nov. 15, 2008 required 14 rounds of shootout competition before a winner was decided. Defenceman Ron Soucie scored the deciding goal, the only tally he ever registered in a Spitfires uniform.

Appendix

All-Time Spitfires Roster

Legend
h-Hockey Hall of Famer
n-NHLer
o-Olympian
s-Stanley Cup champion

Russ Adam-n 1977-78
Akil Adams 1993-95
Rick Adolfi 1982-83
Akim Aliu 2005-06
Jamie Allan 1987-89
Jamie Allison-n 1991-92
Peter Allison 1991-93
Jack Anderson 1975-76
Jay Anderson 1996-97
Jim Anderson-n 1949-51
Brett Angel 2000-02
Matt Anthony 2001-04
Al Arbour-hns 1949-53
John Armelin 1983-84
Brent Armstrong 1978-79
Jason Asadorian 1998-99
Ryan Aschaber 1999-2003
Gord Astles 1946-47
Peter Aston 2005-06
Shawn Babcock 1979-81
Tim Bacik 1992-93
Chad Badawey 1988-90
Bob Bailey-n 1949-50
John Bailey 1949-50
Josh Bailey-n 2006-08
Pete Bakovic-n 1983-85
Ryan Baldwin 2006-08; 2009-10
Terry Banjavic 1998-99
Blair Barnes-n 1977-80
John Barrett-n 1976-78
T.J. Battani 2006-07
Mike Battista 1983-84
Gerald Beaulieu 1981-83
Paul Beauparlant 1983-84
Paul Beazley 1993-95
Bruce Bell-n 1983-84
Brad Belland 1983-84
Jean Belliveau 1979-80
Geoff Benic 1985-88
Robert Benjamin 1984-85
Rod Benkovich 1980-81
David Benn 1992-93
Brian Bennie 1980-82
Paul Bezzo 2009-10
Bryan Bickell-ns 2005-06
Craig Binns 1991-93
Marek Biro 2006-08
Jesse Blacker 2007-10
Brian Blad 1984-87
Brady Blain 1991-94
Rob Blain 1995-96
Bryan Blair 1998-99
Mike Bogden 1992-93
Graeme Bonar 1982-84
Ted Bonham 1975-76
Dave Bonner 1988-89
Tom Boroski 1975-76
Paul Bortignon 2003-05
Ruslan Boryschenko 2001-02
Charles Bosnyak 1975-76
Mark Botell-n 1979-80
Robin Boucher 1997-2001
Bill Bowler-n 1991-95
Scott Bowles 2006-07
David Bowman 2000-04
Steve Boyd 1988-89
Earl Brandy 1946-47
Matthew Bragg 2007-08
Jeff Bramham 1990-92
Austen Brassard 2009-10
Kip Brennan-n 1996-98
Marv Brewer 1951-52
Chuck Brimmer 1982-83
Jay Brodie 1980-81
Bobby Brown 1950-53
Tim Bryan 1995-97
Gord Buckley 1947-48
Tim Burgess 1983-85
Andy Burnham 1997-99
Sean Burns 1988-91
Archie Burton 1952-53

Cummy Burton-n 1952-53
Jim Burton-o 1979-82
Tim Burton 1980-81
Eddie Busch 1947-48
Mike Bushby 2004-07
Ed Cadot 1951-52
Kelly Cain 1987-88
Sheldon Camp 1979-80
Cory Campbell 2001-02
Ken Campbell 1976-77
Reg Campbell 1951-52
Scott Campbell 2003-04
Jim Campeau 1979-80
Marc Cantin 2009-10
John Capel 1982-83
Ryan Carlisle 2007-08
Mike Carson 1979-81
Collin Carwardine 2005-07
Reuben Castella 1991-93
Maurizio Catenacci 1982-83
Craig Chapman 1976-77
Kyle Chapman 1998-2001
Jordan Cheechoo 2005-07
Don Cherry-n 1951-52
George Chin 1946-47
Bob Chittle 1977-78
Stanislov Choumakov 1996-97
Cameron Church 1947-48
John Cilladi 1998-99
Jared Cipparone 2003-06
Jason Cirone-no 1990-91
Luke Clowes 1992-95
Paul Coffell 1990-91
Aaron Coles 1996-98
Jason Coles 1992-94
Ken Collins 1951-53
Steve Collins 1983-84
Mark Connelly 1975-76
Matt Cooke-ns 1995-98
Rolland Cooney 1947-48
David Cooper 1975-76
John Cooper 1993-95
John Copland 1984-85
John Copley 1990-92
Gerald Corriveau 1951-52
Steve Cote 1984-86
Ryan Courtney 1998-2001
Sean Courtney 2004-05
Justin Coutu 2003-04
Michael Cox 2003-04
Glen Craig 1989-90
Derrick Crane 1992-93
Ron Craven 1951-53
Glenn Crawford 1994-98
Ron Creamer 1980-81
Brian Cross 1976-77
Trent Cull 1990-92
Mark Cundari 2006-10
Glen Cutting 1979-81
John Danlovich 1949-51
Dave Davidson 1987-88
Patrick Davis-n 2005-06
Peter DeBoer-n 1985-89
Scott Defoe 1979-82
Mike Delich 1949-50
Mike Deodato 1979-80
Marty Deschamps 1975-76; 1977-78
Ryan Dickie 2002-04
John-Scott Dickson 2000-05
Lou Dietrich 1952-53
Jason Dixon 2002-05
Ryan Donally 2001-05
Glen Doncaster 1976-77
Darren Dougan 1989-90
Steve Downie-n 2003-06
Greg Dries 1990-91
Dan Drouin 1988-89
John Drury 1948-49
Ben Dubois 2008-10
Craig Duininck 2009-10
Robert Dunham 1951-52
Richie Dunn-n 1976-77
Steve Dunn 1980-82
Mitch Dunning 2009-10
Pierre Dupuis 1983-85
Mike Dwyer-n 1975-77
Tyler Eady 2000-01
Murray Eaves-n 1977-78
Peter Ekroth 1978-79
Matt Elich-n 1995-98
Brian Ellacott 1975-77
Ryan Ellis 2007-10
Mark Emerson 1979-80
Rick Emmett 1994-95
Andrew Engelage 2006-09
Tyler Ertel 1990-91
Cory Evans 1993-95
Carl Evon 1946-47
Kevin Falesy 1988-89
Glen Featherstone-n 1985-88
Fedor Fedorov-n 1999-2000
Drew Felder 1996-98
Bob Ferguson 1978-79
Tim Findlay 1994-97
Gerry Fink 1978-79
George Finn 1981-84
Patrick Finnegan 1998-2000
Jake Fischer 2005-06
Ray Flaherty 1982-83
Jason Flick 1997-98
Rob Flynn 1986-88
Darren Forbes 1997-99
Brian Forestell 1988-91
Roger Fortier 1951-52
Jamie Foster 1994-95
Roy Foster 1950-52
Bert Fournier 1975-76
Cam Fowler-n 2009-10
Mitchell Fox 2009-10
Daniel Franche 1978-79
Chris Fraser 1989-90
David Frawley 2001-02
Robert Frayn 1991-92

Earl Frezell 1947-48
Tom Friesen 1975-76
Ron Friest-n 1976-78
Rival Fullum 1990-91
Paul Gagne-n 1978-80
Georges Gagnon-n 1976-77
Joe Gallant 1976-78
Scott Gardiner 1982-83
Ryan Garlock 2003-06
Leon Gaudreault 1946-47
Stan Gaudreault 1946-47
Ryan Gelinas 1994-97
Dave Geris 1993-96
Stephane Gervais 2001-02
Mario Giallonardo-n 1976-77
Paul Giallonardo 2001-05
Phil Gibson 2001-04
Steve Gibson 1989-93
Bert Giesebrecht 1947-49
Bruce Giesebrecht 1947-49
Todd Gill-n 1982-85
Dick Giola 1951-52
Tim Gleason-no 1999-2003
Trent Gleason 1988-91
Troy Gleason 1988-89
Steve Gleeson 2008-09
Ernie Godden-n 1978-81
Jason Goldenberg 1997-99
John Goodish 1975-76
Brian Gordon 1976-77
Pat Goreham 1976-78
J.P. Gorley 1984-88
Rick Gosnell 1983-84
David Goverde-n 1987-89
Mark Gowans 1984-85
Ross Graham 1952-53
Jeff Grant 1990-91
Vince Grant 1999-2001
Brad Gratton 1989-90
Josh Gratton-n 2002-03
Greg Gravel 1981-83
Adam Graves 1985-88
Gus Greco 1980-83
David Green 1993-96
Richard Greenop 2006-09
Keith Gretzky 1983-86
Irwin Gross 1949-51
Dan Growden 1998-2001
Philipp Grubauer 2009-10
Anthony Guadagnolo 2005-07
Brian Gustafson 1977-78
David Haas-n 1987-88
Willard Haas 1949-52
Matt Hackett 2006-08
Jason Haelzle 1992-93
Gord Haidy-n 1946-48
Sam Haidy 1987-89
Terry Hagen 1951-52
Glenn Hall-hns 1949-51
Taylor Hall-n 2007-10
Kevin Hamlin 1981-82
Paul Hampton 1985-88
Mark Hamway-n 1978-79
Ken Hanik 1975-76
Dave Hannan-nos 1977-78
Kevin Hansen 1996-98
Mike Hanson 1998-99
Gord Harris 1991-92
John Hartley 1989-90
Mike Hartwick 1991-93
Chris Hawken 1980-82
Dick Hayward 1946-47
Jim Heasty 1975-76
Rolly Hedges 1975-76
Shawn Heins-n 1992-93
Timo Helbling-n 2000-01
Rob Hennigar 2000-04
Adam Henrique 2006-10
Steve Hildenbrand 2000-02
Larry Hillman-ns 1952-53
Lloyd Hinchberger 1949-50
Dave Hirst 1977-80
Justin Hodgins 2002-03
Mike Hodgins 1977-78
Jim Hoffman 1977-78
Jim Hofford-n 1981-84
John Holmes 1975-76
Daryl Holmquist 1978-79
Todd Hooey 1980-83
Gareth Hopes 1997-98
Gerald Horton 1952-53
Fern Houle 1947-48
Vic Howe-n 1949-50
Kevin Hudes 2005-07
Alvin Huggard 1952-53
Kent Hulst 1985-87
Todd Hunter 1990-92
Ray Huot 1950-51
Mike Hurley 1992-93
Brad Hyatt 1986-88
Jeff Iles 1984-85
Peter Ing-n 1986-89
Jerry Ingram 1978-79
Frank Inouye 1975-76
Tyson Isaac 2008-09
Bud Isbister 1975-76
Jamie Israel 1990-91
Boris Ivanov 1998-99
Pat Jablonski-n 1985-88
Craig Jalbert 1997-98
Mike James 1999-2003
Phil James 1994-95
Frank Janicek 1978-81
Cam Janssen-n 2001-04
Brent Jarrett 1978-80
Wes Jarvis-n 1977-78
Jamie Jefferson 1982-85
Tom Jefferson 2003-05
Paul Jeffrey 1979-80
Cory Johnson 1993-94
Craig Johnson 1992-93
Earl Johnson-n 1949-51
John Johnson 1988-90

Stephen Johnston 2009-10
Ross Johnstone 1949-50
Brian Jones 1993-94
Ron Jones 1986-90
Michal Jordan 2007-08
Eddie Joss 1949-51
Terry Joss 1995-97
Ed Jovanovski-no 1992-95
Jason Joyal 1992-93
Scott Judson 2004-05
Claude Julien-n 1978-81
Joe Kalto 1949-50
Tom Kane 2007-08
Jeff Kapitanchuk 1997-99
Vadim Karaga 2003-04
Zack Kassian 2009-10
Elvon Kavanaugh 1946-47
Billy Kawulia 1952-53
Ross Kelly 1951-52
Craig Kennedy 1999-2004
Kerry Kerch 1983-84
Chris Kerr 1995-97
Kevin Kerr 1984-87
Tim Kerr-n 1976-77
Dave Kewley 1948-49
Earl Keyes 1946-47
Denis Khudyakov 2002-03
John Kibyuk 1977-78
Cameron Kincaid 1995-98
Bill Kitchen-n 1976-77
Kyle Knechtel 2003-06
Glenn Knight 1977-78
Ken Knight 1977-78
Richard Kokila 1984-86
Ches Konecny 1950-51
Chris Kotspopoulos-n 1975-76
George Kotsopoulos 1976-79
Jakub Kovar 2007-08
Vladimir Kretchine 1993-96
Jeff Kugel 1997-99
John Kurtz 2006-07
Mark Kurzawski 1985-88
Brad Kutschke 1987-89
John Kwant 1977-78
Todd Kwiecien 1979-80
Rob Kwiet 2007-09
Brent L'Heureux 1997-99
Pat Lahey 1981-83
Jacob Lalonde 2008-09
Ken Lamorie 1952-53
Mike Lankshear 1997-98
Derek Lanoue 2009-10
Jay Larson 1979-80
Scott Laurin 1986-88
Gilles Lauziere 1978-79
Mark LaVarre-n 1984-85
Gerry Lavergne 1948-49
Daryl Lavoie 1992-94
Paul Lawless-n 1981-84
Jeff Leavitt 2002-05
Rob LeBlanc 1986-88
Ryan Leblanc 1998-99
Bob Leeming 1988-90
Michael Leighton-n 1998-2001
Gerry Leroux 1976-78
J.P. Leroux 1978-80
Adam Lewis 1982-83
Chris Lidge 1979-80
Maxim Linnik 1998-2000
Marty Lipman 1982-84
Pete Liptrott 1988-90
Brett Liscomb 2003-06
Matt Livingston 1999-2002
Darryl Lloyd 2001-04
Mike Loach 1993-95
Claude Loiselle-n 1980-83
Andrei Loktionov-n 2008-09
David Lomas 2002-06
Clyde Long 1946-47
Dan Longe 1982-83
Guy Losier 1975-77
Eddie Louttit 1952-53
Chris Lukey 1988-90
Peter Luksa 1976-78
John Lumley 1951-52
Craig Lutes 1991-94
Adam Lyons 1982-83
John Lyons 1982-83
Herb Lundmark 1948-49
Adam MacArthur 2006-07
Matt Maccarone 2000-02
Lane MacDermid 2008-09
Paul MacDermid-n 1980-83
Brian MacDonald 1983-84
Leonard MacDonald 1990-92
Dave MacElwee 1981-82
Gerard MacIntyre 1979-81
Kevin MacKay 1989-92
Shawn MacKenzie-n 1979-82
Scott MacLellan 1982-83
Jim MacPherson 1985-86
Marco Maggio 2006-07
Craig Mahon 1997-2002
Dan Mahon 1983-86
Craig Maki 1979-80
Terry Maki 1983-84
Jason Maleyko 1996-97
Dave Mancuso 1977-78
Dan Mandich-n 1977-78
D.J. Mando 1995-98
Tom Mannino 2003-05
Harry Marchand 1946-47
Gaston Marcotte 1952-53
Kirk Marshall 1975-76
Rick Marshall 1982-83
Brian Martin 1984-86
Jeff Martin 1995-2000
Justin Martin 2000-01
Mike Martin 1992-96
Paul Martin 1982-84
Rob Martin 1990-91
Jeff Mascarin 1987-88
Andy Massa 1992-93

Gerrard Masse 1992-93
Matt Masterson 1995-97
Shawn Mather 1999-2001
Rick Matton 1975-76
Mitch Maunu 2002-06
Paul Maurice-n 1984-88
James Maxwell 1948-49
Marlin McAlendin 1952-53
Kevin McAlpine 1975-76
Ron McAteer 1952-53
Jack McCarthy 1951-52
Darren McCluskey 1985-86
Shayne McCosh 1992-94
Darwin McCutcheon-n 1980-82
Grant McDaniel 1980-82
Randy McDonald 1976-77
Dave McDonnell 1980-81
Terry McDonnell 1985-86
John McDougall 1984-85
Kevin McDougall 1988-90
Rod McElroy 1951-52
Paul McFarland 2004-06
Brock McGillis 2001-02
Cory McGillis 2004-07
Doug McGinn 1948-49
Tom McGrattan-n 1946-47
Doug McKay-ns 1947-49
Dennis McKeegan 1976-77
Brent McKenzie 1996-97
Paul McKenzie 1982-84
Bob McKillop 1987-89
Joe McLean 1992-93
Tom McLeod 1977-78
Derek McNamara 1997-98
Billy McNeill-n 1952-53
Iain McPhee 2002-06
Larry McRae 1975-77
Kevin Meagher 1979-80
Todd Meehan 2000-01
Roland Melanson-ns 1977-80
Jim Mellon 1977-78

Frank Melone 1985-86
Ryan Merritt 1989-91
Scott Metcalf-n 1986-87
Kevin Meyer 1983-85
Mark Middleton 1991-92
Jack Miller 1951-52
Scott Miller 1975-76
Wayne Mills 1975-76
Doug Minor 1990-91
Ted Miskolczi 1988-90
Dale Mitchell 2008-10
David Mitchell 1992-93
Jeff Mitchell 1979-81
Paul Monforton 1946-47
Rheal Mongeon 1952-53
Lane Moodie 2003-04
Dennis Mooney 1948-49
Robert Mooney 1981-82
Dave Moore 1975-76
Patrick Moran 2008-09
Vic Morin 1978-80
Aaron Morrison 1992-93
Craig Morrison 1982-84
Rick Morton 1990-91
Tom Mounsey 1949-50
John Muckler-ns 1950-52
Matt Mullin 1991-94
Craig Muni-ns 1980-82
John Murphy 1979-80
Patrick Murphy 2009-10
David Myles 1989-90; 1991-92
Mike Neill 1983-85
Greg Nemisz 2006-10
Michal Neuvirth-n 2007-08
Dave Nicholls 1980-81
Michael Nishi 2009-10
Ahren Nittel 2000-03
Jerome Noel 1975-76
Jordan Nolan 2006-08
Ben O'Connor 2005-07
John Odam 1979-81

Conor O'Donnell 2007-10
John Offidani 1950-51
Francis O'Grady 1948-49
Sean O'Hagan 1988-91
Jim Olsson 1981-84
Dave O'Meara 1948-49
Ryan O'Neill 1991-93
Ian O'Rear 1984-87
Cal O'Reilly-n 2003-06
Steve Ott-n 1999-2002
George Ouellette 1947-49
Luc Ouellette 1984-85
Kevin Paden 1993-95
Mike Pagnello 1981-83
Ed Palamar 1951-53
Paul Paliani 1983-84
Richard Paliani 1983-84
Matt Paltridge 2006-08
Richard Panik 2009-10
Lou Paolatto 1946-48
Bill Parent 1981-83
Bob Parent-n 1975-78
Louis Parent 1946-47
Blake Parlett 2006-08
Rod Pasma 1991-92
Troy Passingham 2009-10
Ryan Pawluk 1995-97
Wilf Payne 1983-86
Chris Peck 1977-78
Brit Peer 1985-86
Dean Pella 1988-89
Tyler Pella 1988-89
Sal Peralta 2000-03
Mark Perras 1975-76
Alan Perry 1984-86
Bert Peters 1982-83
Steve Peters-n 1979-80
Brian Petterle 1981-82
Chris Peyton 1992-93
Dick Piatkowski 1949-52
Rick Pickersgill 1983-84

Kevin Pitel 1980-81
Mark Plantery-n 1978-79
David Pluck 1992-95
Michal Podolka 1997-98
Glen Poirier 1982-83
Joel Poirier 1993-95
Mike Polano 1989-91
Jason Polera 1997-2000
Terry Porter 1976-77
Saverio Posa 2009-10
Jerry Price 1952-53
Marcel Pronovost-hns 1947-49
Nick Prush 1997-98
Tom Purcell 1987-89
Dennis Purdie 1992-93
Gary Purdon 1975-76
Chris Purves 2005-07
Brent Pye 1993-94
Max Quackenbush-n 1947-48
Joel Quenneville-ns 1975-78
Ivan Rachunek 1999-2000
Joe Ranger 1986-88
Bob Rawlyk 1948-52
Steven Rawski 1999-2001
Al Raymond 1983-84
Shaun Reagan 1983-85
Frank Rediker 2001-04
Tom Reick 1975-76
Elgin Reid 2007-08
Jon Reid 1997-98
Ted Reid 1949-50; 1952-53
Mark Renaud-n 1975-76
Mickey Renaud 2005-08
Jim Revenberg 1987-89
Monty Reynolds 1946-47
Jerry Ribble 1988-89
Mark Ridout 1997-2001
Dennis Riggin-n 1951-53
Luc Rioux 1997-2000
Gerry Rioux-n 1978-79
Don Roach 1978-79

Jim Robertson 1951-52
Marc Robillard 1992-93
Dave Roche-n 1993-95
Scott Roche 1996-97
Tom Roman 1985-86
Brian Rome 1983-84
Mike Root 2005-06
Sandy Ross 1975-76
Michael Rupp-ns 1997-98
Mike Russ 1946-47
Kenny Ryan 2009-10
Dan Ryder 1981-83
Mark Samoyloff 1983-84
Neil Sandilands 1982-83
Peter Sarno-n 1996-98
Terry Sawchuk-hns 1947-48
Shawn Scarfe 1984-85
Joe Scherer 1979-80
Glen Schofield 1983-85
Bo Schryer 1976-78
Lain Schubert 1991-93
Jonathan Sciacca 2004-07
Travis Scott-n 1993-95
Dylan Seguin 2009-10
Andy Self 2004-05
Mike Self 2001-03
Joey Sewell 1998-2001
Darrin Shannon-n 1986-89
Darryl Shannon-n 1985-88
Ryan Shaver 1995-98
Jack Shaw 1977-78
Rob Shearer-n 1993-96
Alexander Shevchenko 2002-03
Pavel Shtefan 1998-2000
Justin Shugg 2007-10
Ben Shutron 2008-09
Jim Sidwell 1979-80
Mike Siefker 1985-87
John Sikura 1976-77
Shawn Silver 1993-94
Brad Simms 1998-99

Jason Simon-n 1988-89
Frank Sinacori 1999-2002
Tim Sinasac 1997-99
Harkie Singh 1997-98
Tim Sittler 1976-77
Charlie Skjodt 1975-77
Paul Skjodt 1976-77
Art Skov 1946-47
Elmer Skov 1949-53
Glen Skov-ns 1946-50
Bob Smilskie 1975-76
Brad Smith-n 1975-78
D.J. Smith-n 1992-97
Don Smith 1949-52
Ed Smith 1984-86
Rick Smith 1996-98
Steve Smith 1990-92
Bradley Snetsinger 2005-08
Aaron Snow 2007-08
Jason Snow 1989-90
Anthony Soboczynski 2006-07
Brian Soso 2003-06
Ron Soucie 2008-09
Mike Speer 1990-91
Jason Spezza-n 2001-02
Earl St. Hilaire 1991-92
Todd St. Louis 1995-96
Eric Stamp 1991-93
Ed Stankiewicz-n 1949-50
Blair Stayzer 1996-2000
Brad Stepan 1986-88
Bill Stephenson 1975-76
Ryan Stephenson 1982-83
Doug Stewart 1983-84
Ryan Stewart 1993-94
Cory Stillman-ns 1990-92
Jamie Storr-n 1994-95
Jason Stos 1988-92
Jon Stos 1989-90
Tom Sullivan 1991-92
Valeriy Svoboda 1995-96

Jeff Szeryk 1990-91
John Tamer 1983-84
Scott Tarkowski 1977-78
John Taylor 1947-48
Karl Taylor 1988-90
Scott Taylor 1987-88
Brad Teichmann 1991-92
Larry Thibeault 1950-52
Doug Thiel 1950-52
Eldor Thomas 1950-51
Mark Thomas 1987-88
Scott Timmins 2008-10
Scott Todd 2004-07
Frank Tomchak 1975-76
Larry Tomie 1951-52
Brad Topping 2004-05
Dick Tourangeau 1975-77
Neil Trineer 1980-81
Stephen Trojanovic 2009-10
Stu Tufts 1990-91
Keaton Turkiewicz 2005-07
Bob Turner 1949-51
Mark Turner 1988-89
Ron Twiss 1975-76
Scott Tyo 1984-85
Jim Uniac 1947-48
Josh Unice 2008-10
J.D. Urbanic 1983-87
Al Van Belleghem 1948-49
Chris Van Dyk 1994-97
Jamie Vargo 1989-90
Michel Vautour 1977-78
Rob Veccia 1982-85
Tyler Verhaeghe 1983-84
Kelly Vipond 1992-93
Craig Voakes 2006-07
Ron Vogel 1996-99
Adam Wallace 2007-10
Ivan Walmsley 1947-48
Trevor Walsh 1988-91
Caleb Ward 1994-95
Jason Ward-n 1997-99
Wes Ward 1994-97
Todd Warriner-no 1990-93
Jeff Washbrook 1996-97
Lorne Watters 1951-52
Austin Watson 2008-10
Curtis Watson 1997-2000
Paul Watson 1994-95
Steve Webb-n 1992-94
Mike Weber-n 2003-07
Scott Weedon 1981-82
Derek Wells 1994-95
Eric Wellwood-n 2006-10
Kyle Wellwood-n 2001-03
Jamie Wentzell 1996-97
Dan West 1993-95
Michael Whaley 2009-10
Bob Wheat 1976-77
Shane Whelan 1985-87
Alex White 2002-03
Bill White 1986-88
K.J. White 1986-91
Dave Wilkins 1975-76
Mark Wilkinson 1975-76
Paul Wilkinson 1987-88
Mike Williams 1984-85
Behn Wilson-n 1976-77
Colin Wilson 1992-94
Don Wilson 1951-52
Garrett Wilson 2007-08
Jeff Wilson 1990-91
John Wilson 1976-77
Johnny Wilson-ns 1947-49
Larry Wilson-ns 1947-49
Mike Wolak 1986-89
Russ Wood 1992-93
James Woodcroft 2007-10
Jack Woods 1982-83
Ken Woods 1952-53
Keith Wynn 2006-07
Andrew Yogan 2007-09
Jason York-n 1988-91
Adam Young 1992-96
Harry Young 2006-10
Nick Young 1998-99
Jeff Zehr-n 1995-98
Jay Zeidel 1983-84
Jason Zohil 1989-91
Joe Zorica 1951-53
Martin Zorica 1949-51

• Spitfires Coaching History

1946-47 Ebbie Goodfellow 5-12-1
1947-48 Jimmy Skinner 29-6-1
1948-49 Jimmy Skinner 34-13-1
1949-50 Jimmy Skinner 34-13-1
1950-51 Jimmy Skinner 32-18-4
1951-52 Jimmy Skinner 3-18-2
1951-52 Len Wilson 0-3-0
1951-52 Mickey Drouillard 6-21-1
1952-53 Jimmy Skinner 16-35-5
1975-76 Doug Johnston 10-33-4
1975-76 Wayne Maxner 2-17-0
1976-77 Wayne Maxner 21-37-8
1977-78 Wayne Maxner 36-24-8
1978-79 Wayne Maxner 32-35-1
1979-80 Wayne Maxner 36-31-1
1980-81 Ron Harris 28-26-0
1980-81 Ron Carroll 5-7-2
1981-82 Marcel Pronovost 22-42-4
1982-83 Marcel Pronovost 2-13-0
1982-83 John Becanic 14-32-0
1982-83 Doug Imrie 3-5-1
1983-84 Bob Boucher 6-22-0
1983-84 Terry McDonnell 2-2-0
1983-84 Wayne Maxner 14-22-2
1984-85 Mark Craig 28-35-3
1985-86 Tom Webster 34-26-6
1986-87 Tom Webster 16-7-1
1986-87 Tony McDonald 15-14-2
1986-87 Jim Rutherford 5-4-2
1987-88 Tom Webster 50-14-2
1988-89 Tom Webster 25-37-4
1989-90 Brad Smith 17-41-8
1990-91 Brad Smith 33-29-4
1991-92 Brad Smith 2-6-2
1991-92 Wayne Maxner 14-16-5
1991-92 Dave Prpich 9-11-1
1992-93 Wayne Maxner 14-25-2
1992-93 Kevin MacIntosh 5-17-3
1993-94 Shane Parker 25-36-5
1994-95 Mike Kelly 41-22-3
1995-96 Mike Kelly 10-20-3
1995-96 Dave Prpich 3-1-0
1995-96 Paul Gillis 8-20-1
1996-97 Paul Gillis 29-29-8
1997-98 Vern Stenlund 3-14-0
1997-98 Dave Prpich 4-5-0
1997-98 Tony Curtale 12-21-5
1998-99 Tony Curtale 10-21-4
1998-99 Dave Prpich 13-18-2
1999-00 Tom Webster 35-30-2-1
2000-01 Tom Webster 34-22-8-4
2001-02 Tom Webster 33-24-6-5
2002-03 Tom Webster 32-23-4-1
2002-03 Mike Kelly 4-3-1-0
2003-04 Steve Smith 23-28-2-6
2003-04 Mike Kelly 4-2-1-2
2004-05 Mike Kelly 13-14-2-3
2004-05 Dave Prpich 13-15-4-4
2005-06 Moe Mantha 1-3-0
2005-06 D.J. Smith/Bill Bowler** 31-26-3-4
2006-07 Bob Boughner 18-43-2-5
2007-08 Bob Boughner 41-15-7-5
2008-09 Bob Boughner 57-10-0-1
2009-10 Bob Boughner 50-12-1-5
2010-11 Bob Jones
**Co-interim coaches

• Spitfires Captains History

1946-47 Paul Monforton
1947-48 Max Quackenbush
1948-49 Bert Giesebrecht
1949-50 Glen Skov
1950-51 Irwin Gross
1951-52 Elmer Skov
1952-53 Elmer Skov
1975-76 Scott Miller
1976-77 Joel Quenneville
1977-78 Joel Quenneville
1978-79 Blair Barnes
1979-80 Claude Julien
1980-81 Ernie Godden
1981-82 Darwin McCutcheon; Greg Gravel
1982-83 Greg Gravel; Claude Loiselle
1983-84 Mike Neill
1984-85 Todd Gill
1985-86 Paul Maurice
1986-87 Paul Maurice
1987-88 Paul Maurice; Paul Hampton; Adam Graves
1988-89 Peter DeBoer
1989-90 Peter Liptrott
1990-91 Jason York
1991-92 Cory Stillman
1992-93 Cory Stillman; Dennis Purdie; Craig Lutes
1993-94 Craig Lutes
1994-95 Bill Bowler
1995-96 Mike Martin
1996-97 D.J. Smith
1997-98 D.J. Mando; Peter Sarno; Jeff Martin
1998-99 Jason Ward; Jeff Martin
1999-2000 Craig Mahon
2000-01 Craig Mahon
2001-02 Craig Mahon
2002-03 Tim Gleason
2003-04 Craig Kennedy
2004-05 Ryan Donally; Mitch Maunu
2005-06 Paul McFarland
2006-07 Mike Weber
2007-08 Mickey Renaud
2008-09 Josh Bailey; Harry Young
2009-10 Harry Young
2010-11 Ryan Ellis

• Spitfires Who've Coached in the NHL

Jim Anderson
Al Arbour
Don Cherry
Peter DeBoer
Claude Julien
Paul Maurice
Wayne Maxner
John Muckler
Marcel Pronovost
Joel Quenneville
Tom Webster
Johnny Wilson
Larry Wilson

• Spitfires Who Played in the World Junior Championship

Canada

Roland Melanson (1979)
Adam Graves (1988-g)
Darrin Shannon (1989)
Tom Webster (coach, 1989)
Ed Jovanovski (1995-g)
Jamie Storr (1995-g)
Matt Cooke (1998)
Jason Ward (1998, 1999-s)
Jason Spezza (2001-b, 2002-s)
Steve Ott (2001-b, 2002-s)
Kyle Wellwood (2003-s)
Ryan Ellis (2009-g, 2010-s)
Taylor Hall (2010-s)
Adam Henrique (2010-s)
Greg Nemisz (2010-s)

Czech Republic

Michal Neuvirth (2008)

Slovakia

Richard Panik (2010)

Switzerland

Timo Helbling (2000, 2001)

United States

Richie Dunn (1977)
Alan Perry (1985, 1986-b)
Mike Wolak (1987)
Pat Jablonski (1987)
Tim Gleason (2001, 2003)
Cam Fowler (2010-g)

Legend

g-gold medallist
s-silver medallist
b-bronze medallist

• Spitfires Who've Played in the Olympics

Jim Burton (Austria) Lillehammer, 1994
Todd Warriner (Canada) Lillehammer, 1994-s
Ed Jovanovski (Canada) Salt Lake City, 2002-g
Jason Cirone (Italy) Turin, 2006
Tim Gleason (USA) Vancouver, 2010-s

Legend

g-gold medallist
s-silver medallist

• Spitfires Award Winners

TEAM

Memorial Cup (Champions of CHL)
  2008-09
  2009-10
J. Ross Robertson Cup (Champions of OHL)
  2008-09
  2009-10
Wayne Gretzky Trophy (OHL Western Conference Champions)
  2008-09
  2009-10
Hamilton Spectator Trophy (Top Regular-Season OHL Record)
  1987-88
  2008-09
Emms Trophy (OHL Emms Division Champions)
  1979-80
  1987-88
Bumbacco Trophy (OHL West Division Regular-Season Champions)
  2008-09
  2009-10

INDIVIDUAL

Memorial Cup

Stafford Smythe Memorial Trophy (Memorial Cup Most Valuable Player)
  Taylor Hall, 2008-09
  Taylor Hall, 2009-10
Ed Chynoweth Trophy (Memorial Cup Leading Scorer)
  Taylor Hall, 2009-10
Memorial Cup All-Star Team
  Darrin Shannon, 1987-88
  Darryl Shannon, 1987-88
  Ryan Ellis, 2008-09
  Taylor Hall, 2008-09
  Cam Fowler, 2009-10
  Taylor Hall, 2009-10

CHL Awards

CHL Scholastic Player of the Year
Darrin Shannon, 1987-88

CHL Sportsman of the Year
Kyle Wellwood, 2002-03

CHL Top Draft Prospect Award
Todd Warriner, 1991-92
Jason Spezza, 2000-01

CHL Brian Kilrea Coach of the Year Award
Bob Boughner, 2007-08
Bob Boughner, 2008-09

CHL Rookie of the Year
Taylor Hall, 2007-08

OHL Awards

Red Tilson Trophy (OHL Most Outstanding Player)
Glenn Hall, 1950-51
Ernie Godden, 1980-81

Eddie Powers Memorial Trophy (OHL Scoring Champion)
Bert Giesebrecht, 1948-49
Earl (Dutch) Reibel, 1949-50
Peter Sarno, 1997-98
Taylor Hall, 2009-10

Max Kaminsky Trophy (OHL Most Outstanding Defenceman)
Darryl Shannon, 1987-88
Ryan Ellis, 2008-09

Emms Family Award (OHL Rookie of the Year)
Cory Stillman, 1990-91
Peter Sarno, 1996-97
Taylor Hall, 2007-08

Dave Pinkney Trophy (OHL Lowest Team GAA)
Andrew Engelage, Josh Unice, 2008-09

Bobby Smith Trophy (OHL Scholastic Player of the Year)
Darrin Shannon, 1987-88
Ryan Ellis, 2007-08

Leo Lalonde Memorial Trophy (OHL Overage Player of the Year)
Bill Bowler, 1994-95

William Hanley Trophy (OHL Most Sportsmanlike Player)
Kyle Wellwood, 2002-03

Matt Leyden Trophy (OHL Coach of the Year)
Bob Boughner, 2007-08
Bob Boughner, 2008-09

OHL Executive of the Year
Warren Rychel, 2008-09

Wayne Gretzky 99 Award (OHL Playoff Most Valuable Player)
Taylor Hall, 2008-09
Adam Henrique, 2009-10

Roger Neilson Memorial Award (OHL Top Academic College/University Player)
Derek Lanoue, 2009-10

• Team Records

Single Season

Most Points: 115 (2008-09)

Most Wins: 57 (2008-09)

Highest Winning Percentage: .846 (2008-09)

Most Home Wins: 31 (2008-09)

Most Road Wins: 26 (2008-09)

Fewest Losses: 11 (2008-09)

Most Goals: 396 (1987-88)

Fewest Goals Against: (171) 2008-09

Fewest Goals (201): 2003-04

Most Goals Against: (470) 1975-76

Longest Winning Streak: 16 games (Jan. 18-March 3, 1988)

• Individual Records

CAREER

Goals: Ernie Godden 152

Assists: Bill Bowler 318

Points: Bill Bowler 467

Games: John Scott Dickson 306

Penalty Minutes: Adam Young 663

Defenceman Goals: Joel Quenneville 61

Defenceman Assists: Joel Quenneville 168

Defenceman Points: Joel Quenneville 229

Goalie Wins: Andrew Engelage 78 (2006-09)

Goals-Against Average: Troy Passingham 2.78 (2009-10)*

Shutouts: Andrew Engelage 7 (2006-09)

Games Coached: Wayne Maxner 564 (1975-80; 1983-84; 1991-93)

Coaching Wins: Tom Webster 294 (1985-89; 1999-2003)

*Based on a minimum 50 games played

SINGLE SEASON

Goals: Ernie Godden 87 (1980-81)

Assists: Bill Bowler 102 (1994-95)

Points: Ernie Godden 153 (1980-81)

Rookie Points: Cory Stillman 101 (1990-91)

Rookie Goals: Taylor Hall 45 (2007-08)

Defenceman Goals: Joel Quenneville 27 (1977-78)

Defenceman Points: Joel Quenneville 103 (1977-78)

Goalie Wins: Andrew Engelage 46 (2008-09)

Goals-Against Average: Andrew Engelage 2.35 (2008-09)

Shutouts: Glenn Hall 6 (1950-51)

Coaching Wins: Bob Boughner 57 (2008-09)

SINGLE GAME

Goals: 5 (Gerry Leroux, Oct. 27, 1977; Paul Gagne, Oct. 11, 1979)

Assists: 6 (Greg Gravel, Oct. 28, 1982)

Points: 9 (Greg Gravel, Oct. 28, 1982)

Powerplay Goals: 3 (Ernie Godden, March 21, 1981; Greg Gravel, Oct. 28, 1982; Bill Bowler, Jan. 23, 1993; Craig Lutes, March 17, 1993)

Shorthanded Goals: 2 (Claude Loiselle, March 8, 1983; Kelly Cain, Dec. 11, 1987; Glenn Crawford, Sept.29, 1995; Shawn Mather, Sept. 28, 2000)

Fastest Opening Goal: 9 seconds (K.J. White, Oct. 4, 1990)

Fastest Goal to Open a Period: 5 seconds (Jason Spezza, Nov. 18, 2001)

Fastest Two Goals by One Player: 7 seconds (Blair Barnes, Nov. 9, 1979)

Fastest Three Goals by One Player: 2:56 (Bill Bowler, March 5, 1994)

• Championship Rosters

2009-10 Memorial Cup and OHL Champions
Marc Cantin, Mark Cundari, Craig Duininck, Ryan Ellis, Cam Fowler, Philipp Grubauer, Taylor Hall, Adam Henrique, Stephen Johnston, Zack Kassian, Derek Lanoue, Dale Mitchell, Greg Nemisz, Troy Passingham, Saverio Posa, Kenny Ryan, Justin Shugg, Scott Timmins, Adam Wallace, Eric Wellwood, James Woodcroft, Harry Young, Bob Boughner (Coach), Warren Rychel (GM).

2008-09 Memorial Cup and OHL Champions
Jesse Blacker, Mark Cundari, Ryan Ellis, Andrew Engelage, Richard Greenop, Taylor Hall, Adam Henrique, Rob Kwiet, Andrei Loktionov, Lane MacDermid, Dale Mitchell, Greg Nemisz, Conor O'Donnell, Justin Shugg, Ben Shutron, Scott Timmins, Josh Unice, Adam Wallace, Austin Watson, Eric Wellwood, Harry Young, Warren Rychel (GM), Bob Boughner (Coach).

1987-88 OHL Champions
Jamie Allan, Geoff Benic, Kelly Cain, Peter DeBoer, Glen Featherstone, Rob Flynn, J.P. Gorley, David Goverde, Adam Graves, David Haas, Paul Hampton, Brad Hyatt, Peter Ing, Pat Jablonski, Ron Jones, Mark Kurzawski, Jeff Mascarin, Tom Purcell, Jim Revenberg, Darrin Shannon, Darryl Shannon, K.J. White, Paul Wilkinson, Mike Wolak, Tom Webster (coach), Jim Rutherford (GM).

• Spitfires Selected in the NHL Draft

1976
103. Larry McRae, Los Angeles Kings
116. Charlie Skjodt, Toronto Maple Leafs

1977
83. John Wilson, Toronto Maple Leafs

1978
21. Joel Quenneville, Toronto Maple Leafs
113. Dave Mancuso, Chicago Blackhawks
129. John Barrett, Detroit Red Wings
213. Wes Jarvis, Washington Capitals

1979
59. Roland Melanson, New York Islanders1
26. Blair Barnes, Edmonton Oilers

1980
19. Paul Gagne, Colorado Rockies4
8. Shawn Babcock, Edmonton Oilers
169. Shawn MacKenzie, Colorado Rockies

1981
23. Claude Loiselle, Detroit Red Wings
55. Ernie Godden, Toronto Maple Leafs
61. Paul MacDermid, Hartford Whalers
66. Gus Greco, Colorado Rockies
120. Todd Hooey, Calgary Flames

1982
14. Paul Lawless, Hartford Whalers
149. Pat Lahey, Detroit Red Wings
178. Greg Gravel, Pittsburgh Penguins

1983
52. Bruce Bell, Quebec Nordiques
114. Jim Hofford, Buffalo Sabres

1984
25. Todd Gill, Toronto Maple Leafs
207. J.D. Urbanic, Boston Bruins

1985
56. Keith Gretzky, Buffalo Sabres
71. Mark Gowans, Detroit Red Wings
252. Paul Maurice, Philadelphia Flyers

1986
22. Adam Graves, Detroit Red Wings
35. Mark Kurzawski, Chicago Blackhawks
36. Darryl Shannon, Toronto Maple Leafs
56. Kevin Kerr, Buffalo Sabres
69. Kent Hulst, Toronto Maple Leafs
73. Glen Featherstone, St. Louis Blues
182. Geoff Benic, Chicago Blackhawks

1988

4. Darrin Shannon, Buffalo Sabres
48. Peter Ing, Toronto Maple Leafs
115. Ron Jones, Winnipeg Jets
196. Brad Hyatt, Los Angeles Kings
237. Peter DeBoer, Toronto Maple Leafs

1989

134. Jim Revenberg, Vancouver Canucks
215. Jason Simon, New Jersey Devils

1990

217. K.J. White, Los Angeles Kings

1992

4. Todd Warriner, Quebec Nordiques
6. Cory Stillman, Calgary Flames
157. Steve Gibson, Edmonton Oilers

1994

1. Ed Jovanovski, Florida Panthers
105. Dave Geris, Florida Panthers
194. Mike Loach, New York Islanders

1995

41. D.J. Smith, New York Islanders
65. Mike Martin, New York Rangers
82. Chris Van Dyk, Chicago Blackhawks
148. Adam Young, New Jersey Devils

1996

118. Glenn Grawford, New Jersey Devils

1997

31. Jeff Zehr, New York Islanders
61. Matt Elich, Tampa Bay Lightning
75. Jeff Martin, Buffalo Sabres
141. Peter Sarno, Edmonton Oilers
144. Matt Cooke, Vancouver Canucks

1998

95. Andy Burnham, New York Islanders

1999

165. Michael Leighton, Chicago Blackhawks
190. Blair Stayzer, Calgary Flames

2000

25. Steve Ott, Dallas Stars
277. Ryan Courtney, Buffalo Sabres

2001

2. Jason Spezza, Ottawa Senators
23. Tim Gleason, Ottawa Senators

2002

85. Ahren Nittel, New Jersey Devils
117. Cam Janssen, New Jersey Devils

2003

97. Ryan Donally, Calgary Flames
118. Frank Rediker, Boston Bruins

2004

45. Ryan Garlock, Chicago Blackhawks
120. Mitch Maunu, Chicago Blackhawks

2005

29. Steve Downie, Philadelphia Flyers
150. Cal O'Reilly, Nashville Predators
213. Scott Todd, Nashville Predators

2006

57. Mike Weber, Buffalo Sabres
155. Peter Aston, Florida Panthers

2007

143. Mickey Renaud, Calgary Flames
156. Richard Greenop, Chicago Blackhawks

2008

9. Josh Bailey, New York Islanders
25. Greg Nemisz, Calgary Flames
82. Adam Henrique, New Jersey Devils
202. Harry Young, New Jersey Devils

2009

11. Ryan Ellis, Nashville Predators
58. Jesse Blacker, Toronto Maple Leafs
112. Lane McDermid, Boston Bruins
165. Scott Timmins, Florida Panthers
172. Eric Wellwood, Philadelphia Flyers

2010

1. Taylor Hall, Edmonton Oilers
12. Cam Fowler, Anaheim Ducks
105. Justin Shugg, Carolina Hurricanes
112. Philipp Grubauer, Washington Capitals

PHOTO CREDITS:

Donna Corston: 164; **Dan Hamilton** (DH): 62, 65, 66, 74, 76, 77, 78, 79, 81, 82, 83, 84, 85, 86, 87, 88, 89, 90, 92, 93, 94, 95, 96, 97, 98, 99, 100, 101, 102, 103, 104, 105, 106, 107, 108, 109, 112, 114, 116, 119, 120, 121, 122, 123, 124, 125, 126, 128, 129, 130, 132, 133, 134, 135, 136, 137, 140, 141, 142, 143, 144, 145, 146, 147, 148, 149, 152, 153, 154, 155; **Rich Hayward**: 20; **OHL/Aaron Bell** (OHL): 159, 160, 162, 163; **OHL/Terry Wilson** (OHL): 161, 163; **Marcel Pronovost** (MP): 9, 10, 11, 12, 14, 19, 22, 23, 24, 27, 30, 31, 32; **Tony Techko Sports Archives, University of Windsor** (TTSA): 14, 16, 37, 40, 49, 54, 58, 63; **Windsor Spitfires Hockey Club** (WSHC): 42, 43, 51, 52, 61, 68, 117, 127, 146; **The Windsor Star** (WS): 8, 18, 20, 21, 22, 25, 26, 28, 29, 33, 34, 35, 38, 44, 45, 46, 47, 49, 50, 53, 55, 56, 57, 59, 61, 67, 69, 70, 71, 77, 156, 157.